THE ANGLO-SAXON KINGDOMS

THE POWER STRUGGLES FROM HENGIST TO ECGBERHT

THE ANGLO-SAXON KINGDOMS

THE POWER STRUGGLES FROM HENGIST TO ECGBERHT

LEONARD DUTTON

Published in 1993 by
SPA

in conjunction with
Leonard Dutton

British Library Cataloguing in Publication Data
A catalogue record for this book is available from the British Library

ISBN 1 85421 197 8

Designed and produced by Images (Publishing) Malvern Ltd.
Printed and bound in Great Britain.

CONTENTS

ILLUSTRATIONS

MAPS

To my Parents
Percy and Ada Dutton

ACKNOWLEDGEMENTS

Phillimore and Co. Ltd. 1. Morris, *The Age of Arthur*.

2. Gildas, *The Ruin of Britain*.

3. Nennius, *Historia Brittonum*.

Basil Blackwell Ltd   James, *The Franks*.

Eyre Methuen   Whitelock, *English Historical Documents, volume I*.

Every attempt has been made to seek permission prior to publication from all copyright holders. Would any copyright holders who have not replied please contact the publisher.

Front Cover Photograph: courtesy of Catherine Whiting: St. Oswald, Gloucester Cathedral.

Back Cover Photograph: Death of St. Oswald, Gloucester Cathedral.

INTRODUCTION

This work describes the political situation in Britain as it evolved after the withdrawal of Roman power in 409. For almost four centuries, Britain had enjoyed the stability provided by a centralised system of government. South of Hadrian's Wall, there was only one sovereign power in the land, that of the Roman governor or *vicarius*. But after 409, the central power was split and divided among more than twenty regional rulers, the British tribal kings. This is a difficult period to describe because of the sparsity of information. The present work assembles available evidence and presents it together with sufficient explanation to bring out its full significance. It shows how the Jutes, Saxons and Angles extinguished the British tribal regimes and established their own regional kingdoms. The division of sovereignty among so many regional rulers led to a patchwork of shifting rivalries, animosities and opposing alliances, inevitably erupting from time to time into open warfare, as each ruler strove to ensure the security of his own realm. The new Anglo-Saxon regimes had to work out a political accommodation not only with one another, but also with the neighbouring Welsh, Scottish and Pictish kings.

At an early stage it was recognised first by the Britons, then by the Saxons and the Angles, that there was a need for a supreme central authority, who would ensure peace throughout the land. The story is taken as far as the reign of Ecgberht, King of the West Saxons 802-839. Ecgberht's reign marks the end of the historical period during which the Saxons and Angles were able to develop their political institutions free from the threat of invasion across the North Sea. As a result of the historical process, Ecgberht was able to establish a pre-eminence based on the strength and traditions of both the West Saxon and Kentish kingdoms. It was the regime built up by Ecgberht which was to take the lead in withstanding the stresses of the next historical period, the period of the Viking assault.

PART 1

EARLY GERMANIC
SETTLEMENTS

THE CLOSING YEARS OF ROMAN BRITAIN

The later years of the Roman occupation of Britain were a time of great political disturbances. There were continual raids by the Picts from Scotland, the Scotti from Ireland and Saxons along the coast. Many of the events of this period affected the migration and settlement of the land by the Angles and the Saxons.

An important trend was the gradual withdrawal of legionary troops from Britain and their replacement by mercenary forces, recruited from tribes beyond the Roman frontiers, often from Germany. British and classical writers often referred to those from Germany indiscriminately as Saxons, regardless of their actual place of origin. Historians distinguish between two main types of mercenary: the *laeti*, who served within Roman units under Roman command; and the *foederati*, who entered as an entire group into a treaty (*foedus*) with the Romans. The *foederati* had the status of allies of Rome and served under their own military leaders. Under the emperor Theodosius the Great (379-395) much greater use was made of *foederati*.

Many of the troops manning the northern defences of Roman Britain were of Germanic extraction. As early as the third century, there is evidence of Frisian units at Burgh-by-Sands and Housesteads along Hadrian's Wall. At the latter fort there was a Germanic unit called *Numerus Hnaudfridi* – Notfried's Troop, and a shrine was set up to tribal gods. One of the earliest records tells of the emperor Probus, who brought Burgundians and Vandals to Britain from east of the Oder in 278 to help the government quell an incipient revolt.

The events of the year 306 show that the leaders of the Germanic troops had come to have considerable influence in the Roman army. The emperor Constantius Chlorus brought a force to Britain to deal with a major problem along Hadrian's Wall. Among his troops was a cohort of Alamannic auxiliaries under their own leader, Crocus, described as 'king of the Alamanni'. Constantius dealt with the situation along the Wall, but in the same year died in the imperial palace at York. His troops proclaimed his son Constantine (later called 'the Great') as emperor in succession to his father. The Alamannic chief, Crocus, took a prominent part in supporting Constantine's nomination as emperor.

In 367 a major crisis occurred, when the defences of northern Britain were overrun by an alliance of Scots and Picts, and this was accompanied by a breakdown of discipline by the troops on Hadrian's Wall. Some, perhaps most, of these were of Germanic extraction. The Duke of the British Provinces – Dux Britanniarum – called Fullofaudes, who commanded the northern forces, was captured and the Count of the Saxon Shore – Comes *Litoris Saxonici* – called Nectarides, was killed. Both of these officers had German-sounding names. Count Theodosius was sent to retrieve the situation in 369. He rebuilt the damaged forts on Hadrian's Wall and reorganised the defence system beyond the Wall by placing the British tribes there under the control of four Roman officials, who probably had the rank of *praefecti*. Their task was to introduce Roman organisation and military methods, so that the tribes would be better fitted to resist the Picts. These tribes virtually became buffer states, which were intended to counter Pictish incursions before they reached the Wall. But the Picts had been by-passing the land defences by mounting sea-borne attacks in their coracles along the east coast. Theodosius' response was to erect a chain of signal stations along the Yorkshire coast as far south as Filey to providing warning of the approach of raiders by sea. These stations were probably manned by Germanic auxiliaries and controlled from a headquarters at Malton (SE 7871), the Roman Derventio. Further south, the perimeter defences of the larger towns were strengthened by the construction of bastions on which artillery pieces could be mounted.

The menace of sea-borne raids along the south and east coasts became a major problem. The Roman response was the construction of a chain of ten massive stone-built forts stretching from Branodunum at Brancaster near Hunstanton to Portus Adurni at Portchester on Portsmouth Harbour, covering a distance of 280 miles. They were under the command of the Count of the Saxon Shore. Four of the ten were located in Kent (Regulbium at Reculver, Rutupiae at Richborough, Dubris at Dover and Portus Lemannis at Lympne), indicating that this was the area most under threat and that the raiders favoured the short sea crossing from the continent.

The Forts of the Saxon Shore.

The Roman-style *praefecti* of the tribes north of the Wall became virtual rulers and founded dynasties, which provided them with a succession of kings. These British states were to play their part in the early history of the Angles, particularly the most easterly, the Votadini. Their territory was divided into two halves, the northern part lying between the Firth of Forth and the river Tweed and the southern part lying between the Tweed and the Wall. The chief centre of the northern Votadini was the large hill fort at Traprain Law (NT 5874), some forty acres in extent, while the chief centre of the southern Votadini was the hill fort Yeavering Bell (NT 9329). The new leaders had Roman names, Paternus, son of Tacitus, over the southern Votadini and possibly Catellius Decianus over the northern Votadini. The original ruler or *praefectus* of the Britons of the Clyde was Quintilius Clemens. His dynasty ruled as kings of Strathclyde until the Norman conquest. Their capital was at Dumbarton, the fortress of the Britons.[1]

The continued presence of Alamannic auxiliaries within Britain was shown in 372, when the emperor Valentinian placed a strong force of Alamanni at an unknown location under the command of Fraomar, who had been king of the Alamanni on the upper Rhine near Mainz. He was given the title of Tribune.

Major weakening of the Roman garrison in Britain occurred in 383, when Magnus Maximus, who may have been the Dux Britanniarum, rebelled, proclaimed himself emperor and marched a considerable force from Britain to Gaul. Among the troops removed were probably the remnant of Legio XX, stationed at Deva, modern Chester. Magnus established his rule over Britain, Gaul and Spain, with his capital at Trier. He was active principally on the continent, but returned to Britain probably in 384 and conducted a victorious campaign against the Picts and Scots. His rule was brought to an end when he was killed in Italy in 388.

In the closing years of the fourth century, the barbarian attacks were continuing. In 396-8 the Vandal general Stilicho organised further action against the raiders, but in 401 he had to withdraw

---

[1] Morris, *The Age of Arthur*. p. 17.

more troops, probably including the garrison at Segontium near Carnarvon. This opened up a serious gap in the defences of the northwest at a time when the raids across the Irish Sea were continuing, and measures were needed to plug the gap. The Historia Brittonum (part of the Nennius documents) reported that at about this time the military leader Cunedag (or Cunedda, an early form of the name Kenneth) was transferred from Manau Guotodin (i.e. Manau of the Votadini) to North Wales with his eight sons. He was the son of Aeternus, son of Paternus, who had been appointed to give military leadership to the southern Votadini. Manau Guotodin is the most northerly part of the land of the Votadini at the head of the Firth of Forth. It was beyond the Antonine Wall and at the extreme limit of Roman controlled territory. It was, in fact, the frontier area facing the land of the Picts. At the time of his transfer, Cunedag, a south Votadinian leader, was deployed in this frontier zone, apparently guarding it against the Picts. After his transfer to North Wales, he had the task of providing military training, organisation and leadership for the Britons of North Wales, so that they would be able to undertake their own defence. This was the task carried out by Cunedag's father and grandfather for the Votadini. The transfer of Cunedag to North Wales was stated to have taken place 146 years before the reign of Mailcunus (in Welsh Maelgwn) the Great, King of Gwynedd.[2] The Welsh Annals report the death of Maelgwn in the annal for 547. This gives the latest date for the transfer of Cunedag as 401 i.e. at about the time when the Roman garrison was withdrawn from Segontium. The Historia Brittonum stated that Cunedag expelled the Irish (Scottos), so that they never returned again. He established the kingdom of Gwynedd and took possession of Deva, which was the most suitable place to act as his capital. He was so successful that his kingdom became the foremost martial power in the west, ready to face the Anglian challenge, when it came. He founded a dynasty, which continued into the thirteenth century and ended with Llewellyn ab Gruffydd. His sons provided similar leadership for other tribes in Wales, where they also founded

---

[2] Nennius, *Historia Brittonum*. para. 62.

royal dynasties.

A few years after 401, the British proclaimed a native emperor, Constantine III, and in 407 he led further troops from Britain to Gaul against an invasion by Vandals, Suebi and Alans, who could have threatened Britain.

ARCHAEOLOGICAL TRACES

It is not known if the Germanic mercenaries and auxiliaries were totally withdrawn when the last units of the Roman army vacated Britain, or if certain of them were left behind, because they were not first line troops. Many of them had raised families, who were settled on land which had been allotted to them. So a number of non-British settlements had come into existence, probably not distant from where the men were serving. Archaeologists have discovered and studied a number of sites in the eastern and southern parts of England, which they have identified as being associated with pagan Germanic people. Features of the sites are: burials which can be identified as pagan, often containing articles (weapons, jewellery, pottery), which provide a connection with sites in northwestern Europe; traces of buildings, characteristic of contemporary buildings in Germany, such as sunken huts (*Grubenhauser*) and post-built halls. Although it is not possible to assign precise dates to these finds, reliable guidance as to the period concerned may be obtained from the dating of corresponding finds on the continent. This indicates that some of these sites were occupied as early as the late Roman period. The geographic location of many of the sites is consistent with this, as they are situated a short distance from a Roman town or road, showing a close connection with the Roman organisation.

These sites can be related predominantly with two main areas in northwestern Europe, the area in the southern part of the Jutland peninsula around the modern town of Schleswig, and the area lying between the estuaries of the rivers Elbe and Weser. Bede called the former Angulus, the latter Old Saxony. It is apparent that many of the Germanic people brought into Britain by the Romans originated from these areas. Although as a general rule northerly sites reveal Anglian associations, while southern sites reveal Saxon associations, some sites have features which suggest both. In East Anglia, Middle Anglia and eastern Mercia brooches and metalwork have been found pointing to a

Saxon rather than an Anglian origin.

North of the Humber, Germanic type urn burials have been found within a mile of the centre of York, one of the most important military centres in Roman Britain. In the area of the Yorkshire Wolds, there are a cluster of sites, some situated close to the road linking Brough-on-Humber (the Roman Petuaria) and Malton (the Roman Derventio). An extensive cemetery at Sancton (SE 903402) contained both inhumations and cremations. The cremation urns have close parallels with corresponding urns from Borgstedt in southern Schleswig and the island Fyn dated fourth or early fifth centuries. Some early pots at Sancton can be matched with pots in Old Saxony near Cuxhaven. Other Sancton urns reflect forms and decoration among the Alamanni and the Franks of the middle Rhineland. It appears, therefore, that this cemetery was used by people who originated in Angulus, Old Saxony and the middle Rhineland. A fourth century brooch of south German origin was found in a mid-sixth century Anglian grave at Londesborough (SE 8645) and a spearhead and pottery similar to south German types were found at Driffield (TA 0257). These south German traces may probably be related to the mention of the Alamannic leaders Crocus (at York in 306) and Fraomar (in 371).

In Lincolnshire an early cremation cemetery is located near Ancaster close to the Roman road from Lincoln. Close to Leicester (Ratae Coritanorum, the cantonal centre of the Coritani), a cemetery is located at Thurmaston (SK 6109). At Loveden Hill (SK 907458) and Newark, Nottinghamshire, pottery had styles and decoration of Anglian types. In East Anglia two very early cemeteries outside Venta Icenorum, the cantonal centre of the Iceni, at Markshall and Caistor-by-Norwich imply the presence of two communities, which had official functions for the protection and support of Venta. The finds at Markshall include early urns of Saxon type, while Caistor contains both Anglian and Saxon vessels. A site at West Stow (TL 8271) contains the remains of an Anglo-Saxon village dating from the early part of the fifth century to the middle of the seventh century. The foundations of about eighty buildings, sunken huts and post-built halls have been identified. Some replica huts have been erected on the site and may be viewed. Another similar village has been identified at Pakenham (TL 9367). At

Spong Hill, North Elmham (TF 983195) a cemetery has been discovered from which two thousand cremation urns have been recovered.

Replica Anglo-Saxon Huts at West Stow.

A site at Highdown Hill (TQ 092043) near Worthing and another at Mucking (TQ 6882) near Tilbury in Essex are considered to have accommodated a unit to provide early warning of raiders along the southern coast and the Thames estuary, similar to the units along the Yorkshire coast. Pottery found at Mucking corresponded closely with that found at Feddersen Wierde on the river Weser.

An area which played a key role in the Saxon settlement was the middle Thames valley. Here a number of Germanic settlements sprang up between the late fourth and early fifth centuries centred upon Dorchester-on-Thames. As a Roman town Dorchester was located where the road between Towcester (Lactodorum, a junction with Watling Street) and Silchester (Calleva Atrebatum) crossed the Thames. Originally founded as a fort in the early years of the Roman conquest, it never acquired a greater importance than as an administrative centre for the region. Nevertheless, it was provided with its own town defences, and in the later fourth and early fifth centuries a unit of Germanic mercenaries, probably with the status of *foederati,* was drafted in to man the town's defences, to replace a Roman unit withdrawn to the continent. The unit was allocated a number of areas in the vicinity for the settlement of families. Traces of them have been found at the following locations (distances shown from Dorchester): (See map 5)

Abingdon (SU 4997) 6 miles northwest, cemetery containing 203 individuals.

Berinsfield, Wally Corner, 1 mile north, cemetery containing 111 individuals, male and female, weapons and jewellery dated 5th–7th centuries.

Brighthampton (SP 3803) 13 miles northwest.

Clifton Hampden 2 miles north, cemetery of 11 – 20 burials.

Cuddesdon (SP 5902) 5 miles north, 6 – 10 burials.

East Shefford (SU 3975) 15 miles southwest.

Frilford (SU 4496) 9 miles west.

Harwell (SU 4989) 7 miles southwest.

Long Wittenham (SU 5793) 2 miles west, cemetery of 234 burials.

Lowbury Hill (SU 5482) 8 miles south.

Milton (SU 4892) 6 miles west.

Radley, Barrow Hills (SU 5398) 5 miles northwest, over 400 buildings.

Sutton Courtney (SU 5093) 3 miles west, 11 – 40 buildings.

Wheatley (SP 5905) 7 miles north.

BRITAIN ALONE

The date usually accepted for the final withdrawal of Roman power is 409-410. According to the Greek historian Zosimus, the Roman administrators were not so much withdrawn as expelled by the Britons. This suggests that the Roman military presence had shrunk to a point where the British leaders were able to take such action. In 410 the emperor Honorius wrote a rescript to the British civitates, telling them to undertake their own defence. The fact that this communication was sent to the British tribal authorities and not to the Roman commander or civil governor confirms the absence of Roman authority. The British civitates continued to operate intact, but their leaders became the sovereign authority within the tribal area and resumed the status of kings, which they had possessed before the Roman conquest.

One of the sources of information about this period is the British cleric, Gildas, who wrote his treatise entitled *De excidio et conquesto Britanniae* – The Destruction and Conquest of Britain – in about 545. He describes how a *superbus tyrannus* came to lead the Britons. This expression can be rendered as supreme leader, but the word tyrannus also has the sense of a usurper. The superbus tyrannus could, therefore, designate the man who had usurped the supreme Roman power. There is evidence that a difference of opinion emerged among the Britons as to how the country should be run, and it seems that two schools of thought came into being: what may be termed a Roman party, favouring the restoration of the link with Rome, and a British party, presumably led by the *superbus tyrannus*, favouring the maintenance of independence.

The eviction of Roman officials by the Britons had an important consequence for the status of the Germanic settlements. It has already been explained that some of their leaders had entered into a treaty relationship with the Romans and had become allies of Rome. The treaty would have given legal authority to the senior Roman representative, the *dux* or the *vicarius*, for the overall control of the Germanic people settled in Britain. Upon the departure of the Roman officials the treaty obligations of the Germanic leaders would have lapsed. These leaders had entered into no treaty obligations to the tribal kings or to the *superbus tyrannus* and in the absence of Roman authority they were left free to do as they pleased. This situation may not have been foreseen by the Britons, but it meant that the British kings and the *superbus tyrannus* had no control over the Germanic enclaves, which became a law unto themselves.

The great Anglo-Saxon cleric and historian, the Venerable Bede of Jarrow, writing in 731, identified the *superbus tyrannus* with Vortigern, although Gildas never used the name. The *Historia Brittonum* reported that Vortigern was ruling in Britain in the consulship of Theodosius and Valentinian (dated to 425) and in the fourth year of his reign the Saxons came to Britain.[1] In this statement, the word Saxons is used in the wider sense given to it by classical and British writers as signifying Germanic people in general. It cannot be taken to refer to the first arrival of Anglo-Saxons in Britain, as it was shown above that a number of Germanic settlements were already in existence by this time. It is more likely to refer to an armed incursion of Saxon raiders. By this time the protection afforded by the Saxon Shore forts was no longer effective and raiders would be able to penetrate inland without opposition.

In 428 or 429 Bishop Germanus of Auxerre paid a visit to Britain in company with Bishop Lupus of Troyes. The purpose of the visit was to give advice to the British church about the problems caused by the Pelagian heresy. Bede tells that while the two bishops were in Britain the Britons were troubled by the invasion of a large combined force of Picts and Saxons. The Britons asked the bishops to help them and Germanus assumed command of the British army. The two sides came to confrontation in a valley and when the bishops led the Britons in three shouts of Alleluia, the enemy took fright and fled.[2] It is possible that the Saxons who joined forces with the Picts were the Saxons reported in the *Historia Brittonum*. In view of Bede's statement that the bishops restored peace to the island and overcame its enemies, it appears that

---

[1] Nennius, *Historia Brittonum*. para. 6.
[2] Bede, *Historia Ecclesiastica*. part I ch. 20.

the Pictish and Saxon raiders were driven back.

The Alleluia battle had shown that the Britons were unable to deal with the barbarian incursions without outside help. The two 'parties' within Britain were agreed on the need to appeal for outside help, but differed completely on how this was to be done. The 'Roman party' naturally looked to Rome, but this was anathema to the 'British party'. The *Historia Brittonum* stated that: 'Vortigern ruled in Britain and during his rule in Britain he was under pressure from fear of the Picts and Irish and of a Roman invasion and not least from dread of Ambrosius.'[3] The last-named was probably the leader of the 'Roman party'. It may be taken that, whereas Vortigern was stated to be king of the Britons, Ambrosius and his supporters did not acknowledge the authority of Vortigern and, like Gildas, regarded him as a usurper of the legitimate Roman power. Ambrosius became involved in hostilities with an unidentified Vitalinus at Wallop during the twelfth year of Vortigern's reign.[4] Wallop may be identical with the Wallop villages in Hampshire. Overlooking them are the earthworks of the hill fort of Danebury (SU 3237). If 425 is accepted as the date for the accession of Vortigern, the battle of Wallop can be dated 437.

Vortigern was in a serious dilemma. Although he had seized the supreme political power, he possessed no armed forces under his own direct control to enforce his decisions. Such forces were essential, so that he could deploy them against external threats or internal insurrection. The Roman *vicarius*, acting through or with the *dux Britanniarum*, had been able to deploy regular Roman troops or auxiliaries. But the only forces available to Vortigern were the British tribal levies, who were inexperienced, untrained and under the control of the tribal leaders.

Two Gallic chronicles give brief entries about the Saxons. One, compiled in 452, stated that Britain was subjected to the domination of the Saxons in the nineteenth year of Theodosius, computed to 441. The other, compiled in 511, reported that Britain passed into the power of the Saxons in the sixteenth year of the joint rule of Theodosius and Valentinian, computed to 440. None of this information can be confirmed

---

[3] Nennius, *Historia Brittonum*. para. 31.

[4] Gildas, *The Ruin of Britain*. paras. 19-23.

from other evidence.

In 445-6 Bishop Germanus made a second visit to Britain. The account of this visit given by Germanus's biographer, Constantius, is important for the light it throws upon conditions in southern Britain. The purpose of the visit, like the first visit, was to deal with the theological problem of the Pelagian heresy. Constantius tells that Germanus had dealings with British ecclesiastical and civil personalities. Although Germanus had become involved in a Saxon and Pictish raid during his first visit, there is nothing to suggest that hostilities involving the pagan Saxons, Picts or Irish were taking place during his second visit. A journey through a war-stricken area would surely have been mentioned. The account of Germanus's second visit throws serious doubt upon the entries in the Gallic Chronicles that Britain was in the power of the Saxons by 440 or 441.

Gildas reported that the Britons continued to be so seriously harassed by the barbarians that finally they 'sent off a letter again, this time to the Roman commander Aetius in the following terms: "To Aetius, thrice consul: the groans of the British." ' Further on came this complaint: 'The barbarians push us back to the sea, the sea pushes us back to the barbarians: between these two kinds of death we are either drowned or slaughtered.' But they got no help in return. Aetius had been appointed consul for the third time in 446 and for the fourth time in 454. The letter from the Britons must have been sent some time between these dates, presumably by Ambrosius and members of the 'Roman party'. In Bede's account of this letter, he added that the Britons received no help because Aetius was engaged against Attila, king of the Huns. This was an accurate statement of the military situation in Europe at the time. Gildas reported that the invasions continued until the Britons 'convened a council to decide the best and soundest way to counter the brutal and repeated invasions and plunderings by the peoples I have mentioned. Then all the members of the council, together with the proud tyrant, were struck blind: the guard – or rather the method of destruction – they devised for our land was that the ferocious Saxons (name not to be spoken!), hated by man and God, should be let into the island like wolves into the fold, to beat back the peoples of the north. Nothing more destructive, nothing more bitter has ever befallen the land. How utter the blindness of their minds! How desperate and crass the stupidity! Of their own free will they invited under the same roof a people whom they feared worse than death.' The composition of the council is not stated, but it seems to have consisted of the British tribal leaders. Although Gildas mentions only the threat from the invaders in the north and west, the *Historia Brittonum* had stated that Vortigern feared not only the Picts and Scots, but also an invasion by the Romans. After the council Vortigern had the authority to engage a force of Germanic mercenaries, with the results described in the following chapter.

PART 2

THE FOUNDING OF THE KENTISH, SAXON AND ANGLIAN KINGDOMS

THE ARRIVAL OF HENGIST

Gildas continued his narrative as follows: 'Then a pack of cubs burst forth from the lair of the barbarian lioness, coming in three keels, as they call warships in their language . . . On the orders of the ill-fated tyrant, they first of all fixed their dreadful claws on the east side of the island, ostensibly to fight for our country.' The Historia Brittonum, expanded upon the event: 'Then came three keels, driven into exile from Germany. In them were the brothers Horsa and Hengist . . . Vortigern welcomed them and handed over to them the island that in their language is called Thanet, in British Ruoihm.'[1] This source then gave a date which is erroneous and cannot be used. The use of Anglo-Saxon words – keels and Thanet – indicates that both sources were using some Anglo-Saxon information.

Bede based his version upon Gildas, but also supplied an indication of the time scale. 'In the year of our Lord's incarnation 449, Marcian became emperor along with Valentinian, the 46th from Augustus, and ruled for seven years. Then the nation of the Angles or Saxons, being invited by the aforesaid king, arrived in Britain with three warships, and received by the order of the same king a place of settlement in the eastern part of the island, as if they were to fight on behalf of the country, but really intending to conquer it.'[2] He repeated the same information in the chronological summary in his final chapter. The Anglo-Saxon Chronicle gave the same information as Bede, but added that Hengist and Horsa landed at Ebbsfleet (TR 3362) on the Isle of Thanet.

The year 449 has conventionally come to be accepted as the actual date for the arrival of Hengist and Horsa, but none of the early sources actually gives this date. On the authority of Bede, there is a period of seven years 449-456 during the reign of the emperor Marcian. In 449

---

[1] Nennius, *Historia Brittonum*. para. 31.

[2] Bede, *Historia Ecclesiastica*. part I ch. 15.

Aetius was still assembling a force of Roman and allied troops strong enough to block the progress of Attila and his Huns. Aetius was hard pressed and needed every man. In this year there was no possibility of the return of Roman troops to Britain. But in 451 events moved to a climax when the Huns entered Gaul and came into confrontation with Aetius's combined forces. A major battle took place on the Catalaunian Fields (near Chalons) and although Attila was not defeated his army was diverted from Gaul. The strategic situation in Gaul was transformed by the removal of the threat from the east. The significance of the battle was probably not lost on Vortigern. He must have known that Ambrosius and his followers were seeking to persuade Aetius to send a military force back to Britain. The freedom from Roman rule which they had enjoyed for forty years would suddenly have become in immediate jeopardy. It was a vital matter about which he and the British kings could take no chances. It could have been this as much as the threat from the north which caused them to meet in council and agree unanimously to recruit professional mercenaries capable of engaging Roman troops in battle. For these reasons, the year 451 seems the most likely date for the arrival of Hengist and Horsa.

The sources quoted above agree that Hengist arrived with a small group of only three boats. The boats of the period had only a limited capacity and Hengist's boats were probably similar to the longboat discovered at Nydam near Schleswig. Built of oak, it was seventy-seven feet long and less than eleven feet wide. It had neither sail nor mast, but was propelled by fifteen oars on each side. If a complement of two men to each oar is assumed, the total crew of such a ship would be about sixty men. On that basis, Hengist's party could have amounted to some 180-200 men, consisting of Hengist's counsellors, personal retinue and body-guard. They represented the immediate response to the invitation by Vortigern and were admitted only to the Isle of Thanet, which at this time was a genuine island separated from the mainland by the river Wantsum. Ebbsfleet, where Hengist is stated to have landed, could have been the normal place for landing on Thanet, as it was here that Augustine arrived in 598. Hengist with this three boats had arrived to discuss Vortigern's proposal that they should enter his service as mercenary soldiers.

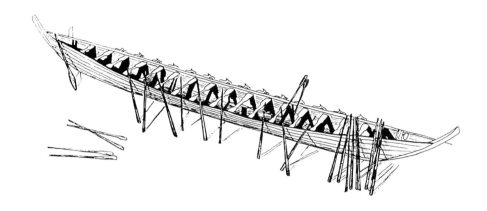

Reconstruction of the Nydam Boat.

The Historia Brittonum describes Hengist as: 'experienced, shrewd and skilful' and portrays him as outwitting Vortigern. It quotes Hengist as saying, presumably during the negotiations on the Isle of Thanet: 'We are few, if you wish we can send home for more men, to raise a larger number to fight for you and your people.' The two men finally came to an agreement and 'envoys were sent across the sea, and returned with sixteen keels full of picked men.'[3] They could have transported about 960 men.

There is no direct evidence to show how this force was to be utilised, but an important element in the situation was the presence of the Roman fort of Rutupiae at Richborough. At the time it stood on a small island in the middle of the river Wantsum, two miles south of Ebbsfleet. It was the main base from which the Emperor Claudius launched his assault in 43 A.D. Forty years later the Romans erected a tall marble arch within the base as a memorial to their successful invasion campaign. Rutupiae became in effect the Gateway to Britain and the network of Roman roads started there. During the third century, a strong stone-built fort was erected on the site, one of the forts of the Saxon shore. The extensive ruins of this fort and the foundations of the arch are still to be seen at Richborough. Vortigern knew that if Aetius wished to send Roman troops back to Britain he would first need to re-

---

[3] Nennius, *Historia Brittonum*. para. 37.

occupy Rutupiae. For Vortigern it was vital to prevent this by making its defences impregnable. Vortigern's agreement with Hengist gave him professional soldiers, whom he could deploy to ensure the proper defence of Rutupiae.

THE SETTLEMENT IN KENT

The Historia Brittonum reported that in one of the sixteen ships 'came Hengist's daughter, a beautiful and very handsome girl. When the keels had arrived, Hengist held a banquet for Vortigern, and his men and his interpreter, whose name was Ceretic, and he told the girl to serve them wine and spirits. They all got exceedingly drunk. When they were drinking, Satan entered into Vortigern's heart, and made him love the girl. Through his interpreter he asked her father for her hand, saying, "Ask of me what you will, even to the half of my kingdom". Hengist took counsel with the elders from the island Oghgul (unidentified) to decide what they should ask of the king for the girl, and they all agreed to ask for the country that in their language is called Canturguoralen, in ours Kent. So he granted it to them, although Gwyrangon was ruling in Kent and did not know that his kingdom was being handed over to the heathens and that he himself given secretly into their power on his own. So the girl was given in marriage to Vortigern and he slept with her and loved her deeply.'

'Hengist said to Vortigern, "I am your father and will be your adviser. Never ignore my advice and you will never fear conquest by any man or any people, for my people are strong. I will invite my son and his cousin to fight against the Irish (Scotti), for they are fine warriors. Give them lands in the north about the Wall that is called Guaul". So he told him to invite them, and he invited Octha and Ebissa, with forty keels. They sailed round the Picts and wasted the Orkney Islands, and came and occupied many districts beyond the Frenessican Sea, as far as the borders of the Picts.'[1]

On the basis on this evidence, a fleet of forty ships, transporting a force of some 2,400 warriors under the joint command of Hengist's son and nephew (perhaps the son of Horsa), sailed up the east coast to the

---

[1] Nennius, *Historia Brittonum.* para. 38.

Orkney islands, which they sacked, and then south along the west coast. The Frenessican Sea is unidentified, but could be the Solway Firth. One of their centres, perhaps their main centre, was at Dumfries, the name of which means the fortress of the Frisians.

Some historians are sceptical of the story about Hengist's daughter, but whether it is regarded as historical fact or fiction, it represents the British view that Hengist gained control of the kingdom of Kent by subterfuge. The British source alleges that Vortigern used his supreme power as overlord to instal Hengist as king of Kent over the existing British incumbent. This may seem a remarkable action, but there would have been good strategic sense for it. The military resources of the local British king would have consisted of untrained tribal levies, which would have been incapable of offering effective resistance to the Roman legions if they attempted to land at Rutupiae. By installing Hengist as king of Kent, Vortigern gave him a personal stake in the defence of the gateway to Britain. British sovereignty was unimpaired, as Vortigern remained as supreme overlord.

The defence against the Picts and Scotti was a second priority and responsibility for this was delegated to Hengist's son and nephew, who must have been very young and without experience. The decision to deploy a force of mercenaries to the Solway area was strategically sound. The withdrawal of Roman troops had left the defences of the north weakened and the Picts and Scotti were taking full advantage of the changed military situation. Cunedag's descendants were defending the Welsh and northwestern coasts from their base at Chester, but the Solway Firth was beyond their effective range. This waterway was offering an easy route for the Scotti sailing from Ulster to penetrate into Britain. The mercenary force at Dumfries was well based to prevent this and also to interdict Pictish raids in the western sector.

Bede reported that Hengist's men 'engaged with the enemy, who had come from the north to give battle and the Saxons had the victory. When this was announced in their homeland, as well as the fertility of the island and the cowardice of the Britons, a more considerable fleet was quickly sent over, bringing a stronger force of armed men, which added to the band sent before, made up an invincible army. The newcomers received by the gift of the Britons a place to inhabit among them, on

40

condition that they should wage war against their adversaries for the peace and security of the country, and the Britons were to give them the pay due to soldiers. They came from three very powerful tribes of the Germans, namely the Saxons, the Angles and the Jutes. From the stock of the Jutes are the people of Kent and the people of Wight, that is, the race with holds the Isle of Wight, and that which in the province of the West Saxons is to this day called the nation of the Jutes, situated opposite that same Isle of Wight. From the Saxons, that is, from the region which now is called that of the Old Saxons, came the East Saxons, the South Saxons, the West Saxons. Further, from the Angles, that is, from the country which is called Angulus and which from that time until today is said to have remained deserted between the provinces of the Jutes and the Saxons, are sprung the East Angles, the Middle Angles, the Mercians, the whole race of the Northumbrians, that is, of those people who dwell north of the river Humber, and the other peoples of the Angles.'[2] It was shown in an earlier chapter that by the time of Hengist's arrival groups of Anglo-Saxons were already settled in scattered enclaves throughout the eastern half of the country south of the Wall. Since Roman times there may well have been some movement of individuals and small groups across the North Sea, as a result of which the enclaves may have been able to expand. Although early sources provide considerable detailed evidence about Hengist and his mercenaries, their activity is shown to have been confined to Kent and the Solway area. There is no evidence to show that fresh mercenary troops arrived north of the Thames in the mid-fifth century and were given land by the Britons to settle there. The sources show that Vortigern and Hengist had deployed the mercenaries to the areas under immediate threat: Kent and Solway.

Bede stated that the people settled in Kent were Jutes. This is generally accepted in view of the strong archaeological evidence for the presence of Jutish people in Kent at this period. It is, however, not known how a people from distant Jutland came to settle in Kent. A possible explanation is to be found in a passage of the epic poem Beowulf, in which Beowulf's followers are told of the exploits of earlier

---

[2] Bede, *Historia Ecclesiastica.* part I ch. 15.

heroes. They are told about a Dane called Hengest, who was a thegn of the Danish king and accompanied him on a visit to Finn, king of the Frisians. During the visit fighting broke out between the Danes and Finn's retainers, who included a contingent of Jutes. The Danish king was killed and Hengest took over leadership of the Danes. Although peace was restored Hengest plotted revenge and subsequently revolted against Finn and slew him. This story appears more legendary than factual, but there is a case for equating the Hengest in the Beowulf story with the Hengist who migrated to Kent. The episode in Beowulf places Hengist and his Jutes in an area where Vortigern could have easily made contact with them. If Hengist's continental base was in Frisia, this would explain the reference to islands (i.e. the Frisian islands) in the Historia Brittonum. It would also explain why Hengist's northern base near the Wall became known as the Fortress of the Frisians.

THE WAR IN KENT

After a while the accord between Hengist and Vortigern came under strain. An important fact is that major changes were taking place in the military situation in Europe. Attila died in 453 and Aetius was murdered in 454. In Italy an internal struggle was raging for control of the imperial government. Any possibility of a return of Roman troops to Britain had completely disappeared. Hengist's army in Kent had served its purpose for Vortigern and had become an expensive embarrassment to the Britons. Gildas stated that the barbarians 'again complained that their monthly allowance was insufficient, purposely giving a false colour to individual incidents, and swore that they would break their agreement and plunder the whole island unless more lavish payment were heaped on them. There was no delay: they put their threats into immediate effect.'[1] William of Malmesbury (writing in the twelfth century) gives the following account of how the treaty came to an end: 'Vortimer, the son of Vortigern, thinking it unnecessary longer to dissemble that he saw himself and his Britons circumvented by the craft of the Angles, turned his thought to their expulsion and stimulated his father to the same attempt. At his suggestion, the truce was broken seven years after their arrival.'[2]

The Anglo-Saxon Chronicle gives a date of 455 for the first battle between Hengist and the Britons. 'Hengist and Horsa fought against King Vortigern at the place which is called Aegelesthrep, and his brother Horsa was killed there; and after that Hengist and his son Aesc succeeded to the kingdom.' Aegelesthrep is usually taken to be identical with modern Aylesford (TQ 7359). The next battle was reported in the annal for 456. 'Hengist and his son Aesc fought against the Britons in the place which is called Creacanford and killed 4,000 men; and the Britons then deserted Kent and fled with great fear to London.'

---

[1] Gildas, *The Ruin of Britain*. para. 23.

[2] Malmesbury, *The Kings before the Norman Conquest*. para. 8.

Creacanford is modern Crayford (TQ 5175). No further battles are reported until the annal for 465. 'Hengist and Aesc fought against the Britons near Wippedesfleot, and there slew twelve British chiefs, and a thegn of theirs was slain there whose name was Wipped.' A fourth battle was reported in 473, when 'Hengist and Aesc fought against the Britons and captured countless spoils and the Britons fled from the English as from fire.'

The Historia Brittonum provides a more detailed account of the war in Kent as seen from the British side, but provides no dates. 'Vortigern's son Vortimer fought vigorously against Hengist and Horsa and their people, and expelled them as far as the aforesaid island called Thanet, and there three times shut them up and besieged them, attacking, threatening and terrifying them. So they sent envoys overseas to Germany to summon keels with a vast number of fighting men. And afterwards they used to fight against the kings of our nation, sometimes victoriously advancing their frontiers, sometimes being defeated and expelled. Vortimer fought four keen battles against them. The first battle was on the river Darenth. The second battle was at the ford called Episford in their language, *Rhyd yr afael* in ours, and there fell Horsa and also Vortigern's son Cateyrn. The third battle was fought in the open country by the Inscribed Stone on the Gallic Sea. The barbarians were beaten and he was victorious. They fled to their keels and were drowned as they clambered aboard them like women. But Vortimer soon after died. Before he died he told his followers to set his tomb by the coast, in the port from which (the English) had departed, saying, "I entrust it to you. Wherever else they may hold a British port or may have settled, they will never again live in this land".[3] No details were provided about the fourth battle.

It will be seen that there is a strong similarity between the four battles reported by the Anglo-Saxon Chronicle and the four battles reported by the Historia Brittonum. The main difference between the two sources is that the first two battles have been transposed. The correct chronological sequence seems to be that given in the Anglo-Saxon Chronicle. By merging the information provided by the two chronicles it

---

[3] Nennius, *Historia Brittonum*. paras. 43-4.

is possible to gain a fuller picture of the war in Kent. The battle of Aegelesthrep is clearly identical with the battle of *Rhyd yr afael*. Aylesford stands where the pre-historic trackway along the crest of the North Downs crosses the river Medway, some twenty-five miles west of Canterbury. The military situation appears to be that Vortimer was leading his army from the west along the crest of the North Downs towards eastern Kent, which was held by Hengist and his forces, but was defeated by them at the river crossing. It is to be noted that upon the death of Horsa, his place as joint leader was taken by Hengist's son Aesc. He was also known as Octha and had shared command of the contingent, which had been sent north to fight off the Picts and Scots.

The battle on the river Darenth probably formed part of the same activity as the battle at Crayford. The Roman road from Canterbury to London (Watling Street) crosses the river Darenth at Dartford and two miles further west it crosses the river Cray at Crayford. The battle was fought for the possession of these two river crossings. Hengist's victory left him master of all of Kent as far as Crayford. The road was open to London, but there is no evidence that he attempted to capture the city.

Evidence from other sources supports the evidence of a major British defeat in Kent at about this time. In his description of the tribulations of the Britons, Gildas stated that some made for lands beyond the sea. Gaulish sources reported the arrival of 12,000 British fighting men in northern and central Gaul during the period 458-460. A bishop of the British was also reported to be in Gaul in 461. The co-incidence of the arrival of such a large number of British fighting men in Gaul and the major defeat of a British army in Kent suggests that the former was a consequence of the latter.

According to the time-scale of the Anglo-Saxon Chronicle there was no further major military activity until the third battle in 465. The Chronicle did not represent the battle of Wippedesfleot as a victory for Hengist, while the Historia Brittonum provided enough detail to show that it was a decisive victory for the Britons. Some useful clues are provided for the location of this battle. It involved the capture of a port, from which the barbarians were expelled. Vortimer, as we have seen, instructed his followers that he was to be buried there, so that the barbarians should not regain it, even if they still held other ports. This port was on the coast, by the Inscribed Stone on the shore of the Gallic Sea. The Latin *portus* was the word used to refer to the forts of the Saxon Shore. The full names of Richborough, Lympne and Portchester were Rutupiae Portus, Portus Lemanis and Portus Adurni. Although we have come to think of them primarily as fortresses, because of their massive stone defences, they were in fact fortified ports, where warships and other ships had a defended harbour. This passage shows that the forts of the Saxon Shore were involved in the fighting and that Vortimer's troops had succeeded in recapturing one of them from the barbarians. The mention of the Inscribed Stone confirms that a Roman structure was involved. The Historia Brittonum stated explicitly that Vortimer drove Hengist's army as far as the Isle of Thanet, where they were shut up and besieged. Two of the Saxon Shore forts stand opposite the Isle of Thanet: Regulbium (Reculver) and Rutupiae (Richborough). Of these only the latter stands on the shore of the Gallic Sea. Rutupiae was the port where the third battle took place.

The Anglo-Saxon Chronicle called the site Wippedesfleot, but this word has been lost as a full name. The second part fleot, modern fleet, has the meaning of a shallow tidal passage or creek and survives in the name Ebbsfleet, only a mile from Richborough. According to tradition, St Augustine crossed from the Isle of Thanet to mainland Kent at Richborough. He was received there by King Aethelberht and to mark the spot a chapel, the remains of which may still be seen, was erected in the northeast corner of the fort and given the name St Augustine's in Fleet. To this day the farm adjoining the Richborough fort is called Fleet Farm. It is likely that Wippedesfleot was the part of the river Wantsum adjoining Rutupiae, where Hengist's men fled to their boats and were drowned as they did so.

This battle showed a remarkable turn-about in the military situation since the British disaster at Crayford. Credit for the British success at Richborough must go to Vortimer. It may be presumed that he had been able to raise a new British army, which overpowered Hengist's army and drove it along Watling Street from Crayford past Canterbury to Richborough. Hengist lost his foothold in mainland Kent and for a while his very survival in Britain depended on his defence of the Isle of Thanet. For a number of years (from 465 to 473 according to the Anglo-

46

Saxon Chronicle) both sides would have attempted to establish a bridgehead on the opposite bank of the river Wantsum. Vortimer three times shut them up there. Eventually the fourth battle took place, as a result of which Hengist's army was able to re-establish itself on the Kentish mainland.

The Historia Brittonum continued: "The barbarians returned in force, for Vortigern was their friend, because of his wife, and none was resolute to drive them out . . . So it came to pass after the death of Vortimer, son of king Vortigern, and after the return of Hengest and his hosts, they instigated a treacherous plan to trick Vortigern and his army. They sent envoys to ask for peace and make a permanent treaty. Vortigern called a council of his elders to examine what they should do. Ultimately one opinion prevailed with all, that they should make peace. The envoys went back, and the conference was convened, where the two sides, British and Saxons, should meet, unarmed, to confirm the treaty. But Hengist told all his followers to hide their daggers under their feet in their shoes, saying, "When I call out to you and say Draw your knives, take your daggers from your shoes and fall upon them and stand firm against them. But do not kill the king; keep him alive, for my daughter's sake, whom I wedded to him, for it is better for us that he be ransomed from us". So the conference assembled, and the Saxons, friendly in their words, but wolfish in heart and deed, sat down, like allies, man beside man. Hengist cried out as he had said, and all the three hundred seniors of king Vortigern were murdered, and the king alone was taken and held prisoner. To save his life, he ceded several districts, namely Essex and Sussex, together with Middlesex and other districts that they chose and designated.'[4]

This incident is usually considered legendary, rather than a valid historical event. In this passage the chronicler claims that soon after Hengist had re-established his position on the Kentish mainland as a result of the fourth battle, he set about making plans to extend his domain from Kent into the adjoining areas to the north, south and west. Again the chronicler attributes the loss of British territory not to military defeat, but to treachery by Hengist. By the murder of so many

---

[4] Nennius, *Historia Brittonum*. paras. 45-6.

British leaders, Hengist was allegedly seeking to weaken the British leadership to such an extent that the neighbouring British kingdoms would submit peacefully to his dominion.

The early sources provide no evidence of further fighting in Kent after 473 and Hengist's hold on Kent was apparently secure. The Chronicle states in its annal for 488 that Aesc succeeded to the kingdom of Kent, presumably on the death of Hengist. There is a certain confusion among the early sources about the name of Hengist's successor. Bede makes an important statement. Spelling was not standardised and he spells the name as Oisc and adds that it was the family name (cognomen) of Oeric, who was the son at Hengist. As Oisc was the family name, the kings of Kent, who were descended from Oeric, were known as the Oiscings.[5] On this evidence it appears that the activity attributed to Aesc by the chronicler was in fact carried out by Oeric, whose full name would be Oeric Oisc or alternatively spelt Aeric Aesc. Oeric is an early form of the Scandinavian name Eric, which is consistent with all the other evidence about the Jutish or Danish origin of Hengist. In connection with these events, the Historia Brittonum contains no mention of Aesc, Oisc or Oeric, but in their place has the name Octha, who is stated to be the son of Hengist. It added that upon the death of Hengist (no date given), his son Octha came from the north of Britain to Kent and that the kings of Kent are sprung from him. The name Octha is identified by Bede as the name of Oeric's son and most of the early sources agree with this. The Historia Brittonum has apparently confused Octha with his father Oeric.

On Bede's evidence the names Oeric and Octha are the personal or given names of two members of the Aesc/Oisc family. None of the early sources has explained how Hengist and Horsa acquired their distinctive names. In the Germanic languages, Hengist means a stallion and Horsa means a horse or mare. Unlike Oeric and Octha these do not appear to be valid personal names, but they could be *noms de guerre,* based on the emblems portrayed on their war banners. The tradition is so strong that a horse continues to be the emblem of the county of Kent.

---

[5] Bede, *Historia Ecclesiastica.* part II ch. 5.

THE UPRISING BY THE GERMANIC ENCLAVES

The evidence so far expounded concerns fighting only in Kent. Before 477 the Anglo-Saxon Chronicle contains no reports of combat outside Kent, but according to Gildas, fighting spread throughout the country. His graphic description is as follows: 'In just punishment for the crimes that had gone before, a fire heaped up and nurtured by the hand of the impious easterners spread from sea to sea. It devastated town and country round about, and, once it was alight, it did not die down until it had burned almost the whole surface of the island and was licking the western ocean with its fierce red tongue . . . All the major towns were laid low by the repeated battering of enemy rams; laid low, too, all the inhabitants – church leaders, priests and people alike, as the swords glinted all around and the flames crackled. It was a sad sight. In the middle of the squares the foundation-stones of high walls and towers that had been torn from their lofty base, holy altars, fragments of corpses, covered (as it were) with a purple crust of congealed blood, looked as though they had been mixed up in some dreadful wine-press. There was no burial to be had except in the ruins of houses or the bellies of beasts and birds . . . So a number of the wretched survivors were caught in the mountains and butchered wholesale. Others, their spirit broken by hunger, went to surrender to the enemy; they were fated to be slaves for ever, if indeed they were not killed straight away, the highest boon. Others made for lands beyond the sea . . . Others held out, though not without fear, in their own land, trusting their lives with constant foreboding to the high hills, steep, menacing and fortified, to the densest forests, and to the cliffs of the sea-coast.'[1]

The evidence on the war in Kent showed that Hengist's army did not proceed further west than Crayford. They cannot, therefore, be held responsible for the widespread havoc described by Gildas. In that case, who were the plunderers who ravaged the country? It was reported

---

[1] Gildas, *The Ruin of Britain*. paras. 24-5.

above that when the Romans departed they left behind a number of settlements occupied by the families of Germanic mercenary soldiers. They were directly subordinate to the Roman power, and after its removal they were under no obligation to recognise the authority of Vortigern or any of the British tribal kings, and had become a law unto themselves. With the ending of subventions from the Roman authorities they could have been experiencing genuine hardship. Pillaging at the expense of the Britons would help to make good some of their shortages.

It appears likely that when fighting broke out in Kent this triggered a general uprising of the people in the Germanic settlements, who then proceeded to sack British towns and cities. These settlements were usually located near Roman military highways, and were well placed to despatch raiding parties far and wide throughout Britain. It is not known if there had been any contact between the settlements and Hengist. The uprising could have been entirely spontaneous or collusion could have taken place. In either case, Gildas had the impression that the fighting by the newcomers and the sacking of the towns was all part of the same calamity. From the investigations of archaeologists it has become apparent that some of the Roman cities had, indeed, been sacked in the post-Roman period. In some cases, as in London, Gloucester and Bath, the destruction was so extensive that the original Roman street plan was to a great extent obliterated.

'After a time, when the cruel plunderers had gone home, God gave strength to the survivors.' Gildas's statement shows that the purpose of the barbarians was the acquisition of plunder, not the conquest of land for settlement. The raiders returned with their plunder to the settlement areas in the east. The leader of the Britons 'was Ambrosius Aurelianus, a gentleman who, perhaps alone of the Romans, had survived the shock of this notable storm; certainly his parents, who had worn the purple, were slain in it.' The wearing of the purple was a mark of the emperor. The possibility arises that Ambrosius Aurelianus was identical with or related to the Ambrosius who fought Vitalinus in 437 at the battle of Wollop and was feared by Vortigern. Under Ambrosius Aurelianus 'our people regained their strength and challenged the victors to battle. The Lord assented and the battle went their way. From then on victory went now to our countrymen, now to their enemies.'[2] The *Historia Brittonum* confirmed that Ambrosius was the great king among all the kings of the British.[3] William of Malmesbury's opinion was that the Britons 'would have perished altogether, had not Ambrosius, the sole survivor of the Romans, who became monarch after Vortigern, quelled the presumptuous barbarians by the powerful aid of the warlike Arthur.'[4] The name of Ambrosius has been preserved in Welsh tradition in the modern form Emrys.

---

[2] Gildas, *The Ruin of Britain.* paras. 25-6.

[3] Nennius, *Historia Brittonum.* para. 48.

[4] Malmesbury, *The Kings before the Norman Conquest.* para. 8.

HE CONQUEST OF SUSSEX

After 473, the Anglo-Saxon Chronicle contains no further entries about the fighting in Kent and the scene of military activity shifts to the south coast. The annal for 477 reports the arrival of Aelle with his sons Cymen, Wlencing and Cissa in three ships at Cymenesora, where they fought the Britons and drove them into the forest called Andredeslea. The last-named was the Sussex Weald. Cymenesora has been identified with a place known as the Owers, now covered by the sea south of Selsey Bill. The Anglo-Saxon word *ora* has the meaning of a bank or beach and the name Owers is derived from it. It would have been the spot where Aelle's party made landfall and beached their boats. Cymenesora was located in the western part of the *civitas* created by the Romans for their loyal ally, King Cogidubnus, out of the territory of the British tribe of the Atrebates. The people of the *civitas* were known as the Regnenses. Their capital was at Noviomagus Regnensium, modern Chichester, only eight miles from Cymenesora. From the entry in the Chronicle it is clear that there was no question of the Britons ceding their territory peacefully to Aelle.

The next entry for Aelle occurs in the annal for 485, which reported that he fought the Welsh near Mearcredesburna. This place is unidentified, but the word has the sense of a frontier stream. It may be inferred that it was a stream which separate two territories, that the Saxons were proceeding from one territory to another and that the defenders of the second territory were trying to prevent them crossing the stream and gaining entry to their territory. The Saxons appear to have been advancing along the coastal strip in an easterly direction. The stream where this battle took place was probably one of the streams which flow south from the South Downs into the sea.

In the annal for 491, the chronicler reported that Aelle and Cissa besieged Andredesceaster and killed all inside, with not a single Briton left alive. Andredesceaster is the Roman fort of Anderida (or Anderita) at modern Pevensey (TQ 6504), one of the forts of the Saxon Shore. The

Britons put it to the use for which it was intended, when the Romans built it in about 340, for defence against the Saxons. It is different from the other Saxon Shore forts. They have a geometrical site-plan, (quadrilateral or pentagonal), whereas Anderida has an irregular site-plan, conforming to the shape of the promontory on which it stood. Its walls (thirty feet high and twelve feet thick) stood higher and the enclosed area of about ten acres was larger. The water level at Pevensey has changed since Roman times. The promontory on which the fort stands was originally surrounded on three sides by the sea, which gave it good natural protection. Access to the mainland was provided by the west gate, which was guarded by two massive bastions. North of the fort was a large estuary, now completely dry land, which could be used by ships of the Roman fleet, the Classis Britannica. Access to the harbour was given by the east gate.

Henry of Huntingdon, writing in the twelfth century (700 years later), provided a detailed account of the fighting: 'Aelle laid siege to Andredesceaster, a strongly fortified town. The Britons swarmed together like wasps, assailing the besiegers by daily ambuscades and nocturnal sallies. There was neither day nor night in which some new alarm did not harass the minds of the Saxons; but the more they were provoked, the more vigorously they pressed the siege. Whenever they advanced to the assault of the town, the Britons from without falling on their rear with their archers and slingers drew the pagans away from the walls to resist their own attack, which the Britons, lighter of foot, avoided by taking refuge in the woods; and when they turned again to assault the town, again the Britons hung on their rear. The Saxons were for some time harassed by these manoeuvres, till, having lost a great number of men, they divided their army into two bodies, one of which carried on the siege, while the other repelled the attacks from without. After this the Britons were so reduced by continual famine that they were unable any longer to withstand the force of the besiegers, so that they all fell by the edge of the sword, with their women and children, not one escaping alive.' It is not known how factual this account is; it has a degree of plausibility and Henry may have had access to sources now lost. His use of the word 'pagans' to refer to the Saxons indicates that some of his information came from a British source. If so, it is noteworthy that it agrees with the Anglo-Saxon chronicler that the Britons within the fortress were slaughtered to the last man, woman and child. According to this report the battle took the form of a siege, with an external British force trying to drive off the Saxon besiegers. This is the second of the Saxon shore forts shown to have been used in the fighting between Britons and the Germanic invaders.

Militarily, the capture of Andredesceaster was important for the Saxons, as it gave them possession of the large defended harbour which could be used for the reception of vessels bringing reinforcements from Old Saxony. No further battles are reported and serious resistance by the Britons cannot have continued long after 491. Politically, the British kingdom of the Regnenses would have been replaced by the kingdom of the South Saxons. Bede described Aelle as king of the South Saxons. The fate of the tribal centre at Noviomagus is not reported. By 894 it was known as Cissaceaster, having apparently been renamed after Aelle's son Cissa. The reason for this can only be conjectured: perhaps it was Cissa who captured it; perhaps he became king and made it his capital.

ARTHUR'S EARLY VICTORIES

In reporting the death of Hengist, the *Historia Brittonum* stated: 'Then Arthur fought against them in those days, together with the kings of the British; but he was their leader in battle.' The source provided details of the twelve battles fought by Arthur and added: 'He was victorious in all his campaigns.' His first six battles were given as follows: 'The first battle was at the mouth of the river called Glein. The second, the third, the fourth and the fifth were on another river called Dubglas, which is in the country of Linnuis. The sixth battle was on the river called Bassas.'[1] None of the place-names quoted can be readily identified, but it will be noted that all three locations were on the banks of rivers. It was at the mouths of rivers and estuaries that the Romans had built the Saxon shore forts. It is apparent that the river Dubglas played a key role in Arthur's early battles as four consecutive battles were fought on its banks. 'Dubglas' is of Celtic origin and has the literal meaning Blackwater, which is the name of one of the main rivers in Essex. It has a long and wide estuary and it must be significant that on the southern shore of its estuary stood the Saxon shore fort Othona, known to the Saxons as Ythancaestir and located near modern Bradwell-on-Sea (TR 0308). Little of the fort remains today to be seen. The seaward side has disappeared and only part of one side is exposed. The walls were originally fourteen feet thick. As evidence has been set out to show that two of the Saxon shore forts, Rutupiae and Anderida, were involved in the fighting between Britons and the invaders, it is likely that other forts in the combat area also became similarly involved. There is, therefore, a distinct possibility that the river Dubglas is identical with the river Blackwater in Essex and that Arthur fought four battles around the fort of Othona.

The value of Othona to the Britons was that it was a stronghold which not only gave a place of refuge for the local population, but also

---

[1] Nennius, *Historia Brittonum*. para. 56.

enabled them to extend defence to the surrounding area. For the invaders, Othona would have been a bridgehead from which to launch their attack inland and also a fortified harbour for the protection of their ships. From this British source, it is apparent that the Saxons had launched an attack on the area north of the Thames, but were repeatedly defeated by the Britons under Arthur's leadership. The silence of the Anglo-Saxon Chronicle on activity in Essex at this time may be due not only to the natural reluctance to record defeats, but also to the fact that the Saxon participants, who would have remembered and recorded it, were either killed or drowned or driven back across the sea. Subsequent evidence set out in a later chapter is consistent with the foregoing by showing that the East Saxons were unable to establish their kingdom until the mid-sixth century.

Campaigns in the Southeast 455-491.

The only indication of the timing of Arthur's battles is that they started at about the time of Hengist's death, probably 488. It was at this time that Aelle was conducting a successful campaign along the south coast. The possibility arises, therefore, that at about the time when Aelle was

56

attacking Anderida, Arthur was engaged at Othona. The scenario at Othona would have been similar to that at Anderida: the British families in the area had taken refuge in the fort, which was besieged by the Saxon invaders. Four times Arthur drove off the siege force and brought relief to the fort's defenders.

It is apparent from the foregoing that the war between the Britons and the invaders had spread from Kent into the neighbouring areas to the north and south. This was the strategic plan attributed to Hengist in the report about his treachery at the conference with British leaders in or about 473. This conference is generally considered legendary rather than historic, but in either case the combined evidence from British and Anglo-Saxon sources indicates that a war plan for the conquest of Sussex and Essex was being implemented. The author of this would surely have been Hengist.

During the 480s, there would have been three invading armies, one each in Kent, Sussex and Essex, each under its own commander. Additionally, there was still the Kentish contingent in the area of Hadrian's Wall. Supreme command would have been in the hands of Hengist, who acted as the counterpart of Ambrosius Aurelianus, the British supremo. But Hengist had become an old man, and when he died in 488 the war was still raging and there would have been an urgent need for a successor to take over the supreme command.

At about this time documents start to report a new supreme post, spelt variously as Brytenwalda, Bretenanwealda, Brytenwealda or Bretwalda. The first element Bryten or Breten probably refers to Britons or Britain. The second element is derived from the Anglo-Saxon verb *wieldan*, meaning to have power over, control, tame, subdue, conquer, seize; it is the predecessor of the modern English verb to wield. Thus the meaning was probably 'conqueror of the Britons'. Upon the death of Hengist, Aelle was the most experienced and most successful war leader on the Saxon side. He had won two victories against the Britons at Cymenesora in 477 and at Mearcredesburna in 485, whereas the Saxon attacks against Othona at the mouth of the river Blackwater were repeatedly repelled by Arthur. Aelle was. therefore, appointed to succeed Hengist as supreme commander with the newly invented title Bretwalda. After Aelle there were seven other holders of the post of Bretwalda, each of whom was also king of one of the Anglo-Saxon kingdoms.

THE ARRIVAL OF THE WEST SAXONS AND THE SOUTHERN JUTES

Some time after the arrival of Aelle and his sons, two further invasions of the south coast were carried out at points further to the west. They both represented incursions into the British kingdom of the Belgae. The Anglo-Saxon Chronicle reported in the annal for 495: 'Two ealdormen, Cerdic and his son Cynric, came with five ships to Britain at the place which is called Cerdicesora, and they fought against the Britons on the same day.' Cerdic and Cynric are identified later as West Saxons. The annal for 501 reported that: 'Port and his two sons Bieda and Maegla came to Britain with two ships at the place which is called Portsmouth; and there they killed a young British man of very high rank.' The use of a different landing place indicates that they were separate from Cerdic's expedition. Bede's statement quoted above reported that the area surrounding Portsmouth was originally conquered and settled by Jutes.

The West Saxons named the place where they made landfall after their leader Cerdicesora, literally Cerdic's beach or bank. As in the similar case of Cymenesora it was a place with a gentle sloping shore, where ships could be easily beached. Some local historians consider that Cerdic's group first landed at Calshot Spit and there is a good basis for this view. The spit is a natural shingle bank with a depth of over forty feet and was probably in existence in Saxon times. On the north side, there is a beach sheltered from the open sea. Calshot Spit would have been one of the first features on the mainland encountered by Cerdic as he led his small force up the Solent. The Spit also had the advantage of being easily defended during the crucial early days. There is some support from place-name evidence for the identification of Calshot Spit as Cerdic's first landing place. The name Cerdicesora has not survived in full, but the place name Ower, derived from *ora*, survives for the location where the Spit joins the mainland. The group led by Cerdic as reported by the chronicler does not give the impression of a serious invasion force and for this reason some writers consider that this entry and that of

Aelle and Port lack credibility. But it is necessary to keep in mind that the purpose of the chroniclers was not to provide a comprehensive record for the benefit of posterity, but to record the activities of the king.

The chronicler recorded in the annal for 508 that: 'Cerdic and Cynric killed a British king, whose name was Natanleod and 5,000 men with him. Then the land up to Charford was called Netley after him.' Allowance may be made for exaggeration by the chronicler, but to inflict casualties approaching this scale Cerdic would have needed a larger army. It follows that he must have received considerable reinforcements from across the sea since he landed thirteen years previously. This victory is important, because it enabled Cerdic to establish his force securely in territory twelve miles inland from his starting point.

The arrival of reinforcements for Cerdic is reported in the annal for 514: 'The West Saxons came into Britain with three ships at the place which is called Cerdicesora; and Stuf and Wihtgar fought against the Britons and put them to flight.' Stuf and Wihtgar are later said to be relatives of Cerdic and Cynric. It is of interest that nineteen years after the first landing Cerdicesora was still being used by the West Saxons for beaching ships arriving from Old Saxony.

The annal for 519 reported an important political development: 'Cerdic and Cynric succeeded to the kingdom; and in the same year they fought against the Britons at a place called Charford.' At this time the area controlled by Cerdic was still quite small, only a fraction of the modern county of Hampshire and it was still beset on most sides by hostile Britons, but he must have felt sufficiently secure to proclaim a Saxon kingdom independent of British rule. In 527 another battle by Cerdic and Cynric against the Britons took place at Cerdicesleag (unlocated).

After the annal for 501, the Anglo-Saxon Chronicle provides no further entries concerning the campaigns waged by the southern Jutes against the Britons. But if there is no information from the Jutish side, it is possible that British bards recorded activity remembered by British participants. A Welsh poem has preserved the memory of a battle in the south during Arthur's time:

Before Geraint, the enemy's scourge,
I saw white horses, tensed, red.
After the war cry, bitter the grave . . .

In Llongborth, I saw the clash of swords,
Men in terror, bloody heads,
Before Geraint the Great, his father's son.

In Llongborth I saw spurs
And men who did not flinch from spears,
Who drank their wine from glass that glinted . . .

In Llongborth I saw Arthur's
Heroes who cut with steel.
The Emperor, ruler of our labour.

In Llongborth Geraint was slain.
Heroes of the land of Dyfneint,
Before they were slain, they slew.

Under the thigh of Geraint swift chargers,
Long their legs, wheat their fodder,
Red, swooping like milk-white eagles . . .

When Geraint was born, Heaven's gate stood open;
Christ granted all our prayers;
Lovely to behold, the glory of Britain.[1]

The name Llongborth cannot be related to any modern place-name, but
it has the meaning in Welsh 'port of warships'. This describes exactly the
Roman forts of the Saxon shore. The most westerly of these and hence
the nearest to Dyfneint, the Roman Dumnonia, now Devon and
Cornwall, was Portus Adurni, modern Portchester, overlooking
Portsmouth harbour, where, according to the Anglo-Saxon Chronicle,

---

[1] Morris, *The Age of Arthur.* pp. 104-5.

Port and his sons made landfall. Their arrival so close to one of the Saxon shore forts may have been more than a matter of chance. Like the Saxons at Othona they would have needed a fortified harbour, where their ships could be beached or berthed and which could be used as a base for their advance into the interior. An attack on Portchester could not, of course, be undertaken with a force of two ships. These transported only the advance guard or the personal entourage of Port. The chronicler did not consider it necessary to mention the force under Port's command; that went without saying. The activity described by the Welsh bard may well have been the British response to the Jutish attack on Portus Adurni. Geraint, prince of Dumnonia, led a mounted force from his kingdom in the west, and joined forces with Arthur to relieve the besieged defenders of the fort. In the fierce combat Geraint lost his life. The reference by the chronicler to the young British man, a very noble man, is a quite suitable description of Geraint. The battle scene would have been similar to that at Othona and Anderida, but this was not one of Arthur's victories and is not included among his twelve battles listed in the *Historia Brittonum*. It is not clear if Port had arrived from across the North Sea or from Kent, but the chronicler's statement that he came to Britain implied the former. Some scholars have serious reservations about the annal of 501, but if there may be doubts about the personal names, the size of the force or the accuracy of the date the analysis set out above gives sufficient grounds for considering it as the record of a valid historical event, which should not be discarded in its entirety.

Having secured a port at Portchester, the Jutes would have been able to bring in further reinforcements and extend their area of conquest. Archaeological investigations have provided good evidence of the existence of a people in the Isle of Wight and southern Hampshire akin to the Jutish people of Kent. A Jutish cemetery on Chessell Down (SZ 4085) on the Isle of Wight contains more than a hundred and thirty graves and is considered one of the richest in England. A smaller cemetery at Bowcombe Down (SZ 4687), southwest of Carisbrooke, contained at least eleven interments. On the mainland a Jutish cemetery was discovered at Droxford (SU 6018) above the Meon valley. The seizure of these areas by people of Jutish origin may be viewed as a further manifestation of Hengist's central war-plan to extend the area of conquest north, south and west from his original base in Kent. It was the next stage after Aelle's landing at Cymenesora.

ARTHUR'S LATER VICTORIES

In the north a serious situation had developed. Bede reported that the barbarians 'entered into a temporary league with the Picts, whom by this time they had driven away by warfare, and began to turn their weapons against their allies.'[1] This referred to the Kentish contingent in the Solway area. It appears that when war broke out in Kent hostilities also erupted in the north between the Kentish contingent and the local Britons, causing the former to make an alliance with the Picts. The Kentish contingent was still in existence at the time of Hengist's death in 488, as his son Octha travelled from the north back to Kent. The situation in the north demanded Arthur's attention. The Historia Brittonum reported that his seventh victory took place in Celyddon Forest i.e. the Caledonian Forest, apparently against the alliance of Picts and the men of Kent. This would have occurred some time after 488. The Kentish contingent was probably scattered or destroyed by Arthur, as there is no subsequent evidence of their continued presence in the north.

Arthur's remaining victories consisted of the eighth in Guinnion fort, the ninth in the city of the Legion, the tenth on the bank of the river Tryfrwyd, the eleventh on the hill Agned, the twelfth on Badon Hill, where 960 men fell from a single charge of Arthur's. The location of the eighth, tenth and eleventh battles cannot be determined. The city of the Legion, the location of Arthur's ninth battle, is the early name for both Chester and Caerleon. It is not known which of the two is intended here. Their westerly location may indicate that Arthur's opponents on this occasion may not have been Saxons, but raiders across the Irish Sea, who laid siege to the city until Arthur arrived and drove them off.

More is known about Arthur's twelfth battle, but difficulties arise in determining both its location and date. Linguistically the Latin *Mons Badonis* is probably represented by the modern Badbury, of which there

---

[1] Bede, *Historia Ecclesiastica.* part I ch. 15.

are several. The most likely of the places with this name is probably the hill fort at Badbury Rings (ST 9702) in Dorset. Even today it is a most impressive site. It stands at a height of 327 feet and has three rings of ramparts and ditches with elaborate entrances at the east and west ends. Some of the ditches are more than 60 feet deep. The outermost ring is almost a mile in circumference. According to Gildas, the fighting against the barbarians 'lasted right up till the year of the siege of Badon Hill, pretty well the last defeat of the villains, and certainly not the least. That was the year of my birth; as I know, one month of the forty-fourth year since then has already passed.'[2] As Gildas is considered to have written his book in about 545, this statement indicates that the battle took place within a few years of 500. But the Welsh Annals contain an entry for the battle in the annal for 516. It is difficult to establish which of these two dates is correct. No entry for the battle is given in the Anglo-Saxon Chronicle. If the equation of Mount Badon with Badbury Rings is accepted the date of about 500 cannot be reconciled with the time-scale of the Anglo-Saxon Chronicle, in which no invaders could have penetrated so far west by that date. But the later date of 516 is possible, as both the southern Jutes and the West Saxons had established a considerable military presence in the neighbouring territory of the Belgae by that date.

On available evidence, the attackers at Mount Badon/Badbury Rings could have been the southern Jutes or the West Saxons or a combination of both. The chronicler had, however, shown that the West Saxons were extending their area in a northerly direction and by 519 had reached Charford. Their subsequent activity continued to show an intention to advance towards the north, and therefore they appear to be less likely than the southern Jutes as Arthur's adversaries at Mount Badon. The latter could have advanced from the area of the New Forest in a westerly direction until they entered the land of the Durotriges (approximately modern Dorset), where the defenders would have prepared for the threatened invasion by re-activating and strengthening their hill forts. The southern Jutes would have continued their advance up the valley of the river Stour until they encountered the main

---

[2] Gildas, *The Ruin of Britain.* para. 26.

Durotrigan resistance at Badbury Rings, one of the strongest of their hill forts. The battle scene could well have been similar to that at the Saxon shore forts: the Durotriges were besieged within the hill fort, but Arthur came to their relief by repeated charges against the siege force. The invaders would have been expelled from the territory of the Durotriges back into Belgic territory, probably approximately along the line of the historic (pre-1974) county boundary between Hampshire and Dorset.

If it is considered that the evidence for a date in about 500 is to be preferred, it becomes necessary to revise the date given by the chronicler for the arrival of the Jutes in Portsmouth harbour to a date probably soon after the arrival of the South Saxons in 477. The chronicler is certainly poorly informed about the activities of the southern Jutes and this could be the reason why the Chronicle has preserved no memories of the battle at Badon Hill.

It is relevant that under the year 665 the Welsh Annals report 'the second battle of Badon'. It will be shown in the appropriate chapter that a location at Badbury Rings is fully consistent with the situation at the time.

 PERIOD OF
PEACE

According to the *Historia Brittonum*, the battle of Badon Hill was the twelfth of the twelve victories gained by Arthur, and Gildas was consistent with this when he described the battle as almost the last defeat of the villains. Arthur lived on until 537 but is not reported in any further battles against the Saxons. Gildas stated explicitly that at the time he was writing his book foreign wars had stopped, but civil strife continued. The war between the Britons and Saxons had ceased soon after the battle of Badon Hill i.e. soon after 500 or 516, and peace had continued and was still in force at the time Gildas was writing in about 545. The evidence from the Anglo-Saxon Chronicle is consistent with the situation described in the British sources. After the battle of Charford in 519, only one further battle against the Britons is recorded, at Cerdicesleag in 527, until the annal for 547.

Gildas ruefully described the conditions during the period of peace: 'The cities of our land are not populated even now as they once were; right to the present they are deserted, in ruins and unkempt. External wars may have stopped, but not civil ones. For the remembrance of so desperate a blow to the island and of such unlooked for recovery stuck in the minds of those who witnessed both wonders. That was why kings, public and private persons, priests and churchmen, kept to their own stations. But they died and an age succeeded them that is ignorant of that storm and has experience only of the calm of the present. All the controls of truth and justice have been shaken and overthrown, leaving no trace, not even a memory, among the orders I have mentioned; with the exception of a few, a very few.'[1] Gildas's aim in writing his book was to attack the evils which had grown up in conditions free from the menace of warfare. He denounced five of the British kings, whom he characterised as tyrants or usurpers.

This long period of peace, lasting some thirty years or more, was the

[1] Gildas, *The Ruin of Britain.* para. 26.

fruit of the hard campaigns waged by the Britons, frequently under the leadership of Arthur. The internal revolt of the Germanic enclaves had been suppressed and they had been brought under the rule of the British kings. The Britons had been unable to prevent the Jutes and Saxons establishing themselves in the southeast – they were left in possession of Kent, Sussex, southern Hampshire and the Isle of Wight – but had defeated two major attempts to extend the area of conquest. After this the Jutes and Saxons lost their offensive spirit and fighting ground to a halt. After Badon, the Britons showed no desire to mount a counter-offensive to regain these areas. Arthur had proved himself a brilliant military commander in a defensive war, but he had no political authority. The British tribal kings were quarrelsome and parochial in outlook. Central leadership had been provided first by Vortigern and then by Ambrosius Aurelianus, but after him there is no sign of a central figure who could provide leadership in a united offensive to expel the Saxons and Jutes from the southeast. On the Saxon side, Aelle was the supreme war leader as Bretwalda, but after his death (date unknown) a successor was not appointed and the post of Bretwalda remained vacant until the second half of the sixth century. During the period of peace neither the Britons nor the Saxons had a supreme war leader, because the need for one no longer existed.

Some important developments took place during this period within Britain and in the adjacent territories in Europe. An unusual situation had arisen in southern Hampshire. As explained above, two kindred Germanic peoples had seized territory in the area. After the battle of Badon Hill the southern Jutes had withdrawn to the area, but their army had been defeated and many of their leaders slain. The West Saxon army, however, was intact and it was inevitable that the southern Jutes on the mainland should come under West Saxon protection and domination. On the Isle of Wight the situation was different; the West Saxons had not occupied the island and despite their military defeat the Jutes remained in control. This changed in 530, when Cerdic and Cynric seized the Isle of Wight and killed a few men in Wihtgarabyrig, now known as Carisbrooke. There are two striking features about the version of this in the Anglo-Saxon Chronicle. First, the chronicler did not specify the nationality of Cerdic's opponents, whereas in other entries he invariably stated that they were Britons. There can be little doubt that in this entry they were the southern Jutes. Second, the mention of a 'few men' is unusual. The chronicler never under-estimates the achievements of the king and this statement should therefore be taken at its face value. It appears that Cerdic gained control of the Isle of Wight from the Jutes against only light opposition. After 530 the West Saxon kings ruled the Jutes on both the Isle of Wight and the adjacent mainland.

The chronicler reported that in 534 Cerdic and Cynric gave the Isle of Wight to their relatives Stuf and Wihtgar. The same year Cerdic died, but there is nothing to suggest that he fell in battle. A former barrow, Cerdicesbeorg, long since disappeared, but recorded in an eleventh century charter at Stoke (SU 4152) near Hurstbourne in northwestern Hampshire, is generally regarded as the burial place of Cerdic. The location of Cerdic's barrow at Stoke shows that by 534 the West Saxons had absorbed all of the Jutish territory and made considerable progress further inland. It is possible that Cerdic had been buried on the limits of his kingdom, so that his departed spirit could still protect the land from its enemies. Cerdic's barrow was well north of the Belgic capital at Venta (modern Winchester), and probably in the frontier area between the Belgae and the Atrebates. The military situation at the time of Cerdic's death appears to be that the West Saxons had taken possession of all or most of Belgic territory and were now confronting the Atrebates. The Atrebatan forces were fresh and, as the period of peace was still unbroken, the West Saxons appear to have been unable to assemble a strong enough army to mount an offensive against them.

A valuable facility which the West Saxons gained was the Roman fortress and port of Clausentum, modern Bitterne (SU 4412), on the river Itchen. It had obvious advantages over the exposed site at Cerdicesora, which disappears from records after 514. Documents started to refer to Hamtun, which, on the evidence of the Burghal Hidage, was the Saxon name for Clausentum.

The chronicler recorded that Wihtgar died in 544 and was buried at Wihtgarabyrig (Carisbrooke).

The lack of offensive spirit among the Saxons and men of Kent could be attributed in part to Arthur's victories, but another important factor was the changed situation across the Straits of Dover. After the battle of the Catalaunian Fields in 451, Roman power in Gaul continued to disintegrate and was gradually replaced by that of the Franks. A dynamic leader, Clovis, emerged; he succeeded in uniting all the Franks and started to extend his rule from northern Gaul towards the south. This brought him into confrontation with the Visigoths, who had occupied southern Gaul. In a crucial battle at Vouillé in 507, he extended his power south of the river Loire and the Visigoths were confined to Spain and a coastal strip in Languedoc. After his death in 511, his four sons were able to continue his conquests into adjoining areas not only in the south and east, but also to the north. In 521 Hygelac, King of the Geats, a people living in southern Sweden, felt sufficiently threatened by the Franks to launch an attack against Frankish territory at the mouth of the river Rhine. King Theuderic, one of Clovis's sons, sent his son Theudebert to deal with the attack and in the ensuing battle Hygelac was killed and his army defeated.

There is no direct evidence about the conquest of northwest Europe by the Franks. King Theudebert, grandson of Clovis, wrote to the Emperor Justinian in Constantinople in about 540 and represented himself as ruler over many peoples, including the Visigoths, Thuringians, Saxons, Jutes and Norsavi (unidentified). A panegyric of King Chilperic of the Franks (reigned 561-84) stated effusively: 'You protect vast lands. The Goth and the Basque tremble, as does the Dane; the Euthian (probably Jute) trembles too, and the Saxon and Breton . . . You are the terror of the Sueves (Swabians) and the Frisians, who are confined to the sea . . . and admit your domination.'[2] This may well be suspected of exaggeration, but it was consistent with the earlier letter by Theudebert and together they indicate that the lands as far north as the Jutland Peninsula and the Danish islands had come under Frankish rule. The Frisians, Saxons, Angles, Jutes and Danes all became subject peoples.

There is no evidence, however, to show that the Franks reached beyond the Danish islands into Sweden. As reported above, the king of the Geats in southern Sweden felt sufficiently threatened in 521 to launch an attack against Frankish territory. It was probably at about

---

[2] James, *The Franks*. p. 166.

this time that Frankish power reached the western shores of the Sound, the narrow stretch of water, which separated the Danes from the Geats on the Swedish mainland.

The Anglo-Norman writers Henry of Huntingdon in his *Historia Anglorum* and Roger of Wendover in his *Flores Historiarum* provide important evidence about the situation in Britain during the period when Frankish power was spreading in the lands across the North Sea. They record an extract from a lost original about an influx of Angles and they both entered it for the year 527. Henry wrote that 'large bodies of men came successively from Germany and took possession of East Anglia and Mercia; they were not yet reduced under the government of one king; various chiefs contended for the occupation of different districts, waging continual wars with each other.' If the date 527 is to be accepted as valid, fighting cannot have broken out with the Britons as early as this, because it was still during the peace. The date 527 is within six years of the battle at the mouth of the river Rhine in which Hygelac, king of the Geats, was defeated and killed by Theudebert of the Franks. The influx of Angles into Britain which was stated to have taken place in 527 appears to have been a direct consequence of the changed military situation in the Anglian homeland. By 527 the Franks had probably extended their rule further north and seized Angulus, which appears to have triggered a migration of Angles across the North Sea to Britain in an attempt to escape from Frankish domination. The movement would have been spontaneous and consisted of family groups, who moved into the enclaves already occupied by Anglo-Saxon people. At this stage no political changes ensued and the enclaves remained under the domination of the local British tribal kings. As the migration was not an armed invasion the period of peace continued undisturbed. Gildas, living somewhere in the west, knew nothing about it or, if he did, did not consider it a breach of the peace.

Evidence from two foreign sources throws important light on how the internal situation in Britain developed. The Greek historian Procopius of Caesarea was active at the court of the Emperor Justinian (reigned 527-565) in Byzantium. In his history of the Gothic Wars he stated that Britain was occupied by three nations, the Angles, Frisians and Britons. 'And so great appears to be the population of these nations that every year they emigrate thence in large companies with their women and children and go to the land of the Franks. And the Franks allow them to settle in the part of their land which appears to be the more deserted, and by this means they say they are winning over the island. Thus it actually happened that not long ago the king of the Franks, in sending over some of his intimates on an embassy to the Emperor Justinian in Byzantium, sent with them some of the Angles, thus seeking to establish his claim that this island was ruled by him.'[3]

A similar note is struck by a German chronicler in the seventh century, when he wrote: 'The Saxon people . . . leaving the Angli of Britain, urged on by the need and desire to find new homes, sailed to Hatheloe on the German coast when King Theodoric of the Franks was at war with the Thuringian leader Hermanfred . . . Theodoric sent envoys to these Saxons, whose leader was called Hadugat . . . and promised them homes for settlement in return for victory.'[4] Hatheloe is identical with modern Hadeln near Cuxhaven at the mouth of the river Elbe. Theodoric's war against the Thuringians is known to have taken place in 531, indicating that the Saxons had arrived at Hatheloe during or just prior to the year 531. This was within four years of the annal reporting the arrival of migrants in East Anglia.

The two sources agree that at about this time a reverse migration of families was in progress across the North Sea to the land of the Franks. Procopius's mention of over-population is echoed by the German statement about the 'need and desire to find new homes.' As an explanation of this evidence, it appears that soon after the first arrival of the migrants in East Anglia in 527 the Anglo-Saxon enclaves, which can have had only a limited capacity, reached saturation point. Further newcomers could not be accommodated and were turned away. The Britons would not have permitted them to settle on British territory. Immigrant families who could find nowhere to settle were left with no choice but to return across the North Sea, giving the impression that the land was over-populated.

The third nation mentioned by Procopius was the Frisians. This must

---

[3] James, *The Franks*. p. 103.

[4] Morris, *The Age of Arthur*. p. 291.

be a mistake for Saxons. It seems possible that the Saxons reacted to the Frankish conquest of their land in a similar way to the Angles and the Saxon families fled across the North Sea seeking a refuge in the enclaves south of the Stour. On the basis of the analysis set out above, Essex and Middlesex were still under British rule and, indeed, had not yet come into existence as Saxon kingdoms. As shown in the evidence of the German chronicler quoted above, Saxon migrants were given a reception similar to that in the Anglian lands. But Kent, Sussex and Wessex were already established and there would have been no difficulty about accommodating new arrivals from Old Saxony, who would have provided a welcome addition to the Saxon or Jutish component of the population.

To recapitulate, the evidence set out above supports the following sequence of events:

521   Frankish seizure of Jutland and the Danish islands threatened
        or carried out.
527   Families leave Angulus and sail across the North Sea to
        enclaves within Britain. Similar movement from Old
        Saxony, possibly somewhat earlier.
530-1   Families unable to obtain accommodation in Britain return to
        the land of the Franks.

The re-emergence of an aggressive power across the Straits of Dover was a matter of immediate concern to the kings of Kent. During the time of Hengist he had a rear base in Frisia and repeatedly was able to draw reinforcements from it, thus concentrating all his efforts on the struggle against the Britons. By the 520s the situation confronting Hengist's successors had changed. Hengist's son Oeric reigned for twenty-four years and was succeeded by his son Octha, who was succeeded by his son Eormenric. These kings had to take into account not only the intentions of the Britons, now quiescent, but also those of the kings of the Franks, who had started to claim sovereignty over Britain.

The very name of Eormenric shows that the kings of Kent were not indifferent to the situation in Gaul. This was the name of Eormenric, a famous king of the Goths. The choice of his name for a Kentish prince, who was probably born at about the start of the century, could indicate sympathy with the Goths, if not a diplomatic or dynastic linkage with them, at a time when the Visigoths were still a major power south of the river Loire and an obstacle to Frankish ambitions.

Archaeologists have discovered artefacts of Frankish design at a number of places in Kent, testimony of close contact and commerce between the people of Kent and the Franks during this period. There is no evidence that the kings of the Franks ever attempted to establish a military presence in Kent. The blocking of any such attempt would have become a primary objective of early Kentish diplomacy.

THE ANGLIAN KINGDOMS

The period of peace did not endure long after Bede had completed his book. The Anglo-Saxon Chronicle reported in its annal for 547: 'Ida, from whom the royal family of the Northumbrians took its rise, succeeded to the kingdom (of Bernicia). And he reigned twelve years; and he built Bamburgh, which was first enclosed with a hedge and afterward with a wall.' Bamburgh (NU 1834) stands on a rocky outcrop 150 feet high on the northeastern coast forty-five miles north of Hadrian's Wall. Named Dinguerin by the British, it was located in the territory of the British tribe of the southern Votadini. The Romans had never stationed Germanic auxiliaries on a permanent basis in this area and for this reason no Anglian immigrants would have found shelter there.

Castle on Rock at Bamburgh.

The *Historia Brittonum* also contained an entry about Ida: 'Ida, son of Eobba, held the countries in the north of Britain, that is north of the Humber Sea, and reigned twelve years and joined Dinguerin to Bernicia. At that time Outigern fought bravely against the Anglian people . . . King Maelgwn the Great was reigning among the British in Gwynedd.'[1] The identity of Outigern is not given, but the sense indicates that he was king of the southern Votadini, who resisted Ida's armed invasion of his kingdom. The reference to Maelgwn provides a check to the date 547 given by the Chronicle, as the Welsh Annals report his death from yellow plague in the annal for 547. The *Historia Brittonum* and the Anglo-Saxon Chronicle both set out Ida's genealogy, showing considerable agreement in their versions. The former source stated: 'Ida was the first king of Bernicia.'

When the East Angles first arrived in Britain in family groups from about 527, the land north of the river Stour was occupied by two British peoples. The northern two-thirds was occupied by the Iceni, the southern third by the Trinovantes. One of the principal places of Anglian settlement was at Spong Hill near North Elmham. Others were at West Stow and Caistor-by-Norwich. At first they lived peacefully under British rule until the East Anglian kingdom was established. As in the case of Kent, early sources present some confusion about the founder of the East Anglian royal dynasty. According to the *Historia Brittonum* the first king to rule over the East Angles was called Wehha, who had a son Wuffa.[2] Bede does not actually say who founded the East Anglian kingdom, but states that the East Anglian royal dynasty was known as the Wuffings after Wuffa.[3] By analogy with Oisc and the Oiscings, Wuffa may be the family name (cognomen) of the East Anglian royal dynasty, the founder of which was Wehha (given name) Wuffa (surname). The *Historia Brittonum* had mistakenly recorded Wehha Wuffa as two persons, father and son. Henry of Huntingdon reported that Wuffa became king in 571 i.e. forty-four years after the Angles started their migration to East Anglia. He reigned until 578, when he was succeeded by his son Titel or Tytila, who was succeeded by his son Raedwald in 599. Wuffa's name survives in the name of the small village of Ufford (TM 2953) at a ford across the river Deben.

The Angles living north of the Humber came to be known collectively as the Northumbrians, but originally they consisted of two separate

---

[1] Nennius, *Historia Brittonum*. paras. 61-2.

[2] Nennius, *Historia Brittonum*. para. 59.

[3] Bede, *Historia Ecclesiastica*. part II ch. 15.

groupings, the Bernicians in the north and the Deirans in the south. The latter had their kingdom of Deira situated in the area of the Yorkshire Wolds. The original British inhabitants were the Parisi, who probably had their own kingdom with its capital at Petuaria, modern Brough-on-Humber (SE 9326). As reported above, the Romans established a number of settlements in the area for the use of the families of their Germanic mercenaries. An important development took place in 369-371, when Count Theodosius set up a line of observation/signal stations along the Yorkshire coast to give warning of the approach of Pictish sea-borne raiders. A unit known as the Anticipators was moved from Petuaria to Derventio, modern Malton (SE 7871), to man the system of signal stations. Roads radiated from Derventio, which appears to have been the command centre and supply base.

Geographically, there is continuity between the settlers of the late Roman period and the later Anglian people of Deira. Bede reported that the Deiran centre for their pagan religion was at Goodmanham (SE 8842), three miles north of Sancton, one of the main sites of the original settlers.[4] The derivation of the name Deira has not been definitely established. The Deirans were originally known as Dere, which suggests that they took their name from their principal town, Derventio. This indicates that the Deirans were descended from the Anticipators, stationed in and around Derventio. The name Derventio survives into modern times as the name of the river Derwent, on which the town of Malton stands. In 685 the chronicler referred to the monastery at Beverley (TA 0339) as in Derawudu – in the wood of the Deirans.

The *Historia Brittonum* states that the Deirans had their own royal dynasty and it sets out their genealogy, showing a different line from Ida's.[5] This evidence shows that from the outset Deira and Bernicia were ruled by separate and unrelated dynasties. The Anglo-Saxon Chronicle gives its version of the Deiran royal dynasty, showing considerable agreement with the *Historia*. In its annal for 560, the Chronicle stated that, Ida having died, Aelle succeeded to the kingdom of the Northumbrians and reigned for thirty years. The Chronicle was

---

[4] Bede, *Historia Ecclesiastica*. part II ch. 13.

[5] Nennius, *Historia Brittonum*. para. 61.

poorly informed about the situation in Northumbria and this entry is muddled; it is mistaken in reporting that the kingdom of Northumbria had been formed as early as this and erroneously represents Aelle (in Deira) as succeeding Ida (in Bernicia). As Ida was said to have reigned twelve years from 547, his death would have occurred in 559. Aelle succeeded his father Yffi as king of the Deirans in 560. In its genealogy of the Deiran royal dynasty, the *Historia Brittonum* makes the comment that Soemil, who preceded Aelle by five generations, first separated Deira fron Bernicia. This evidence is important, because it identifies Soemil in Deira in Britain, not in continental Angulus. No dates are quoted, but if Aelle reigned from 560 Soemil could hypothetically have reigned about 445-470, on an assessment of twenty-five years for each reign. On this basis, Soemil could have been leader or king of the Germanic settlers in the area of the Yorkshire Wolds at the time of the general uprising of the settlements in about 460. The cryptic remark about separating Deira from Bernicia could relate to this event, and it forms further evidence that Deira had continuity stretching back into Roman times. There is no evidence, as in the case of East Anglia and Bernicia, that the Royal dynasty of Deira started with an armed invasion in about the middle of the sixth century.

The area bounded by the Humber in the north, the river Witham in the south and the Trent in the west plus the Island of Axholme, lying between Trent and the Don, formed a separate kingdom, known as Lindsey. Little is recorded about its early history. The name of the kingdom was derived from the name of its chief city, Lindum Colonia, modern Lincoln, which was founded about 47 AD as the base of the Roman IX Legion, but when the Legion was redeployed it became a Colonia for the settlement of time-expired soldiers and their families. Although little is known about the activities of the kings of Lindsey, a complete genealogical line has survived. Among the early kings is one Caedbed, a British name. This, together with the retention of a Roman name for the kingdom, suggests that Lindsey, like Deira, had continuity stretching back to Roman times.

The Middle Angles are a people for whom there is a total lack of documentary evidence concerning their early struggles and their early rulers. Their area of settlement, originally occupied by members of the

Iceni, Coritani and Catuvellauni tribes, included the valleys of the Ouse, the Nene and the Welland and stretched as far south as the river Thames. The entry in the Anglo-Saxon Chronicle for 571 shows that the Catuvellauni had still not succumbed to the invaders, as the Britons (presumably the Catuvellauni) were reported to be in combat with the West Saxons in the area of the Chiltern Hills.

The most westerly of the Anglian peoples were the Mercians. The area they occupied became a buffer zone separating the Anglian kingdoms in the east and the still independent British kingdoms in the west. Theirs was a march or frontier area and instead of being called the West Angles they became known as the Mierce or Mercians, the people of the frontier. According to Henry of Huntingdon, the kingdom of the Mercians was founded about 584, when Crida was appointed king. The genealogy provided for Crida shows a line stretching back to the original kings of Angulus: Offa, Angeneot, Eamer, Icel, Cnebba, Cynewald, Crida. In the Life of Saint Guthlac, written in about 740, Icel was regarded as the founder of the Mercian royal line, which was known as the Iclingas.[6] As Bede had reported that the land of Angulus was left empty, it follows that the king and royal family had also vacated Angulus. As the kingdoms of Deira and Lindsey were already in situ they proceeded from the Humber along the river Trent beyond the land of Lindsey, and during their advance inland up the Trent they would have had to overcome the resistance of the British tribes of the Coritani. No record has survived of battles between the Mercians and Britons. The establishment of a new kingdom in Britain was a great achievement for the Icling kings. From British territory they had succeeded in carving out a new power base, where they could rule free from Frankish dominion. Unlike their forefathers in continental Angulus, the Icling kings no longer ruled all the Anglian people, only those within the new Mercian kingdom. In the course of the migration to Britain the Anglian people had become scattered and the greater proportion of them now came under the rule of other regimes, which did not recognise the suzerainty of the Icling dynasty. Crida reigned until 600, when he was succeeded by his son Pybba. Ceorl or Cearl, a cousin of Pybba, came to

---

[6] Ed. Whitelock, *English Historical Documents*. item 156.

the throne in 610, ruling probably until 633.

As the early period of the Anglian kingdoms unfolds, unmistakeable signs of Swedish influence emerge, for which an explanation is necessary. Clear evidence of a strong Swedish connection became apparent from the examination of the East Anglian ship burial, discovered at Sutton Hoo (TM 2947) in 1939. The ship used for the royal burial had been hauled from the river Deben on to a plateau on the east bank and then covered in a large mound of earth. This style of burial was also used for the burial of Swedish chieftains or kings of this period at Vendel and Valsgarde near Uppsala north of Stockholm. This association was re-inforced when it was discovered that the styles and workmanship of some of the articles found at Sutton Hoo, particularly the helmet and shield, were remarkable not only for their high quality, but also for their close similarity with artefacts found in the Swedish graves. The balance of opinion now favours Raedwald, who died in about 624, as the king buried at Sutton Hoo. The name of his grandfather, Wuffa, is Scandinavian in origin and, in the modern form Uffe, is still in use in Sweden and Denmark.

Nine miles northeast of Sutton Hoo, another ship burial was discovered in 1862 at Snape (TM 3959) on the north bank of the river Alde. Its date was estimated as the second half of the sixth century. The close proximity of Snape, Sutton Hoo and Ufford indicates that this area was the original heartland of Wehha and his warriors. Here they entered Britain by sailing up the estuaries of the rivers Deben and Alde, on whose banks they made their first settlements. This location, so near to the coast, contrasts with the internal settlements at West Stow, North Elmham and Caistor-by-Norwich, which had first been settled under Roman auspices.

Another waterside burial was the mound on the north bank of the river Thames at Taplow (SU 9082). The name Taplow is derived from the Anglo-Saxon Taeppahlaew, Taeppa's barrow. The mound was excavated in 1883 and found to contain burial articles appropriate for a king; although not as numerous, they bore comparison with those found at Sutton Hoo in value and artistic merit. Included were a gold buckle, a lyre, decorated drinking horns and the remains of clothing decorated with gold thread. The date of the burial was estimated at about 600. The mound and its contents suggest strongly that Taeppa had been one of the early kings of the Middle Angles, and its location on the northern bank of the Thames could mark the limit of his kingdom at the time of his death.

Unmistakeable evidence of Geatish influence in early Anglian history is found in the great epic poem Beowulf, which was a work of Anglian origin. The theme of the epic is the struggles of the eponymous hero against an evil monster, which was afflicting the hall of the Danish king; Beowulf succeeded in destroying the monster and afterwards the monster's mother, so relieving the king of the menace which tormented him. In the circumstances of the time, the malign presence at the Danish royal hall would have been a Frankish one, exacting tribute from the Danes. The political reality was the threat to the Geats by the advance of Frankish power to the Danish islands, and behind the Beowulf saga could lie attempts by Geatish nobles to help their Danish neighbours to overthrow Frankish dominion. The poem shows where Anglian sympathy lay. The passage in the poem about the death and burial of Beowulf establishes a link with the waterside burials at Sutton Hoo, Snape and Taplow. It tells that after the cremation of Beowulf, his followers built a high and broad mound as a monument to the dead hero, erected on a promontory so that it could be seen by seafarers; they filled it with rings and jewels and built a splendid wall around it.

It is apparent from the foregoing that some of the early Angles had a close acquaintance with Geatish/Swedish customs and history. The most likely way in which this was acquired would have been as a result of a sojourn in the land of the Geats. As an area free from Frankish oppression southern Sweden would have been as inviting as Britain and indeed more accessible. At a time when some Anglian families, particularly those along the west coast, were taking to their boats and sailing across the North Sea to Britain, other Angles, particularly those in eastern Angulus, were crossing in their boats on the shorter and easier sea crossing to southern Sweden in the area still known as Goetland. A colony (or colonies) of Angles settled here and in due course a new generation grew up with experience and memories only of the land of the Geats. It appears that it was from this colony (or colonies) that armed bands set out across the North Sea to seize land from the

Britons. The first such band was led by Ida, who, according to the Anglo-Saxon Chronicle, arrived in the land of the Votadini in 547, and a second band led by Wehha arrived in the area of the river Deben in about 570. Another band sailed into the Wash, but the date of its arrival and the name of the leader are not known.

The movements of the Anglian royal family can be traced only with difficulty. As Bede had reported that the land of Angulus was left empty, it follows that the king and royal family had vacated Angulus at an unknown date. The genealogical line reported for the Mercian kings shows unbroken continuity with the kings of Angulus, including Offa. On this evidence, it was in the heart of Britain that the Anglian royal family finally settled. But the date provided for the foundation of the Mercian kingdom by Crida is not until 584, which indicates that Mercia was the last of the Anglian kingdoms to take shape. This is consistent with the area chosen by Crida for settlement; it was the most westerly of the Anglian kingdoms, an indication that the other kingdoms were already established. On this analysis, the group led by Crida was the last to arrive in Britain i.e. in or just before 584.

The problem of the identity of Icel remains. It was he who gave his name to the Mercian royal dynasty, the Iclings. By analogy with Oisc and the Oiscings, Icel would have been a family name (cognomen), not a given name. But the Mercian royal genealogy enters Icel's name three generations before that of Crida, the first Mercian king, and after Eamer, the son or grandson of Offa. If this evidence is to be trusted, it shows that Icel founded the royal line of the Iclings some sixty to seventy-five years before the arrival of Crida in Britain. This brings Icel into the period when the Angles were fleeing their ancient homeland before the conquering Franks. On this analysis, it was Icel who led the Anglian royal family from Angulus and re-established a fragmented Anglian kingdom on Geatish soil during the mid or late 520s. There they remained until they departed for Britain in about 584.

In the annal for 547, the chronicler provides the names of Ida's ancestors. Information of this kind is usually of little historical value as a primary source, but may be worth considering in the light of other information, such as that given in the previous paragraphs. Ida's father is named as Eoppa and his grandfather as Esa. A separate source had reported that Esa was the first of his dynasty to come to Britain. The names of twelve other ancestors are stated (including Woden), but two of them merit further consideration, Finn and Geat. The former is the king of the Frisians, who figures in the Beowulf saga, and so this name can be excluded here. Probably relevant is Fyn, a large island east of Jutland, which contains archaeological traces of occupation by the Angles. Ida's genealogical list was probably composed some time after his death on the basis of names of his immediate predecessors, which could still be remembered correctly. Geat and Finn appear only as names, whose correct meaning had been forgotten. If it is accepted that Esa was the first of the family to come to Britain, he would have arrived before Ida, crossing the North Sea with the first wave of family groups in or about 527. It is not known if he was able to find a place of refuge or was one of those Angles, who was forced to return to the land of the Franks. At this time Eoppa could have fled in an easterly direction from or via the island of Fyn to the land of the Geats, where Ida was brought up. (It is of interest that the inclusion of Geat in Ida's genealogy has a parallel in the inclusion of Gewis in Cerdic's genealogy in Wessex.) Geatish influence was still apparent in the generations which succeeded Ida, and evidence is presented in a later chapter that fifty years after Ida's arrival a Bernician queen was buried on a Beowulf style of site at Lindisfarne on a high promontory which could be seen by seafarers.

The *Historia Brittonum* gives the British version of events after the battle of Badon Hill, which accords well with the reconstruction set out above. It reports two stages. During the first stage the defeated barbarians sent for help to Germany, with the result that their number continually increased, which was how the British chronicler viewed the influx of family groups in the late 520s. The second stage was when the barbarians brought over their kings from Germany, actually from Geatland, to rule over them.[7] By the 540s further settlement was possible only by means of armed invasion and the forcible seizure of areas already occupied by the Britons. This took place under the leadership of Ida, Crida, Wehha and the unrecorded predecessors of Taeppa.

---

[7] Nennius, *Historia Brittonum*. para. 56.

THE EAST SAXONS AND THE MIDDLE SAXONS

As a result of Arthur's repeated victories at the mouth of the river Blackwater, the kingdom of the East Saxons was not established until about the same time as the East Anglian kingdom. William of Malmesbury wrote that the kingdom of the East Angles was 'nearly co-eval' with that of the East Saxons. According to Henry of Huntingdon, the first king of the East Saxons was called Erchenwin, whose name is given by Florence of Worcester as Escwini. He was succeeded in 587 by his son Sleda. No date is given for the actual foundation of the kingdom, but if Erchenwin/Escwini died in 587, the earliest date for his appointment as king would probably be during the 560s. The course of events in Essex could have been similar to those in East Anglia: an influx of migrants from Old Saxony, fleeing from the rigours of Frankish rule during the late 520s and finding a refuge in the Germanic enclaves, such as Mucking. British rule, however, continued until Erchenwin/Escwini seized power.

Sleda was the first East Saxon king to have a name with an initial 'S' and this became a firm rule for his successors. He married Ricula, daughter of Eormenric, king of Kent, and their son Saberht succeeded to the throne in 597. The earliest mention of the East Saxon kingdom by Bede and the Anglo-Saxon Chronicle is given under the date 604 where it is reported that the East Saxons were ruled by King Saberht, whose capital was the city of London.[1]

From an early date the Middle Saxons became associated with the East Saxons, but they were recognised to have a separate identity. It may be deduced that they entered Britain up the Thames estuary and occupied the area lying west of the East Saxons on the north bank and west of the men of Kent on the south bank. The latter area became known as the Suth rige – the southern area, modern Surrey. The Middle Saxons would have immediately found themselves in a very vulnerable

---

[1] Bede, *Historia Ecclesiastica.* part II p. 3.

position. Numerically small, they were surrounded on three sides by other groupings, albeit of Germanic stock. The forest of the Weald afforded good protection to the south, but apart from that they had no natural features to give a defensible line. Moreover, the river Thames divided their territory into two approximately equal halves. Inevitably, they soon came under the protection of their more powerful neighbours.

The Migration of the Jutes, Saxons and Angles 451-590.

SAXON AND ANGLIAN KINGSHIP

A noteworthy feature of the Saxon kingdoms during the sixth to eighth centuries is the presence of two kings reigning at the same time. They have been called joint kings in this narrative, but ancient documents did not use this term, calling them both king without distinction. The earliest entries in the Anglo-Saxon Chronicle show that the principle of joint leadership was already in operation when the advance parties first arrived on these shores. Normally the joint leaders were close relatives. The first known example was the brothers, Hengist and Horsa, and when Horsa was killed it became a father and son team, Hengist and Aesc. The South Saxons landed under the joint leadership of Aelle and his three sons, which underlined the family nature of Saxon leadership and kingship. The West Saxons were led by father and son, Cerdic and Cynric. When the Isle of Wight was captured in 530, the brothers Stuf and Wihtgar, close relatives of Cerdic, were appointed joint governors at Carisbrooke. The earliest known joint kings of the East Saxons were the brothers Sexred and Saeward, who reigned from 616.

There is no evidence that the Saxons had evolved a monarchical system of a single ruler in their homeland in northwestern Germany. Before their migration to Britain their system of government appears to have been based on a family unit. It was this system which they used and adapted in Britain when they established the early Saxon kingdoms. As late as 692, according to Bede, the Saxons remaining in Old Saxony (between the Elbe and Weser) had still not evolved a system of monarchical government: 'Those Old Saxons have no king, but several magnates set over their nation, and if war breaks out they cast lots impartially, and all follow as commander and obey in time of war whomsoever the lot indicates; but when the war is over, all the magnates again become equal in power.'[1]

The system of joint kingship had definite advantages in the primitive

---

[1] Bede, *Historia Ecclesiastica.* part V ch. 10.

conditions of the period, when a king was more liable to die at short notice and the appointment of a successor would take longer with the poor and slow communications of the time. In the midst of battle, the death or wounding of the king would lead to the immediate loss of command. With a successor already appointed and ready to take over, the continuity of command was ensured. It is not known how the kings divided their responsibilities. In Wessex it is likely that one king had precedence on the grounds of seniority, since the decision and activities of the senior king figure more prominently in the annals, and when the two kings are mentioned together the name of the senior is given first. In Essex, there is evidence of a territorial division of responsibility. Only one case is recorded of a serious difference of opinion between joint kings; this arose in 685 when Lothere and Eadric, joint kings of Kent (uncle and nephew), quarrelled about Kentish policy towards Sussex. Their difference led to war, in which Lothere was killed.

While still in Angulus the Angles had established a strong monarchical state. One of their hero-kings was Offa, who was renowned in Germanic legend. He is celebrated in the Anglo-Saxon poem, *Widsith*, which was probably recited at the Mercian court in the seventh and eighth centuries:

> This is the testimony of Widsith, traveller through
> Kindreds and countries; in courts he stood often . . .
> Attila rules the Huns, Eormenric the Goths,
> Theodric ruled the Franks, Thyle the Rondins . . .
> Offa ruled Angle . . .
> With single sword he struck the boundary against the
> Myrgings, where it marches now,
> Fixed it at Fifeldor. Thenceforward it has stood between
> Angles and Swaefe (Swabians) where Offa set it.[2]

Fifeldor is thought to be the river Eider and the poem records Offa's achievement in fixing his southern frontier along this river.

The author of the epic poem Beowulf knew about Offa and his proud

---

[2] Alcock, *Arthur's Britain*. p. 16.

queen Thryth. He described Offa as 'the best of all men between the two seas', referring to the Jutland Peninsula, lying between the North and Baltic Seas. 'Offa the brave was widely esteemed both for his gifts and his skill in battle; he ruled his land wisely. He fathered Eomer, guardian of thanes . . ., grandson of Garmund, a goliath in battle.'[3] In the Mercian genealogy, Garmund appears as Waermund and Eomer was stated to be the father of Icel.

When the Angles were settling in Britain, it was the system of rule by a single king, a monarch, which they knew and it was this system which they established in the Anglian kingdoms. It will be explained in the following chapters that the Northumbrians and later the Mercians instituted a senior post within their government known as the prefect or patrician, who had special responsibilities and was second in rank to the king. As the name indicates, the post was Roman in origin, had not been imported from Angulus, but had survived after the Roman withdrawal. It is clear that the Saxons and Angles had entirely different ideas and traditions about their systems of kingship when they established their new kingdoms in Britain.

During the pagan era, both Saxons and Angles believed that their kings were descended from the gods and this belief reinforced the royal authority. In witness of their divine descent, all Saxon and Anglian kings were provided with a genealogy tracing their line back to Woden, with the exception of the East Saxon kings, whose line was traced back to the god Seaxneat.

---

[3] Trans. Kevin Crossley-Holland, *Beowulf.* p. 105.

PART 3

EARLY STRUGGLES

THE WEST SAXON ADVANCE TO THE NORTH

By the time of Cerdic's death in 534, the West Saxons appear to have obtained control of most Belgic territory, including the capital Venta, but were prevented from advancing into the land of the Atrebates. A state of military stalemate appears to have arisen and it lasted until 552, when the Anglo-Saxon Chronicle reported that: 'Cynric fought against the Britons in the place, which is called Searoburh and put the Britons to flight.' Searoburh is the Roman Sorviodunum, later known as Old Sarum (SU 137327), an Iron Age hill fort standing 240 feet above the river Avon. Its defences of ditches, earthworks and stockades made it strongly defended and its capture was no mean achievement. To reach it the West Saxons would have advanced a distance of nine miles from their starting point at Charford (now on the Hampshire border) due north up the valley of the Avon.

Before moving off, Cynric would have needed to safeguard the rear area by leaving behind an adequate holding force under a senior commander. He would have been an ealdorman, probably a member of the royal family, and would have been based at Hamtun, which was the military and political centre of the area. In due course it became the capital of the county to which it gave its name, Hamtunscir, modern Hampshire.

The victory at Searoburh brought a fresh expanse of British territory under West Saxon control, consisting at first of land on both sides of the river Avon from Charford to the area of Old Sarum, but it was decided from the start to keep this land under separate administration and not to place it under the control of Hamtun. It formed the nucleus of what later became the county of Wiltshire, named after Wiltun, modern Wilton, the town on the river Wylye at its confluence with the Nadder. The choice of name for the county shows that in those early days Wiltun was its main centre. The significance of Wiltun at that time was that it stood only two and a half miles west of Searoburh, suggesting that it was used in the first place by Cynric to serve as his field headquarters from which to direct the siege. After the capture of Searoburh, he decided not to make use of it and it was abandoned in favour of Wiltun. From Wiltun Saxon rule spread out into the adjoining areas, thereby forming the county of Wiltshire. To the west, Saxon control spread up the river Wylye until it met the natural barrier of the forest of Selwood, now almost completely disappeared. No attempt was made to penetrate further west than this and the land of the Durotriges was spared from Saxon invasion. East of Searoburh stood a line of hill forts at Fosbury (SU 3236), Sidbury (SU 2250) and Figsbury (SU 1934). Their names show that when the West Saxons first encountered them they were operational fortresses (the ending bury having the original meaning of a fortress). The historic boundary between Hampshire and Wiltshire runs to the east of this line of hill forts, suggesting that they had withstood capture by the troops from Hamtun, but were finally taken by troops commanded from Wiltun, into whose area of administration they came.

Cynric's army continued further north along a route, which went further up the Avon valley, over Salisbury Plain, across the Vale of Pewsey and along the ancient Ridgeway. It is not known what kind of opposition was mounted by the Britons, but no further battle is recorded by the chronicler until 556, when Cynric and his son, Ceawlin were reported to have fought the Britons at Barbury (SU 149763). This was another hill fort, standing on the Ridgeway, with strong defences of double ditches and ramparts, enclosing an area of almost twelve acres. The Britons' attempt to block further Saxon progress along the Ridgeway was defeated and the West Saxons were able to continue their advance without further battles until they came to the original area of Germanic settlement in the middle Thames valley. The object of Cynric's long march from Charford now becomes apparent: to liberate the Germanic settlers from servitude to the Britons. He merged the Germanic settlements into the West Saxon kingdom.

Cynric's action raises the question of his and Cerdic's relationship with the settlers in the Dorchester area. It is relevant that the name Cerdic is not a truly Saxon name, but an Anglo-Saxon form of the British name Ceretic. This suggests that he was a native not of continental Saxony, but of Britain and that his parentage was part Saxon, part

94

British. His birthplace could have been in one of the Germanic enclaves, where inter-marriage between Britons and Saxons took place. Cynric's long march to the Dorchester area indicates that it was in this area that Cerdic had his family roots. From this analysis it appears that Cerdic was sent from the Dorchester area to raise an expeditionary force in Old Saxony. Having landed in the Calshot area, he was prevented from reaching Dorchester by the strength of the British resistance, but it is impossible to determine if his activity formed part of a central strategy devised by Aelle as Bretwalda or was a separate enterprise.

The enlarged West Saxon kingdom now consisted of two components: an older part around Dorchester dating back to the introduction of mercenaries by the Romans in the late fourth or early fifth centuries and a more recent part conquered from the Britons stretching as far south as the Isle of Wight. The terminology used in ancient documents reflects this dichotomy. The word Gewissae was frequently used as synonymous with West Saxons and the kings were sometimes entitled 'King of the Gewissae'. Bede stated that the West Saxons were anciently known as the Gewissae.[1] As the term 'West Saxon' was originally used to refer to Cerdic's army in Hampshire, Gewissae is apparently the older expression relating to the early Germanic settlers. In the Anglo-Saxon language, the word Gewissae has the sense of 'confederates', which describes the original status of the settlers when they were allowed to settle in the middle Thames valley as *foederati* under their treaty (foedus) with Rome. It appears that Gewissae was the Anglo-Saxon rendering of the Latin word *foederati* and that the Germanic elders continued to use the word to describe themselves long after the Romans had departed. As late as 901, King Edward the Elder referred in a charter to the councillors of the Gewissae meaning the West Saxons. The Welsh also used the word to refer to the West Saxons: King Alfred was called king of the Gewissi when the Welsh Annals reported his death in 900. When Cerdic's family tree was composed the compiler knew of the word, but apparently not its true sense, and inserted the name Gewis as one of Cerdic's ancestors.

---

[1] Bede, *Historia Ecclesiastica*. part III ch. 7.

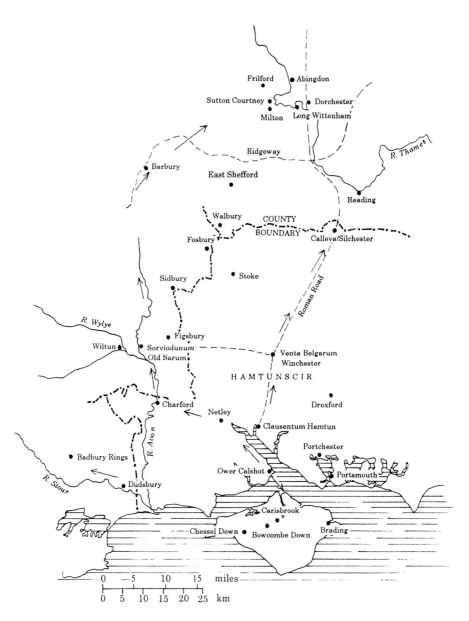

The Jutish and West Saxon Campaigns 495-570.

Cynric was accepted by the Gewissae as their king and he would have taken over Dorchester as the capital of his enlarged kingdom. The original Roman name of the town is not known, but the Saxons drew on it, when they called it Dorcic or Dorciccaestre (as in Bede) or

Dorcecaestre (as in the Anglo-Saxon Chronicle). Cynric died in 560 and was succeeded by Ceawlin. The entries in the Chronicle present a difficulty over Cynric's age. He is first recorded arriving in Britain with Cerdic in 495 and died sixty-five years later, indicating an age in the eighties when he died. Although not entirely impossible, these dates strain the credulity. Some versions of the Chronicle provide an explanation, as they show Cynric not as the son, but as the grandson of Cerdic. Cynric's father is stated to be Creoda, son of Cerdic. In that case Creoda may have predeceased Cerdic, with the result that Cerdic was succeeded in 534 by his grandson, Cynric. This could have misled the early chroniclers into thinking that Cynric was Cerdic's son. The initial K sound of Cerdic's name was retained by the West Saxon royal family with few exceptions as a mark of their descent from Cerdic until the time of Cynewulf (reigned 756-786), the last West Saxon king to have this feature.

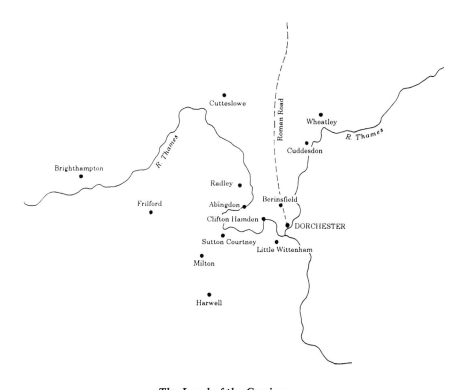

The Land of the Gewissae.

The Gewissae were a martial people and their annexation gave Cynric and Ceawlin a major new source of manpower for their army. The arrival of Cynric was an intrusion, which reversed the military balance in the area. But they had need of a strong army to protect the Gewissean heartland, which occupied an exposed position, confronted on three sides by hostile Britons. Only to the south was it secure from attack. To the west were the Dobunni, to the north the Catuvellauni and to the east the Atrebates. The preponderance of Britons was offset, however, by their lack of unity. No central or co-ordinated leadership was in operation at this time and the tribal kingdoms acted individually.

When Cynric set out on his march to Dorchester in 552, the Atrebatan kingdom was still probably intact. This is shown by the route chosen by Cynric to reach Dorchester. The shortest route from Hamtun to Dorchester was along the Roman military highway, which ran in almost a straight line, and was, of course, paved and ideal for the movement of an army. But the northern half of the Roman highway lay in the land of the Atrebates and passed through their capital, Calleva, modern Silchester, which would have been well defended. This was probably the reason why Cynric moved his army over a less direct route.

After 552 the threat to the Atrebates was growing. In the east, the Middle Saxons were establishing themselves south as well as north of the Thames. The arrival of the West Saxons at Dorchester increased pressure against them from the west. There are no records of a battle or battles, which led to the extinction of the Atrebates, but it is significant that Calleva, the Atrebatan capital, has historically formed part of the county of Hampshire. The county boundary in the north makes a distinct bulge to embrace not only the ancient city, but also its defensive environs to the north. This may be taken to signify that its capture was carried out by troops from Hamtun. Its absence from the Chronicle indicates that it was not one of the achievements of the king, but of a subordinate commander, apparently the ealdorman at Hamtun. Two

British capitals, Venta and Calleva, had now fallen into West-Saxon hands, but the West Saxons had no use for them. The original capital at Dorchester had become the capital of their enlarged kingdom, while Hamtun was functioning satisfactorily as the administrative centre for Hamtunscir. Venta and Calleva both stood largely abandoned and empty; Calleva was never again used as a political centre, and Venta remained unused until in 648 the West Saxon capital was moved there from Dorchester.

The Chronicle recorded in the annal for 568 that Ceawlin and his brother Cutha led an army from the west and came into conflict with Aethelberht, king of Kent, at Wibbandun, modern Wimbledon, where the latter was defeated and driven back to Kent. No mention is made of the Middle Saxons, although the battle took place in the Suth rige, their southern area, which they had captured from the Atrebates only a few years previously, perhaps during the mid or late 550s. The Middle Saxons were not numerically large enough to mount an effective defence of their new homeland and in 568 were unable to prevent its invasion by more powerful neighbours to the east and west. The issue at Wibbandun was to decide whether it was Ceawlin or Aethelberht, who was to be overlord of the Middle Saxons south of the Thames. Although the people of Surrey became subject to West Saxon rule, the identity of their province as a separate political entity was preserved.

The collapse of the Atrebates and the seizure of their former territory removed one threat to the security of the Gewissean homeland, but the Dobunni and the Catuvellauni remained as hostile neighbours. Hostilities broke out with the latter in 571, when the chronicler reported that Cutha fought the Britons at Biedcanford and captured the towns Limbury, Aylesbury, Benson and Eynsham. Cutha died later the same year. The location of Biedcanford, apparently a river crossing, is unknown. Eynsham (SP 4309) lay twelve miles west of Dorchester, Benson (SU 6292) three miles east of Dorchester. The capture of Aylesbury and Limbury (TL 0222 near modern Luton) involved a deep penetration of Catuvellaunian territory and brought the West Saxons into the Chiltern Hills. Their route probably lay along Akeman Street and the Icknield Way, which now formed the frontier separating Saxons and Britons. By this campaign the West Saxons had acquired a large slice of Catuvellaunian territory, but the Catuvellauni had a large kingdom, which continued to exist, although under pressure from the south, north and east.

To the west of Dorchester, the Dobunni had a large kingdom, which stretched from the Bristol Avon to the outskirts of Birmingham and included the Cotswold Hills and the surrounding area. Their capital was at Cirencester, the Roman Corinium. Hostilities with them broke out in 577, when the chronicler recorded that Ceawlin and his son Cuthwine fought the Britons at Dyrham and killed three kings, Conmail, Condidan and Farinmail. They also captured the cities Gloucester, Cirencester and Bath. It is sometimes assumed that the three British kings were kings of these three cities. This is possible, but not necessarily so. As they were fighting together at Dyrham they are unlikely to have been monarchs of independent kingdoms.

A possible scenario which fits the topography is that Ceawlin led his forces from the Dorchester area to Cirencester, which was captured; then along Ermin Street to Gloucester, which also fell. The Dobunnian commanders could have withdrawn their surviving forces south and concentrated them in the hill fort at Dyrham together with a contingent from Bath. The remains of the hill fort are still to be seen on Hinton Hill (ST 741767) near the village of Dyrham. The site covers an area of about twelve acres on a spur of the Cotswold escarpment at a height of 600 feet. The west side was protected by the steep slope of the Cotswold edge, the other sides by lines of defensive ditches and stockaded ramparts.

The West Saxon victory at Dyrham is considered by historians to have major historical significance. The West Saxon kingdom now stretched from the English Channel to the Bristol Channel, and the Britons in the southwest, the Durotriges and the Dumnonii, were cut off from the main body of Britons still free from Anglo-Saxon domination. The former became known as the West Welsh. It was certainly a serious reverse for the Dobunni, who had lost the southern part of their kingdom, three kings and their three principal cities, including their capital. But, as in the case of the Catuvellauni, the battle did not lead to the total collapse of the Dobunni and their kingdom. There is no evidence that Ceawlin's forces advanced far beyond the roads linking

100

Gloucester, Cirencester and Aylesbury. The most northerly point where Saxon traces have been found is Bishops Cleeve (SO 9527). North of this was an expanse of territory nearly forty miles in length, which remained in the possession of the Dobunni. Ceawlin had satisfied his purpose of creating a buffer zone and he had no wish or need to acquire more Dobunnian territory. By his victories in 571 and 577 Ceawlin had advanced his northern frontier, which probably ran along the approximate line Gloucester – Ermin Street – Cirencester – Akeman Street – Aylesbury – Icknield Way – Limbury. This frontier was sufficiently far advanced to enable him to protect the Gewissean homeland from incursions by the surviving Dobunni in the northwest and the still independent Catuvellauni in the northeast. He had in effect established an early example of the *cordon sanitaire*.

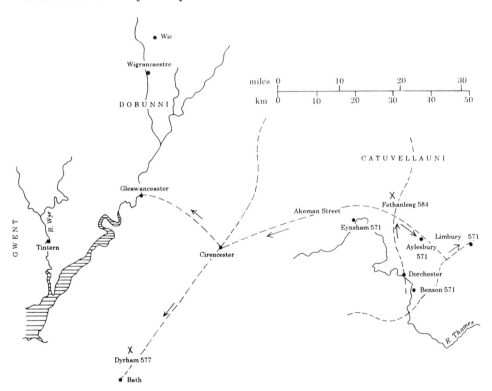

The West Saxon Northern Frontier 571-584.

101

URIEN OF REGED

As Ida was reported to have reigned twelve years, he would have died in 559. Early sources report the situation after Ida's death, but they provide such divergent accounts that it is impossible to reconcile them and present a single consistent version. The *Historia Brittonum* stated that Ida had twelve sons and Simeon of Durham supported this by adding that six sons were begotten in lawful marriage and six were the sons of concubines. Two sources state that after Ida, Glappa ruled for one year. He was not quoted as a son of Ida, which may suggest a dispute over the succession, resulting in the early deposition of Glappa. He was followed by Adda, stated to be the eldest son of Ida, who reigned seven or eight or three years. After Adda other sons of Ida were reported to have reigned: Frithuwald for six or seven years, Theodric for four or seven years, Theodulf one year and Aethelric. Another king called Hussa reigned seven years, but the sources do not identify him as a son of Ida. These kings appear to have ruled in succession, but it is not known in which order, except that Aethelric was probably the last of Ida's sons to occupy the throne.

During the early 570s there is no sign that the northern British rulers were unduly worried about the Anglian invasion at Bamburgh and they were still pursuing their internecine quarrels. The Welsh Annals report an important battle in 573 at Arfderydd, modern Arthuret, ten miles north of Carlisle. The protagonists were Gwendoleu, ruling in the Carlisle area, and the two kings of York, Gurci and Peredur, who gained the victory. However, the principal beneficiary from the battle was Urien, king of Reged, whose rise to power dates from this battle. Reged was a British kingdom west of the Pennines, with its capital probably at Carlisle. Urien extended his rule south to Catterick and became known as Lord of Catterick. His praises were sung by his bard Taliesin: 'Urien of Echwyd . . . sovereign, supreme ruler, all highest, the stranger's refuge, strong champion in battle. This the English know when they tell tales. Death was theirs, rage and grief are theirs, burnt are their homes, bare are their bodies.'[1] It is apparent that Urien was able to assert his suzerainty over other British kings from Galloway to Shropshire, including Solomon, king of Powys, and his arms threatened Calchvyndd (the chalk hills) in the south. Furthermore, his nephew Mouric became king of Glevissig, roughly modern Glamorgan, and through Mouric his influence spread into South Wales. From his position of supremacy he led the struggle against the Anglo-Saxons and became a kind of latter-day Arthur.

During the period of peace the supreme post of Bretwalda among the Saxons had been allowed to lapse, but at an unknown date it was decided to re-activate the post and award it to Ceawlin, who was undoubtedly the most successful of the Anglo-Saxon war-leaders. There must have been a positive reason for this decision and it is likely to have been the need for a supreme commander, who could act as a counterpart to Urien and give central leadership to the Anglo-Saxons.

The Anglo-Saxon Chronicle reported that in 560 Aelle became king of the Northumbrians and reigned thirty years. Actually he became king only of the Deirans. The Welsh Annals reported the death of Gurci and Peredur, joint kings of York, in 580, when they fell in battle at an unlocated place called Caer Greu, against Adda whose identity is not stated. If the date is correctly reported, this battle took place after the reign of Adda, son of Ida. The death of these two British kings may have enabled Aelle to gain possession of York, which became the capital city of Deira. Continuing its report about the Bernician kings, the *Historia Brittonum* gave the names of the British kings who fought against them as Urien, Rhydderch Hen, Gwallawg and Morcant.[2] Rhydderch Hen (Rhydderch the Elder) was king of Strathclyde, Morcant was king of the southern Votadini and Gwallawg was king of the northern Votadini.

In the year 588 some personality changes took place. The Anglo-Saxon Chronicle reported the death of King Aelle and stated that Aethelric reigned after him for five years. The chronicler is again confused about the situation north of the Humber and has convoluted two events: the death of Aelle in Deira and the succession of Aethelric in

---

[1] Morris, *The Age of Arthur.* p. 232.

[2] Nennius, *Historia Brittonum.* para. 63.

Bernicia. Aethelric was known to the Britons as Fflamddwyn – the Firebrand. If Aelle died in 588 this gives him a reign of twenty-eight years, compared with the thirty years stated by the chronicler in the annal for 560.

THE WEST SAXON RETREAT 592

The advance of the West Saxons to the line from Gloucester to Limbury in the north and to the line of the river Severn in the west exposed them to counter-attacks by the neighbouring British peoples. Available evidence reports the continuation of hostilities during the 580s. Welsh and Irish sources report a Saxon invasion of the area west of the Severn during this period; the invaders penetrated as far as the river Wye until they were repelled at the ford of Tintern (SO 5300) by the forces of Mouric, king of Glevissig and nephew of Urien. The Anglo-Saxon Chronicle reported that in 584, 'Ceawlin and Cutha fought against the Britons at the place which is called Fethanleag and Cutha was killed there; and Ceawlin captured many villages and countless spoils and in anger returned to his own land.' The place-name Fethanleag is usually considered to be near Stoke Lyne (SP 5628), four miles north of Bicester. There is a similarity between the campaign to Fethanleag and the campaign to Tintern. Both appear to be drives into enemy territory, not with the object of gaining more land for settlement, but to inflict damage on enemy forces.

The next entry in the Chronicle is terse and cryptic and leaves much unexplained: '592. In this year there occurred a great slaughter at Woden's barrow and Ceawlin was driven out.' It appears from this that a major change in the strategic situation had taken place since 584. Woden's barrow, a pagan name, which was later changed to Adam's Grave (SU 113634), is a Neolithic long barrow on the crest of Pewsey Downs at the southern end of the Ridgeway. One mile to the north, the Ridgeway intersects the eastern part of the Wansdyke at about the midway point of the latter. The original pagan name of the Wansdyke was Woden's Dyke. Originally palisaded, and estimated by archaeologists to have been built about 550, it stretches over ten miles from east to west along the summit of Pewsey Downs and was intended to give defence against an attack from the north. It is apparent that the West Saxon army had been driven back from its advanced positions along Akeman Street, had been expelled from its ancestral territory and driven across the Thames and along the Ridgeway to the Pewsey Downs. The West Saxons had one of the strongest and most successful armies in Britain. To have suffered such a reverse they must have been attacked by a far superior force. The weakened Dobunni would have been quite incapable of mounting such an attack without the aid of substantial allied forces. In the political circumstances of the period the emergence of a British alliance against the Saxons is quite conceivable. A few years previously the West Saxons had clashed with a British force under King Mouric, but failed to destroy it. Mouric remained a threat and may have been able to obtain support or reinforcements from his uncle, Urien of Reged.

The Chronicle does not specify who were Ceawlin's opponents, but William of Malmesbury stated that Ceawlin 'was the astonishment of the Angles, the detestation of the Britons and the destruction of both.' Describing the final days of Ceawlin's reign he added: 'The Angles as well as the Britons conspired against him and, his forces being destroyed at Woden's Dyke, he lost his kingdom thirty-one years after he had assumed it, went into exile and shortly after died.'[1] The statement that the Britons and the Angles had conspired against Ceawlin strains the credulity and is usually discounted, but subsequent developments, as explained below, are consistent with William's evidence that some of the Angles came into conflict with the Saxons. The Angles in question were the Middle Angles, who, having defeated the Catuvellauni, wished to take possession of all Catuvellaunian territory, but found that some of it, stretching from the north bank of the Thames into the Chiltern Hills, was held by the Gewissae. The two kindred peoples came into confrontation and warfare between them became inevitable. At about the same time, the advanced positions of the West Saxons in southern Dobunnia came under attack from British forces advancing from the west and possibly the north. The Britons and Middle Angles became in effect comrades-in-arms against the West Saxons/Gewissae. The latter were overwhelmed by this combined or at least simultaneous assault and driven south of the Thames and along

---

[1] Malmesbury, *The Kings before the Norman Conquest.* para. 17.

the Ridgeway. In their hour of extreme peril they hastily built a defensive line – Woden's Dyke – in imitation of Hadrian's Wall. To avoid being outflanked they extended it five miles on both sides of the Ridgeway, but it proved of no avail. Intensive fighting probably took place at the intersection of the Ridgeway and Woden's Dyke, where the latter was probably breached. The West Saxons fell back to the crest of Woden's Barrow, where a pitched battle took place.

The consequence of this campaign was that the Dobunni regained their lost territory, including Cirencester, Gloucester and Bath; the West Saxons had held it for only fifteen years. The Middle Angles obtained control of the West Saxon lands north of the Thames, including the capital at Dorchester. This was to be a permanent source of dispute between the two peoples for the future.

AETHELRIC OF BERNICIA

Aethelric reigned from 588 until 593 and in this period the Bernicians fought three major battles against the Britons. In the first of these the Bernicians were on the offensive. Urien's bard Taliesin reported that Fflamddwyn – King Aethelric – led four Bernician armies under his sole command and invaded Reged. He demanded hostages, but his large force was defeated by Urien and his son Owain in Argoed Llwyfein, the Forest of Leven. This location cannot be pin-pointed, but is thought to have been in the vicinity of Carlisle. A possible location is near Bewcastle (NY 5674), fifteen miles northeast of Carlisle. It appears that Urien's capital was under direct threat by Aethelric's attack. No precise date is given for this battle.

The second battle reveals that the Bernicians had suffered a serious setback, presumably as a result of the battle in the Forest of Leven. The *Historia Brittonum* reported that Urien blockaded them (the Bernicians) for three days and three nights in the island of Lindisfarne. This was one of the most crucial events in the early struggles in the north and several sources have references to it. It is apparent that a very large force had been deployed against the Bernicians. Urien was not only leading an allied British army, but he had also accepted the support of a force of Scotti. Irish sources reveal that Aedan, king of the Scotti who had settled in Argyll, and Fiachna, king of Ulster (reigned 589-628), fought against the English and that Fiachna seized and occupied Bamburgh. The Bernicians were driven from the mainland and forced to make a last-ditch stand on the near-island of Lindisfarne, which is joined to the mainland only at low tide. They were under the immediate threat of being driven into the sea. The similarity of the predicament of the Bernicians with that of the West Saxons at about the same time will be noted. In both cases the Anglo-Saxon army had been overwhelmed by superior numbers. The Bernician army, however, was saved from destruction when the British kings started to quarrel. The account in the *Historia Brittonum* confirms Urien's position as supremo: 'During this campaign Urien was assassinated on the instigation of Morcant, from jealousy because his military skill and generalship surpassed that of all other kings.'[1] The immediate cause of discord could have been the possession of Bamburgh by Fiachna, which had belonged to the southern Votadini before its capture by Ida in 547, and Morcant would have claimed it as part of his territory. This would have led to a break-up of the alliance and the murder of Urien. The precise date of this battle is not reported, but it would have been after the accession of Fiachna in 589, probably in 590, 591 or 592.

The Bernicians were able to profit from the British discord and re-established themselves on the mainland. They must have still been in a weakened state but there was no longer any central command of the British forces. Urien was succeeded by his son Owain as king of Reged. The Welsh bard Taliesin reported that Owain and Fflamddwyn met in battle at an unknown location and the latter was slain. This battle apparently took place in 593, the year when the Anglo-Saxon Chronicle reported that Aethelfrith, son of Aethelric, succeeded to the kingdom. During this period there is no evidence to show that the Deirans had engaged in military activity against the Britons.

---

[1] Nennius, *Historia Brittonum*. para. 63.

$\mathcal{T}$HE SAXON AND BERNICIAN RECOVERY

Although William of Malmesbury described how Ceawlin's forces were destroyed at Woden's Barrow, subsequent events show that both the West Saxon army and the West Saxon state continued in existence. It is noteworthy that Ceawlin did not fall during the slaughter at Woden's Barrow, although at this period it was a matter of honour that a war-leader should continue fighting to the death. This suggests that the West Saxon army did not suffer total defeat and that some elements survived and continued to fight back. Ceawlin, however, was held responsible for the military debacle and was deposed. The continuation of the West Saxon state was facilitated by the system of multiple kingship practised by the Saxon kingdoms. In 591 Ceola (or Ceolric), the son of Ceawlin's brother Cutha, had been appointed joint king and after his uncle's deposition he continued to reign until 597.

The West Saxon military set-back would have had serious repercussions for all the Saxons and Jutes. With the deposition of Ceawlin the post of Bretwalda became vacant and the Saxon people were left without a supreme military leader at a moment when their need for good leadership was greatest. They turned to King Aethelberht of Kent, who was appointed Bretwalda in succession to Ceawlin. Aethelberht succeeded his father Eormenric in 560 (according to Bede) or in 565 (according to the Chronicle). In a long reign of over fifty years he left an indelible mark on English history. William of Malmesbury summarised his achievements succinctly: 'In the infancy of his reign, he was so much an object of contempt to the neighbouring kings, that, being defeated in two battles, he could scarcely defend his frontier; afterwards, when to his riper years he had added a more discreet knowledge of war, by successive victories, he subjugated every kingdom of the Angles, with the exception of the Northumbrians.'[1] We already know that Aethelberht was defeated in 568 at Wimbledon by Ceawlin

---

[1] Malmesbury, *The Kings before the Norman Conquest.* para. 9.

when he invaded Surrey, and therefore it is possible to place some reliance on William's statement, although there is no information about the second defeat. It is a measure of the seriousness of the situation that in 592 the Saxons had to turn for their military supremo to a king whose military record included two defeats. But he rose to the occasion and led the Saxon and Kentish forces in a campaign which rescued the West Saxons and expelled the Middle Angles from West Saxon territory by means of the successive victories quoted by William of Malmesbury.

According to the the Anglo-Saxon Chronicle in 593, Ceawlin, Cwichelm and Crida perished; the identity of the last two is unknown, but their alliterative names show that they were members of the West Saxon royal house, perhaps sons or grandsons of Ceawlin. The death of all three in the same year and the use of the word perished may suggest that they met a violent death. Two round barrows north of East Hendred (SU 6983), one north of the Ridgeway, the other just south of it and known as Cuckhamsley or Scutchamoor Knob, may be relics of the fighting in 593. The names are derived from the Anglo-Saxon *Cwicelmes hlaew,* meaning Cwicelm's barrow or mound. The annal for 1006 in the Chronicle mentions a strong pagan superstition concerning the dead Cwicelm, who is supposed to have possessed supernatural powers which he could exercise against the invading Danish army. Such powers were attributed to departed kings, held to be descended from the gods. The location of the two barrows suggests the possibility that Cwicelm may have been identical with the Cwichelm, who perished with Ceawlin in 593. If so, it follows that after the slaughter at Woden's Barrow, Cwichelm fought back, driving his opponents along the Ridgeway a distance of thirty miles, until he and one of his companions, perhaps Ceawlin or Crida, fell in combat where the two barrows now stand. The fighting at this spot must have been violent and intense.

In the far north, Aethelfrith inherited a kingdom in 593, which was still weak after its narrow escape from destruction at Lindisfarne, followed by the defeat and death of Aethelric. But early in his reign one of his principal opponents, Owain, son of Urien, died and the kingdom of Reged went into decline. A major event at about this time was the battle of Catraeth, entered in the Welsh Annals as the year 598. It forms the subject of the early Welsh poem, the *Gododdin of Aneirin.* It tells how

Mynydawc and Cynan of Edinburgh despatched a mounted expeditionary force south to Catraeth, which is usually supposed to have taken a circuitous route via Carlisle and the Bowes Pass to Catraeth (Catterick), to avoid Bernician forces. The objective of the operation is not clear, but it turned out to be a complete disaster and the British force was annihilated. The actual location of the battle is often assumed to be at the Iron Age fortress of Stanwick, north of Catterick.

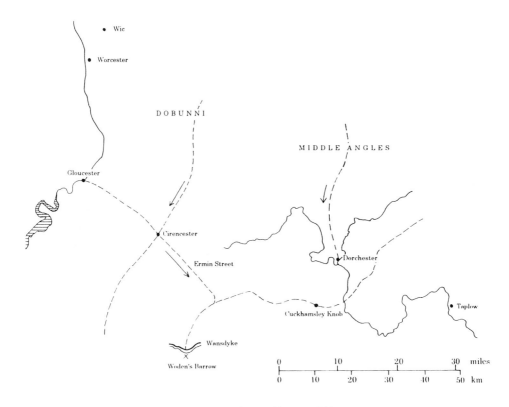

The West Saxon Retreat 592.

Following the decline of Reged, Catraeth was a further set-back for the British cause. The Bernicians were becoming the dominant power in the north, but they still had to reckon with the Scotti. Since 503 they had migrated from Dal Riada in Antrim, northern Ireland, to the west coast and were governed from a centre at Dunadd (NR 837936) on the Kintyre peninsula. They were trying to extend the area under their control, as

112

was apparent at the siege of Lindisfarne. A clash between the Scotti and Bernicians became inevitable and it took place in 603, when the chronicler wrote: 'Aedan, king of the Scots, fought along with the people of Dal Riada against Aethelfrith, king of the Northumbrians, at Degsastan and almost all his army was slain. There Theodbald, Aethelfrith's brother, was slain with all his troops. No king of the Scots dared afterwards lead an army against this nation. Hering, son of Hussa, led the army thither.' In this battle Aedan had the help of Mael Uma, brother of the Irish High King. It is generally accepted that Degsastan is identical with Dawston (NY 5798) in Lidderdale.

There is no direct evidence about the Saxon counter-offensive in the south, but it probably continued throughout the reign of King Ceola. In 597 he was succeeded as king of the West Saxons by his brother Ceolwulf, who 'continually fought and contended either against the Angles, or the Britons, or the Picts, or the Scots,' according to the Chronicle. There can be little doubt that the Angles were the Middle Angles and the Britons included the Dobunni and their allies. It appears that in the first part of Ceolwulf's reign the struggle against these peoples to regain the lost West Saxon territory was still continuing. The mention of Picts and Scots is surprising, but it forms clear evidence that a military alliance had been concluded between the Bernicians and the West Saxons, whose recovery must have become strong enough for them to send a military contingent north. The main battle between the Bernicians and the Scots had been at Degsastan in 603, after which the Scots ceased to be a military threat. It is likely, therefore, that the West Saxons would not send troops beyond their frontier until they had regained their lost lands and were confident of being able to defend them. Hence it appears that by 603 the war against the Middle Angles and Britons had ended in victory for the Saxons and that the West Saxons were again in possession of their ancient lands. Ceolwulf was probably back in the West Saxon capital of Dorchester-on-Thames.

Aethelberht's victory over the Middle Angles not only added to his renown, but it also enhanced the authority and prestige of the office of Bretwalda. He was able to assert his authority over all the Angles except the Northumbrians. The extension of the Bretwalda's realm to the Humber would have led to an increase in the tribute the Bretwalda was able to exact, as he could now tap the resources of the southern Anglian lands.

The appearance of Aethelberht on the Kentish throne shows that a distinctive feature was taking shape in the names of the members of the Kentish royal dynasty. After Hengist the succession had been Oeric (or Aeric) – Octha – Eormenric – Aethelberht, all members of the family Aesc or Oisc. Allowance must be made for vagaries in the early spelling, but there is a strong suggestion that these kings were given a name, which began with the same vowel sound as their family name, probably a form of Eh. Alliteration was an essential element in Anglo-Saxon verse and it was becoming apparent that the Kentish royal dynasty had adopted it when choosing the given names of both male and female members of the royal family. As will be explained below, this feature persisted in the Kentish royal house with few exceptions and became an established Kentish tradition. None of the other royal dynasties followed this pattern.

The Anglo-Saxon Chronicle reported that in 607 Ceolwulf fought against the South Saxons. This is the earliest evidence of friction between the West and South Saxons, presumably over frontier delineation.

KING AETHELBERHT AND ST. AUGUSTINE

An important step taken by King Aethelberht was his decision to marry Berhta, a Christian princess of the royal family of the Franks. Bede naturally interpreted the event in terms of its religious significance and explained that her parents insisted that she should be permitted to practise her faith and, in order to avoid contamination with heathen beliefs, that she should be accompanied by bishop Liudhard. But the determining factor in this dynastic marriage would have been political. Berhta was the daughter of Charibert, a grandson of Clovis and king of Paris 561-7. He must have had strong reasons of state for marrying his daughter to a pagan and these undoubtedly were to strengthen Frankish claims to exercise control over Kent as the gateway to Britain. Aethelberht (or his father Eormenric) may have been under pressure from the Franks to accept a Frankish influence within Kent at this time.

The attention of Pope Gregory had been drawn to the condition of the pagan Anglo-Saxons some time before he became Pope. Bede tells the story of how Gregory had seen boys with fair complexions in the slave market in Rome. Upon enquiring about them he was told that they were Angles from the kingdom of Deira, ruled by king Aelle, and that they were still pagans. Gregory made puns about the names Angles, Deira and Aelle, but he asked the Pope to send a mission to convert the Anglo-Saxon peoples and offered to lead it himself.[1] This was not possible at the time, but when he became Pope in 592 he resolved to put the project in hand. In 596 he sent a mission headed by Augustine to undertake the conversion of the Anglo-Saxons. A party of almost forty men, they arrived in Kent in 597, probably at Ebbsfleet where a cross has now been erected, and were received with great caution by Aethelberht. The occasion recalled the earlier meeting on the Isle of Thanet between Vortigern and Hengist. A few days after his landing King Aethelberht, who could not have been entirely ignorant of the Christian faith in view

---

[1] Bede, *Historia Ecclesiastica*. part II ch. 1.

of his marriage to Berhta, went to Thanet and listened to Augustine's message himself. He allowed Augustine and his followers to come to the Kentish mainland and they were given a house in Canterbury, where they were permitted to preach; in due course Aethelberht accepted baptism.[2]

St. Augustine's Cross, Ebbsfleet.

The conversion of Aethelberht was a great achievement for Augustine, because he was not merely king of Kent, but also Bretwalda and he soon used his supreme authority to encourage the spread of the new religion beyond Kent to other kingdoms. Augustine sent Mellitus into neighbouring Essex, ruled by King Saebert, son of Ricula, sister of Aethelberht, and in 604 he ordained Mellitus as bishop of the East Saxons. Aethelberht built a church dedicated to St Paul in London, which was the capital city of the East Saxons. Also in 604 Augustine ordained Justus to be bishop in west Kent, with his see at Rochester, where Aethelberht founded a church dedicated to St Andrew.

When Raedwald, king of the East Angles, was on a visit to Kent, Aethelberht persuaded him to accept baptism into the new faith, but when he returned home his wife and councillors refused to abandon their traditional religion. The result was that in his temple he had two altars, one for Christian worship, the other for heathen rites.[3]

In his missionary work Augustine encountered a number of problems, about which he wrote to Pope Gregory for guidance. One of these concerned his relations with the British bishops. The British or Celtic church had an unbroken existence dating from Roman times, but since

---

[2] Bede, *Historia Ecclesiastica.* part I ch. 25.

[3] Bede, *Historia Ecclesiastica.* part II ch. 15.

the Roman withdrawal it had developed separately from Rome and no longer recognised the authority of the Pope. Gregory's instruction to Augustine was clear: all the British bishops were to be placed under his authority. Augustine now had the difficult task of approaching them and persuading them to accept this. How was he to arrange a meeting with them? He could not expect them to come at his bidding and expose themselves to the hazards of a journey across hostile Anglo-Saxon territory to Canterbury. He would have had no option but to go west himself to unconquered British territory. Bede explained that in about 603: 'Augustine, with the help of King Ethelbert, summoned to a conference with him the bishops and teachers of the nearest province of the Britons, at the place which to this day is called Augustine's Oak in the language of the English, on the borders of the Hwicce and the West Saxons; and began to persuade them with brotherly admonition that, preserving catholic unity with him, they should undertake for the Lord's sake the common labour of preaching the gospel to the heathens.'[4] It is apparent that the nearest province of the Britons was, in fact, the province of the Hwicce. The significance of meeting on the borders of the Hwicce and the West Saxons was that this was the dividing line between the pagan Anglo-Saxons and the Christian Britons. King Aethelberht had used his authority of Bretwalda to arrange with the West Saxons for the safe passage of Augustine through Wessex as far as the frontier with the Hwicce. The precise location of Augustine's Oak cannot be definitely established, but a good candidate is Down Ampney (SU 1097), because of its location where the Roman road Ermin Street from Silchester to Cirencester (the modern A419) crosses the historic boundary between Wiltshire and Gloucestershire. This could have been the frontier between the Hwicce and the West Saxons in 603. The place-name 'The Oak' marked on a nineteenth century map of Down Ampney could designate the original site, as it would have been geographically the nearest British territory to Augustine's base at Canterbury and he could have journeyed along the Roman roads from Canterbury via London and Silchester to Down Ampney.

This preliminary meeting with the British bishops was followed by a

---

[4] Bede, *Historia Ecclesiastica.* part II ch. 2.

fuller conference attended by seven British bishops and many learned men, who came mainly from their most celebrated monastery at Bangor-is-coed (SJ 31945), but Augustine failed to persuade them to accept his authority and to co-operate in converting the Anglo-Saxons. Augustine made a prophecy that if the Britons did not live with the Anglo-Saxons as brethren, they would have war with them as enemies. The British church continued its existence separately from the new Roman church growing up in the Anglo-Saxon lands.

The evidence about Augustine's meeting with the British bishops at Augustine's Oak indicates strongly that the Hwicce were a British people, presumably those known to the Romans as the Dobunni. Hwicce is a word coined by the Anglo-Saxons and possibly derived from the name of the town Wic, the Roman Salinae, which did not receive its modern name of Droitwich until the reign of Edward III. It was usually the practice of the Anglo-Saxons to name a people after the town from which they were governed. After the loss of Cirencester in 577 the defeated Dobunni were left without a seat of government. In the unoccupied northern part of their territory the only sizeable centre was Salinae, still actively engaged in the production of salt. It also had the advantage of being the centre of an extensive network of roads and tracks along which salt was transported. It appears that the Dobunni re-established their capital at Salinae, where it was furthest from the West Saxon invaders. The Saxon name for Salinae was Wic and the people governed from Wic were known as the Hwicce, also spelt Wicce.

King Aethelberht died on 24 February 616. Bede considered that another of his great contributions to the welfare of his people was the publication of a code of laws written in the English language.

PART 4

THE NORTHUMBRIAN
PERIOD

THE RIVALRY OF THE BERNICIAN AND DEIRAN DYNASTIES

After his victory at Degsastan in 603 King Aethelfrith did not remain inactive for long. The *Historia Brittonum* reported that Aethelfrith the Artful reigned twelve years in Bernicia and twelve years in Deira, making twenty-four years in the two kingdoms. He gave Din Guaire to his wife Bebba, and it was named Bebbanburh, the fortress of Bebba, modern Bamburgh.[1] On this evidence it appears that twelve years after ascending the Bernician throne in 593, Aethelfrith invaded Deira in 605 and annexed it. Little information is available about this important event, but Reginald of Durham stated in his *Life of Oswald* that Aethelfrith assassinated Aelle and drove his son Edwin into exile. On this evidence Aelle died in 605 and not in 588 as stated in the muddled entry by the chronicler. By combining Deira with Bernicia, Aethelfrith created Northumbria, which became the largest and most important kingdom in Britain. The explanation for his transfer of Bamburgh to his wife seems to be that upon his departure for Deira he left her there to rule Bernicia as his personal representative. There is no evidence to explain the reason for his invasion and annexation of Deira, other than the desire for territorial expansion, or alternatively Deira could have been conspiring with Bernicia's British opponents. As a result of Aethelfrith's action the rivalry between his dynasty and the Deiran dynasty for the Northumbrian throne became a dominant factor in the political situation, which affected the south as well as the north. When driven into exile Edwin was about twenty years of age and had formed a dynastic link with Mercia by marrying Coenburg, a daughter of Ceorl, king of the Mercians. While they were in exile she bore him two sons, Osfrith and Eadfrith. Welsh records show that at an early stage Edwin was able to find refuge in the kingdom of Gwynedd.

Aethelfrith spent the next eight years consolidating his hold on Deira and to this end he married Acha, daughter of Aelle and sister of Edwin.

---

[1] Nennius, *Historia Brittonum*. para. 63.

(It is not known if Bebba was still alive at this time.) During this period there is no record that he engaged in military campaigns and his enlarged kingdom appears to be secure. The peace, however, was broken by an important event recorded in the Welsh Annals in its entry for 613 as the battle of Caer Legion (i.e. Chester), where Selyf, son of Cynan and king of Powys, died. The Anglo-Saxon Chronicle also reported this battle, but entered it erroneously in the annal for 605. Bede was interested mainly in the religious significance of the battle, describing how the Britons assembled a large number of monks from the monastery at Bangor-is-Coed to intercede for the victory against the pagan Northumbrians. Although they were unarmed, Aethelfrith had no qualms about deploying his warriors against them and most of them were slain. Ten years previously learned men from this monastery had participated in the conference with St Augustine, when the Britons refused to co-operate in his mission to convert the pagan Anglo-Saxons. Bede saw Aethelfrith's victory as a fulfilment of Augustine's prophecy that as a consequence the Britons would suffer death at the hands of the English.[2]

In the time of the Britons Chester was the chief city of all Venedotia, i.e. Gwynedd, and it was sufficiently important in 601 to have been the venue of a synod of the British church. In its entry for 613 the Welsh Annals also stated that Iago, son of Beli, fell asleep. He was king of Gwynedd and descended from Maelgwyn through Rhun and Beli. (As explained above, Maelgwyn was descended fron Cunedda, who first came to North Wales from the frontier area facing the Picts.) The expression 'fell asleep' suggests death from natural causes, unconnected with Aethelfrith's attack on Chester. Iago was succeeded by his son Cadfan. The kings of Gwynedd probably had their court at Chester and it could have been here that Edwin lived in exile, and so it is not surprising that the capture of Chester appears to have been the main objective of Aethelfrith's campaign. He probably led his forces from York along the Roman road across the Pennines to Manchester (approximately the route of the modern A64 and A62) and then to Chester.

---

[2] Bede, *Historia Ecclesiastica.* part II ch. 2.

It is apparent that three British kings had combined for the defence of Chester – Cadfan and Selyf were joined by Cyndrwyn the Stubborn, king of the Cornovii. Although Aethelfrith's action against Chester seems at first glance to be a case of naked aggression, there is also the possibility that it was directed primarily against Edwin, because he was forming a hostile alliance with the British kings. As a consequence of the military defeat Cadfan was obliged to withdraw from the mainland to the island of Mona (Anglesey), where a new capital was established at Aberffraw (SH 3569). According to Welsh tradition the surviving monks from Bangor-is-coed found refuge on the island of Bardsey (SH 1221), where a Celtic monastery had been founded in the early sixth century. Aethelfrith does not appear to have attempted a military occupation of Mona and Cadfan continued to rule there until he died in 625; he was buried at Llangadwaladr (SH 3869), two miles east of Aberffraw. His tombstone may be seen there, with a Latin inscription, describing him as 'the wisest and most renowned of all kings.' The victory at Chester enabled Aethelfrith to subordinate mainland Gwynedd and the kingdoms of Powys and of the Cornovii to his rule and to exact tribute from them. Bede's assessment of him reflects this extension of his power: 'King Aethelfrith, most eager for glory, ruled over the kingdom of the Northumbrians and more than all the chieftains of the English ravaged the nation of the Britons. For none of the leaders, none of the kings caused more of their lands to pay tribute to the race of the English or be settled by them, after they had exterminated or subdued the inhabitants.'[3]

The Cornovii during Roman times had their own *civitas*, with its capital at Viroconium, the name of which is connected with the nearby hill fort now known as the Wrekin. The extensive ruins of Viroconium can now be seen near the modern village of Wroxeter (SJ 5608), where archaeologists have discovered traces of timber buildings erected on Roman rubble, indicating continued use of the city after the Roman withdrawal. It seems that Viroconium was still the capital of the Cornovii when the Angles first came into contact with them, and so they called them the Wreocensaetan – the people of Viroconium – and the

---

[3] Bede, *Historia Ecclesiastica*. part I ch. 34

town was called Wreocencaestir, which became modified to modern Wroxeter. In 613, Anglian hegemony was established for the first time in the lands, which later became Cheshire and Shropshire.

The military defeat of the Cornovii at Chester had brought Northumbrian power as far south as the northern frontier of the Hwicce, who were not unaffected by the changes in the political balance. The traditions of Glevissig hold that peace on their borders was broken in about 614, some thirty years after the campaign of about 584. There is also a Welsh report of combat in Gwent during the early years of the seventh century. This evidence can only be explained as an advance by the West Saxons into the area west of the river Severn. The chronicler announced an important West Saxon victory in 614, when Cynegils and his son Cwichelm fought at Beandun (or Beamdun) and killed 2,045 Britons. Cynegils was the son of Ceolwulf, whom he succeeded as king of the West Saxons in 611. The location of Beandun cannot be determined, but the battle appears to be the culmination of the campaigns reported by the Welsh sources. It took place within a short time of the battle of Chester and, in view of the military alliance between the West Saxons and the Bernicians, the two battles were probably inter-related. Beandun was another serious set-back for the Welsh and as a result the victorious West Saxon kings may have been able to re-occupy part of the Hwiccian territory. The situation after Beandun may have been similar to the situation after the battle of Dyrham.

After the battle of Chester Edwin probably fled with Cadfan to Mona, where, according to Welsh tradition, he spent part of his youth. Aethelfrith continued to pursue him and his dynasty ruthlessly. Bede reported that a nephew of Edwin's called Hereric took refuge with the British king Ceretic, ruler of the small kingdom of Elmet, lying between the rivers Wharfe and Aire, which at this time still retained a degree of self-government, although probably under Aethelfrith's tutelage. While in banishment Hereric died of poison, and in the circumstances of the time, there must be a strong suspicion that this was a political assassination, engineered by Aethelfrith, perhaps with the connivance of Ceretic.[4]

---

[4] Bede, *Historia Ecclesiastica*. part IV. ch. 21.

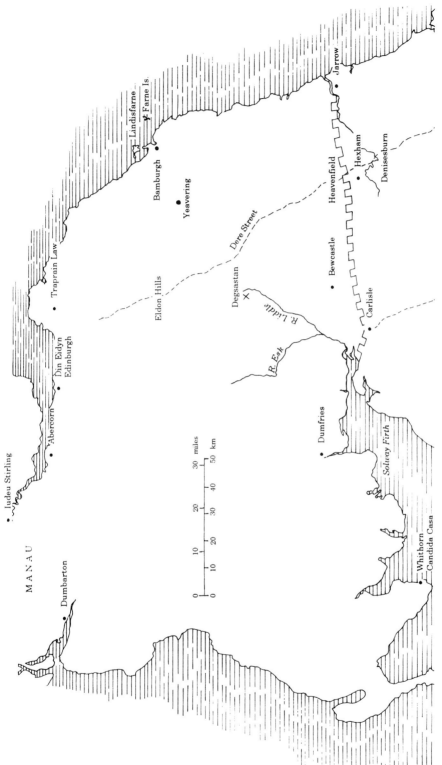

MANAU

Iudeu Stirling

Dumbarton

Abercorn

Din Eidyn
Edinburgh

Traprain Law

Eldon Hills

Dere Street

Lindisfarne

Farne Is.

Bamburgh

Yeavering

Degsastan
×

R. Liddle

R. Esk

Bewcastle

Carlisle

Dumfries

Solway Firth

Whithorn
Candida Casa

Heavenfield

Hexham

Denisesburn

Jarrow

| 0 | 10 | 20 | 30 miles |
| 0 | 10 | 20 | 30 | 40 | 50 km |

The Kingdom of Bernicia.

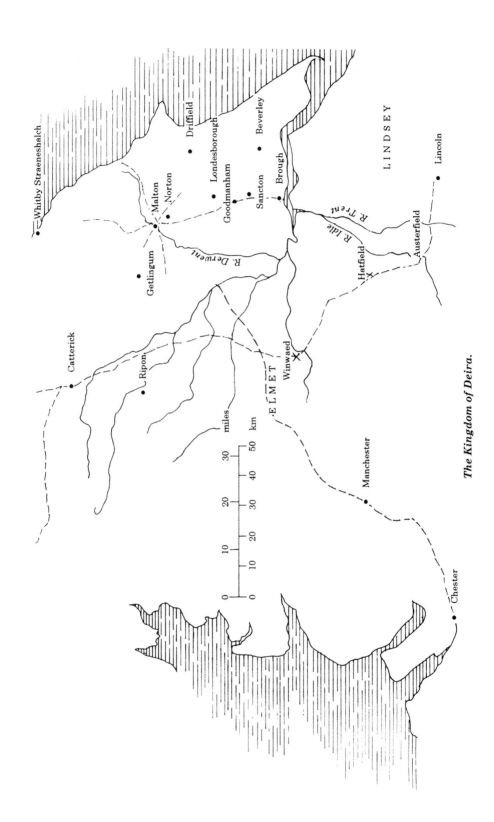

The Kingdom of Deira.

RAEDWALD, KING OF THE EAST ANGLES AND BRETWALDA

Aethelberht's death created a vacancy for the position of Bretwalda. It was apparently considered that despite the defeat of the Britons at Chester and Beandun there was still a need for a Bretwalda. The choice for the appointment went to Raedwald, king of the East Angles, which is interesting for two reasons: Eadbald, son of Aethelberht, failed to obtain the post held by his father, showing that it was not hereditary, and for the first time the appointment went to an Anglian king. The decision was one of the utmost importance. It showed that Raedwald was considered to be the most outstanding Anglo-Saxon military leader of the time and that the other kings south of the Humber had such confidence in him that they were willing to place themselves under his supreme command in battle. How he gained his military renown and the confidence of the other kings is not reported. He is unlikely to have been one of the Angles defeated by Aethelberht; on the contrary, it is more likely that he served with distinction under Aethelberht's command as Bretwalda against the Middle Angles.

The battle of Chester was a great set-back for Edwin's cause, but when there was a change of Bretwalda in 616 he saw a fresh opportunity to obtain support against Aethelfrith. Bede reported that while Aethelfrith was pursuing Edwin, he wandered for many years through various kingdoms in exile and eventually came to Raedwald, who extended a welcome to him and promised to help him. When Aethelfrith learned that Edwin had obtained refuge in Raedwald's hall, he sent messengers with money and gifts to persuade him to put Edwin to death, but Raedwald refused to do so. Aethelfrith sent messengers a second and third time and threatened war if he again refused. Raedwald then quickly mobilised his army and led it north, probably along the Roman road through Lincoln. Bede said that Aethelfrith had insufficient time to assemble the full strength of his army. The two armies clashed where the Roman road from York to Lincoln crosses the river Idle near

Austerfield (SK 6695).[1] The Chronicle reports that this battle took place in the year 617 i.e. within a year of Raedwald becoming Bretwalda, showing that he and Edwin wasted little time in taking action. Aethelfrith was killed in the battle, as was Regenhere, a son of Raedwald. Edwin succeeded to the kingdom of Northumbria and drove out Aethelfrith's family, the athelings Eanfrith, Oswald, Oswy, Oslac, Oswudu, Oslaf and Offa. They and a large band of their supporters found a refuge among the Picts and Scots, traditional enemies of the Britons, establishing strong links which were to exert important influences on the development of the Anglian and Saxon kingdoms to the south. In the first place, Aethelfrith's children were converted to the Christian faith and baptised according to the rites of the Celtic church. Equally important, the sympathy between the Bernician royal house and the Scots and Picts became a significant factor in the rivalries and alignments of the southern kingdoms.

In addition to the sons named above, Aethelfrith had a son Eanhere and a daughter Eabbe. The names of his children present a pattern, which divides into two parts; it is likely that the names beginning Ea . . . were children of Aethelfrith's first wife, Bebba, and that those beginning O . . . were born of his second wife Acha. It is not known how long Bebba ruled at Bamburgh or if she died before Aethelfrith married Acha. There is, however, good place-name evidence about her place of burial. Six miles north of her citadel at Bamburgh the near-island of Lindisfarne projects into the sea. The most striking feature of the landscape of Lindisfarne is the pinnacle of dolorite rock at the southern end, rising to a height of 100 feet. It is known as Beblowe Crag. This unusual and unique name, like nearby Bamburgh (originally Bebbanburh), appears to be derived from Bebba and the Anglo-Saxon word *hleow*, meaning a barrow or mound, hence Bebba's barrow. It is apparent that Queen Bebba was buried in a barrow erected on this rock overlooking the sea and within sight of Bamburgh. All physical remains of Bebba's barrow have long since disappeared and the rock is now crowned by Lindisfarne Castle, founded by Henry VIII. The water-side location of Bebba's barrow provides an association with the burials at Sutton Hoo, Snape

---

[1] Bede, *Historia Ecclesiastica*. part II ch. 12.

and Taplow and with the headland burial of the Geatish hero-king Beowulf. Fifty years after the arrival of Ida, the Bernician royal dynasty was still following a Geatish/Swedish style of burial, which is good evidence that Ida had originated from the Anglian settlers in the land of the Geats.

Beblowe crag, surmounted by Lindisfarne castle.

The victory on the river Idle was won by the Bretwalda's army, since Edwin had no substantial forces of his own. When at the age of thirty-two he ascended the Northumbrian throne he owed his position entirely to Raedwald and had no choice but to acknowledge his suzerainty. For the remainder of Raedwald's reign, a period of eight years, Edwin ruled Northumbria as his vassal, thus extending the area under the Bretwalda's authority to include all of Northumbria. Raedwald became the first ruler to hold sway over all the Anglo-Saxon lands.

When Aethelberht died in 616, his nephew Saeberht, king of the East Saxons, died in the same year. The deaths of these two Christian kings at about the same time was a great set-back for the Christian religion. Aethelberht's son and successor, Eadbald, immediately apostatized from the new faith. Saeberht left three sons to inherit his kingdom and they likewise returned to their pagan beliefs. Bede stated that they paid the price for returning to the worship of devils, for not long afterwards they went into battle against the Gewissae and they were all killed, as was their army.[2] (This battle is another example of the contemporary military practice in which kings, when defeated, fought on to the death.) William of Malmesbury gives the date of this battle as 623 and names the kings as Seaxred and Sigeweard.[3] They were succeeded on the throne by Sigeberht, son of Sigeweard. The battle is not reported in the Anglo-Saxon Chronicle and hence its location is not known. It is clear that the West Saxons and the East Saxons were in physical contact and were in dispute, presumably over territorial delineation. The East Saxons had apparently extended the area under their rule to the west and had probably taken the Middle Saxons under their control. This could have taken place in the course of the war against the Middle Angles during the 590s under Aethelberht's leadership as Bretwalda. Certainly, the West Saxons would have lost control of Surrey as a result of their defeat in 592. The battle of 623 could have taken place north or south of the Thames. In the former case, it is possible that when the West Saxons regained their heartland around Dorchester in about 600 they also recaptured from the Middle Angles the expanse of territory in the Chiltern Hills, which they had originally seized from the Britons in 571; they would then have met the East Saxons on the eastern slopes or approaches of these hills. South of the Thames the two armies could have fought in the western frontier area of Surrey. In either case, the battle of 623 had the important result that it halted the western expansion of the East Saxons.

Eadbald, king of Kent, later returned to his Christian beliefs. Frankish influence in Kent continued during his reign, as, according to William of Malmesbury, he married Emma, daughter of King Theudebert II, who ruled Austrasia, the eastern province of Francia, 595-612.[4] (Theudebert II was a great-great-grandson of Clovis.) King Eadbald reigned for twenty-four years until his death in 640. He and Emma had two sons, Eorcenberht and Eormenred, and the former succeeded to the Kentish throne. There is no evidence that Eormenred shared power with his brother. Eorcenberht married Seaxburh, one of the daughters of Anna, king of the East Angles, and reigned also for

---

[2] Bede, *Historia Ecclesiastica*. part II ch. 5.

[3] Malmesbury, *The Kings before the Norman Conquest*. para. 98.

[4] Malmesbury, *The Kings before the Norman Conquest*. para. 11.

twenty-four years until his death in 664.

King Raedwald died in or about 625. There is considerable agreement that it was Raedwald who was buried in the ship-barrow at Sutton Hoo. The scale and splendour of the buried regalia may be seen as more consonant with the majesty of a Bretwalda than with the style of the ruler of a small provincial kingdom. Among the many objects found in the burial chamber two appear to have been the symbols of Raedwald's authority. One takes the form of what was described as a whetstone, surmounted by a ring and a figure of a stag, and gives the appearance of having been a sceptre. It would have symbolised Raedwald's authority as king of the East Angles. The other takes the form of a wrought iron rod five feet eight inches long with a frame-like structure near the apex. It was of a shape suitable to be held or carried near the king's person in battle or in peace, and was probably a standard to symbolise Raedwald's authority as Bretwalda.

Probable sceptre from Sutton Hoo   *Standard from Sutton Hoo*

131

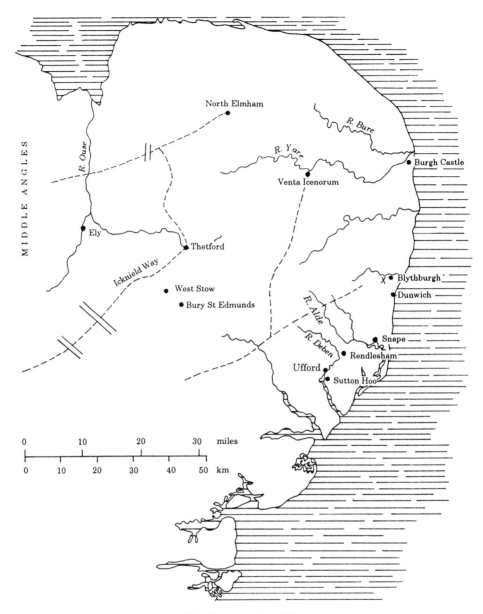

The East Anglian Kingdom.

EDWIN, KING OF THE NORTHUMBRIANS AND BRETWALDA

One of Edwin's first acts as king of the Northumbrians was to invade and take over the small British kingdom of Elmet. The *Historia Brittonum* reports that Edwin drove Ceretic out of Elmet.[1] This appears to be not so much an act of territorial aggrandisement as an act of political vengeance for Ceretic's part in the death of Edwin's nephew Hereric. The Welsh Annals state that Ceretic died in 619.

When Raedwald died in about 625, Edwin advanced a claim to succeed him as Bretwalda. Two of the Anglo-Saxon kingdoms, however, refused to give him their allegiance, Kent and Wessex. To bring Kent within his domain Edwin sought a dynastic marriage with Aethelberga, a daughter of King Aethelberht. Bede relates how Edwin sent suitors to King Eadbald, brother of Aethelberga, in 625 to ask for her hand in marriage, but Eadbald's reply was that it was not lawful for a Christian maiden to marry a pagan, lest her faith be profaned. Edwin was not to be deterred and he sent a promise to Eadbald, that he would do nothing to prevent Aethelberga and her companions from practising their Christian faith. Moreover, he undertook to discuss with his councillors the advisability of accepting the Christian religion himself. Eadbald accepted these assurances and agreed to the proposed marriage. On 21 July 625 Archbishop Justus ordained Paulinus as bishop to accompany Aethelberga and her party to Northumbria and to support them in their religious life.[2] It may be supposed that after these arrangements had been completed, King Eadbald withdrew his opposition to Edwin as Bretwalda.

The West Saxon kings remained true to their alliance with the Bernicians and strongly opposed the extension of Edwin's power. When he tried to assert his suzerainty over Wessex, the kings decided to take direct action to remove him from the scene. Bede tells that in 626 King

---

[1] Nennius, *Historia Brittonum.* para. 63.

[2] Bede, *Historia Ecclesiastica.* part II ch. 9.

Cwichelm of the West Saxons sent an assassin called Eomer, armed with a poisoned two-edged dagger, to Edwin's royal residence near the river Derwent. He arrived on the first day of Easter and gained access to Edwin by claiming to have a message to deliver. But he suddenly pulled out the dagger and attempted to strike Edwin. One of the king's thegns was able to interpose his own body and he received the fatal blow. In the ensuing tumult, Edwin was wounded, while the assassin and another king's thegn were killed.

On the same night Queen Aethelberga gave birth to a daughter, who was named Eanflaed. Bishop Paulinus assured the king that by his prayers he had been able to ensure the safe delivery of the child. Edwin was impressed and promised to serve Christ if he were granted life and victory in a campaign to pursue and punish the king who had sent the assassin. As a pledge for this promise, he delivered Eanflaed to Bishop Paulinus to be dedicated to Christ. At Pentecost she was baptized and became the first Northumbrian Christian. When he had recovered from his wounds, Edwin called up his army and marched into Wessex, which he would have ravaged – the Chronicle said that he killed five kings. Their identity is not stated, but they were probably minor members of the royal house, as Cynegils and Cwichelm survived and continued to rule the kingdom.

In fulfilment of his promise, King Edwin and all his nobles received the Christian faith on Easter Day (12 April) 627 at York in the church dedicated to St Peter, which Edwin himself had hastily built of wood. At the same time he established an episcopal see under Bishop Paulinus. It is clear that the Britons had a distinct memory of Edwin's baptism and their chroniclers recorded their version of it. The Welsh Annals entered it for the year 626 and stated that Edwin was baptised by Rhun, son of Urien. The *Historia Brittonum* also reported that Edwin and twelve thousand men were baptised by Rhun, son of Urien, and by Paulinus, archbishop of York, and they went on baptising all the Northumbrians for forty days. One of the sources for this information was stated to be Elfoddw, archbishop of Gwynedd in the period 768-809 i.e. within about fifty years of the event. On the strength of this testimony, Rhun, the son of Urien, the former king of Rheged, participated with Paulinus in the baptism of Edwin and the Northumbrians. Such collaboration may at first seem unlikely, as Rhun belonged to the Celtic church and Paulinus to the Roman. As an explanation, it is possible that Paulinus may have baptised the Anglian Northumbrians, while Rhun baptised British Northumbrians, who were still pagan. An understanding and friendship between Edwin and Rhun would be in accordance with the political alignments of the time, as they shared a common antipathy towards the Bernician regime.

The Northumbrians converted to Christianity at the time of Edwin's baptism at York would have been Deirans. But Edwin and Paulinus also took the new religion into Bernicia. Bede reported that they went with the queen to the royal residence at Yeavering, and for thirty-six days Paulinus was fully engaged in instructing the people in the new faith and baptising them in the nearby river Glen.[3] The location of Yeavering (NT 9330), fifteen miles west of Bamburgh, is significant. It stands beneath the hill fort of Yeavering Bell, considered to have been the early governmental centre of the southern Votadini and is probably related to it in some way. The site stands on an open wind-swept hill-side and could not have been chosen as a place of comfort. Outigern, the first British leader to take up arms against Ida in 547, could have made use of the hill fort and/or the lower site at Yeavering. In 1953-8, the latter was thoroughly excavated by Dr B. Hope-Taylor, who identified five separate phases of occupation. At the peak of its importance it contained a large hall (the villa regia) in which a throne would have stood. In an early phase it contained a temple, but later a church was built. A remarkable find was the foundations of a timber grandstand, which could have seated 320 persons, and may have been used by Paulinus when he was instructing his converts about the new religious faith. Bede added that later kings abandoned Yeavering and established a residence at Maelmin, probably modern Millfield (NT 941339), two miles from Yeavering. Paulinus also baptised in the river Swale near Catterick in the province of Deira. A church was built at the royal seat at Campodonum, unlocated but probably on the river Don. Paulinus also took his mission into the kingdom of Lindsey, and his first converts were in Lincoln, where he built a splendid stone church.

---

[3] Bede, *Historia Ecclesiastica.* part II ch. 14.

Upon the death of Raedwald, the vacant East Anglian throne went to his son Eorpwald, who acknowledged Edwin as Bretwalda. William of Malmesbury reported that the East Anglians swore obedience to Edwin, who granted Eorpwald 'the empty title of king, himself managed all things as he thought fit.'[4] Bede related how Edwin persuaded Eorpwald to accept the Christian faith, but not long afterwards he was killed by a pagan called Ricberht.[5] William of Malmesbury said that Eorpwald was baptised in 627 and in the same year was slain by Ricberht, who usurped the throne for three years.[6] There can be little doubt that this was a political assassination carried out (like the attempt on Edwin's life in the previous year) by Edwin's political opponents (the Bernicians and West Saxons), and for three years East Anglia was aligned against him. Ricberht's right to occupy the throne (if at all) is not known, but in 630 he was replaced by Sigeberht, who was a half-brother of Eorpwald on the maternal side. He had been banished to Gaul by Raedwald and while in exile had embraced the Christian faith. His accession in 630 as a Christian king probably represented the return of East Anglia to the suzerainty of the Bretwalda. The political change was matched by corresponding religious changes. Sigeberht immediately set about the conversion of his kingdom and was assisted in this task by Felix, who was Burgundian in origin. Felix was ordained as bishop in 630 and was given an episcopal see in the city of Dommoc, probably Dunwich. He presided over the East Angles as their bishop for seventeen years.

Bede was full of praise for Edwin as a Christian monarch and painted a glowing picture of his reign. He considered that as a sign of divine favour Edwin was able to extend his earthly kingdom to include not only English but also British provinces. This statement accords with the evidence set out above that Edwin enjoyed good relations with the Britons, who gave him support while in exile. The presence of Rhun at his baptism also suggest that he was attempting to integrate the Britons peacefully into his realm. Bede illustrated the peaceful conditions within Britain during Edwin's reign by quoting a proverb that a woman with her newborn babe could wander from sea to sea without molestation. He

---

[4] Malmesbury, *The Kings before the Roman Conquest*. para. 48.

[5] Bede, *Historia Ecclesiastica*. part II ch. 15.

[6] Malmesbury, *The Kings before the Roman Conquest*. para. 97.

tells how Edwin ordered that bronze cups should be fixed near springs of drinking water for the use of travellers and no one dared to interfere with them. When he proceeded in state, whether in peace or war, he was accompanied by a standard bearer, who bore a banner known as a tufa.[7] This banner may well have been similar to the standard found at Sutton Hoo and considered to be a symbol of the authority of the Bretwalda.

In 628 a new dynamic figure appeared on the political scene in the southwest Midlands. He was Penda, son of Pybba (reigned 600 – 610). Cynegils and Cwichelm fought Penda at Cirencester, but afterwards they came to an agreement with him. Florence of Worcester agreed: 'Cynegils and Cwichelm, kings of the West Saxons, fought with Penda, king of the Mercians, near Cirencester, and afterwards, having made peace and confirmed it, retired.' The statement that Penda was king of the Mercians in 628 is not supported by Bede, who gave 633 as the date of his accession to the Mercian throne. It is possible that in 628 Penda was contending for the throne in opposition to Cearl, who appears to have recognised Edwin as Bretwalda. It was suggested above that as a result of the battle of Beandun in 614 the West Saxons had been able to re-occupy the southern part of the Hwicce. The northern part was probably still held by the Hwicce, but their army had been severely weakened. Penda's objective in 628 appears to have been to prevent any further advance by the West Saxons towards Mercia or even to expel them completely from Hwiccian territory and to bring the weakened Hwicce under his protection. Available evidence indicates that the fighting was not pursued to the point of defeat of one side by the other and that an agreed settlement was reached, after which the West Saxon kings withdrew from the Hwicce and returned to Dorchester. In the absence of a military victory, the agreement at Cirencester was probably a compromise, which has not been explicitly reported, but some idea of its provisions may be gained by the events which followed it. The main consequences of the agreement were that:

1. The kingdom of the Hwicce continued to exist intact;
2. It gained a new regime of rulers belonging to the Bernician royal dynasty.

---

[7] Bede, *Historia Ecclesiastica.* part II ch. 16.

A passage in Bede implied that two brothers, Eanfrid and Eanhere, were Christian rulers of the Hwicce, who were themselves Christian. The cumulative evidence indicates that this Eanfrid is identical with the Eanfrith who was Aethelfrith's eldest son, head of the Bernician royal dynasty and rival claimant to the Northumbrian throne. After eleven years spent in exile in Scotland, Eanfrith was still seeking to regain his father's throne in 628. His efforts would have received strong backing from his father's allies, the kings of the West Saxons, particularly after the ravaging of their kingdom by Edwin in 626. It appears that as a result of the Cirencester agreement, the West Saxon kings were able to install Eanfrith on the throne of the Hwicce, perhaps with his brother Eanhere as joint king. This was a brilliant diplomatic move, as a result of which the kingdom of the Hwicce was brought into the alignment against Edwin. Eanfrith received a power base from which to carry on his struggle. By 628 the West Saxon kings had formed a solid bloc of states opposed to Edwin's rule, consisting of Wessex, the Hwicce under Eanfrith and East Anglia under Ricberht. Penda, who was probably sympathetic to the political alignment against Edwin, had achieved his immediate aim of limiting the extension of West Saxon power towards Mercia and may have agreed to withdraw his army at the same time as the West Saxon withdrawal.

The historical significance of the Cirencester agreement was that it marked a turning point for the Hwicce: they ceased to be a British kingdom and became part of England. It can be safely assumed that as soon as Eanfrith and Eanhere ascended the Hwiccian throne, the country was opened up to Anglian, mainly Bernician, influences. The two new kings would have brought with them their personal followers and military companions, who had been sharing their exile. To ensure the loyalty of their retinue, the kings would have made them grants of landed estates in Hwiccia, which would soon have become settled by Bernician immigrants. The estates would have been given Anglian names and the process of Anglicisation had begun. The Hwicce, as a defeated people, probably played little or no part in the Cirencester agreement, but their kingdom continued as a political entity and it is possible that their new rulers married Hwiccian princesses, so ensuring the continuity of the original Hwiccian royal dynasty. It was convenient that the new rulers belonged to the Celtic church, as did the Hwicce themselves.

It is known that Eanfrith had at least one son and a daughter. The son was born of Eanfrith's first wife, a princess of the Pictish royal house. He eventually became king of the Picts (reigned 653-7) and was known as Talorcen mac Anfrith. He never became directly involved in Hwiccian affairs, but the role he was to play in the Anglian power struggle is explained below in the chapter on King Oswy. Eanfrith's daughter, brought up in Hwiccia, was called Eabae, and her mother could have been Eanfrith's Hwiccian queen. In due course she married Aethelwalch, king of the South Saxons, a convert to Christianity and an ally of Mercia. Bede confirmed this: 'The queen, Eabae, by name, had been baptised in her own province, that of the Hwicce. For she was the daughter of Eanfrith, the brother of Eanhere, both of whom were Christians with their people.'[8]

After Edwin became Bretwalda and had gained unrestricted power his relations with the British kings started to deteriorate. When Cadfan died in about 625 his kingdom was still limited to the island of Mona and his memorial stone may be seen at Llangadwaladr near his capital at Aberffraw. He was succeeded by his son Cadwallon, who would have known Edwin from the time of his exile in Gwynedd. Any hopes that Edwin would repay the hospitality he had received by restoring Chester and the lost lands to Gwynedd had faded. This could be the reason why the Welsh poem *Moliant Cadwallon* (In Praise of Cadwallon) spoke of the great treachery of Edwin. It implies that Edwin had broken his agreement with Cadfan, but Edwin may have considered that any agreement he had made with the Welsh kings was invalid as he had regained his throne without their assistance. By about 629 Cadwallon renounced his allegiance to Edwin and he appears to have defiantly assumed leadership of the other regional kings. This was in accordance with the status of *primus inter pares* enjoyed by the kings of Gwynedd since the time of Cunedda. Cadwallon's challenge to Edwin's authority was so serious that Edwin had to respond quickly.

Edwin took his forces across the Menai Strait, drove Cadwallon out of

---

[8] Bede, *Historia Ecclesiastica.* part IV ch. 13.

Mona and took possession of the island. Welsh sources described Edwin as one of the three great oppressions of Mona, nurtured within the island. The Welsh Annals report in the annal for 629 that King Cadwallon was besieged in the island of Glennauc. This is also known as Puffin Island, a small island off the east coast of Anglesey. Cadwallon was able to escape to Ireland. Bede said that Edwin brought not only Anglesey, but also the Isle of Man, under his control. Cadwallon soon returned from Ireland and raised another army, as the Welsh Annals reported that in the year 633 Cadwallon was victorious at the battle of Meigen. It erroneously stated that Edwin and his two sons were killed in the battle, but it may be correct that Edwin suffered defeat at Meigen, traditionally placed on the borders of Powys. Welsh bards described one of Edwin's battles, perhaps Meigen, as one of the three pollutions of the Severn, because the blood of those killed reddened the river from its source to the estuary. As a result of his victory at Meigen, Cadwallon would have regained all the lost territory and his capital at Chester. Edwin withdrew his army across the Pennines.

In 633 Penda became king of the Mercians and at about the same time concluded a military alliance with Cadwallon. There is no evidence to explain how Penda was able to obtain the Mercian throne from Cearl, but a violent seizure would by typical of his methods. The *Historia Brittonum* stated that Penda was the first Mercian king to separate Mercia from Northumbria, the implication being that Penda's predecessor had accepted the overlordship of Edwin as Bretwalda.[9] The immediate aim of the military alliance was the destruction of Edwin's power. At first Cadwallon seemed to be the dominant member of the alliance. Their combined armies pursued Edwin across the Pennines. The Chronicle reported that on 14 October 633 King Edwin and his son Osfrith were slain at Hatfield, which is situated seven miles northeast of Doncaster. At about the same time all the buildings and the church at the royal seat at Campodonum in the Doncaster area were destroyed. Edwin was forty-eight years old at the time of his death. His other son Eadfrith fell into Penda's hands and was subsequently put to death by him.

---

[9] Nennius, *Historia Brittonum*. para. 65.

The land of the Hwicce

OSWALD, KING OF THE NORTHUMBRIANS AND BRETWALDA

The battle of Hatfield led to the end of Edwin's attempt to establish a political system in which British, Anglian and Saxon kingdoms could co-exist peacefully under his supreme rule as high-king. The immediate result was the destruction of his army and government, followed by chaos and anarchy throughout Northumbria, and the new Christian diocese which he had founded collapsed. Bede stated that there was such confusion within Northumbria that there was no safety except in flight. Bishop Paulinus took Queen Aethelberga with him back to Kent by ship, taking with them Edwin's daughter, Eanflaed, his son Uscfrea, and Yffi, the king's grandson.[1]

The political unity of Northumbria was unable to withstand the shock of defeat and the kingdom divided again, as told by Bede. The new king of Deira was Osric, the son of Aelfric, an uncle of Edwin's, who had been converted to the Christian faith by Paulinus. The kingdom of Bernicia passed rightfully to Eanfrith. As already explained, in 628 Eanfrith had been placed upon the throne of the Hwicce by agreement between Penda and the West Saxon kings, and by 633 he had achieved the unique distinction of becoming king of two kingdoms in different parts of the country. It may be assumed that he led his followers north from the Hwicce to claim his father's throne. Neither Eanfrith nor Osric were to hold their thrones for long. According to Bede they soon apostatized after gaining their earthly kingdoms. The following summer, probably in York, Osric besieged Cadwallon, who promptly sallied out and destroyed his attackers. He then led his army against Eanfrith, who was forced to sue for peace. When approached by Eanfrith with only twelve of his thegns to discuss peace terms, Cadwallon seized him and put him to death.[2]

This immediately created a problem concerning a successor as head

---

[1] Bede, *Historia Ecclesiastica.* part II ch. 20.

[2] Bede, *Historia Ecclesiastica.* part III ch. 1.

of the Bernician royal dynasty. Eanfrith's son Talorcen had been born while he was in exile among the Scots and Picts and in 634 could not have been more than about sixteen years of age. In the critical situation of the time it was essential to have someone who could lead the Bernicians in battle against Cadwallon. The choice went to Oswald, who was the eldest of the sons born by Acha, Aethelfrith's second wife. He was, therefore, Eanfrith's half-brother, but he had the advantage that through his mother he had a legitimate claim to the Deiran throne, which was also vacant. He lost no time in marching the Bernician army south along Dere Street. Cadwallon's forces were probably deployed along a section of the Wall to block Oswald's entry into Deira. While still north of the Wall and when he knew that a battle was imminent, Oswald set up a cross at a place called Hevenfelth – the heavenly field – and prayed for victory. Bede reported that Oswald advanced against Cadwallon, who was defeated and killed in battle at Denisesburn, the brook of Denis.[3] The battle is also recorded in the Welsh Annals as the battle of Catscaul, literally the battle within the Wall. Denisesburn is usually identified with Rowley Brook, south of Hexham (NY 9364).

Oswald's victory enabled him to take over Deira and to re-unite the two halves of Northumbria. He became the most powerful ruler in Britain and at the age of about thirty was appointed Bretwalda. Unfortunately, the emergence of a re-united Northumbria under the strong leadership of Oswald was a development which was unacceptable to Penda and the British kings. Penda, now head of the Mercian royal dynasty, which traced its lineage through Icel back to Offa, was determined not to accept a position of subordination to Oswald and refused to recognise him as Bretwalda. The British kings were equally opposed to accepting the rule of a Northumbrian overlord. They had lost their leader in Cadwallon and, in the absence of an obvious British successor, found no difficulty in transferring their support to Penda. The British/Mercian alliance held firm and the aim of its struggle was re-directed against Oswald. The result was a shift in the political divide. Before the battle of Hatfield it had been between the supporters of Bernicia and those of Deira. After the battle of Denisesburn it was

---

[3] Bede, *Historia Ecclesiastica*. part III ch. 2.

between the supporters of Northumbria and those of Mercia under the respective leadership of Oswald and Penda. This change affected the relations between Mercia and Wessex, which now found themselves in opposing camps. This point marks the beginning of the long period of hostility between Mercia and Wessex.

According to Bede: 'Oswald, as soon as he received the kingdom, desired that all the nation which he began to rule should be imbued with the grace of the Christian faith . . . and sent to the chief men of the Scots . . . asking them to send him a bishop, that the nation of the English whom he was ruling might by his teaching and ministry both learn the gifts and receive the sacraments of the faith of the Lord. Nor were they slow in granting what he asked; for he received Bishop Aidan . . . On the arrival of the bishop, the king gave him a place for an episcopal see on the island of Lindisfarne.' This place had already acquired a special status as the location of the burial mound of Queen Bebba, Oswald's step-mother, on the rocky height of Beblowe Crag. Aidan founded a monastery on the site now occupied by the ruins of the Benedictine Abbey, and a statue of St Aidan has been erected there to commemorate this great figure in early Anglo-Saxon history. 'The king industriously applied himself to building and extending the Church of Christ in his kingdom . . . From that time there came many day by day from the region of the Scots to Britain and preached the word of the faith with great devotion to those provinces of the English over which Oswald reigned . . . Churches were built in various places; . . . possessions and estates were given by gift of the king for the founding of monasteries; English children, as well as older people, were instructed by Scottish masters in study and the observance of monastic discipline.'[4] As explained below, there is evidence of Celtic-style monasteries in East Anglia and Sussex, which were probably founded as a result of the work of Oswald and St Aidan.

The East Angles quickly felt the effects of the political changes, which had taken place. As explained above, King Sigeberht had probably given his allegiance to Edwin as Bretwalda. Bede stated that during Sigeberht's reign a holy man called Fursa arrived in East Anglia from

---

[4] Bede, *Historia Ecclesiastica.* part III ch. 3.

Ireland. He was received with honour by Sigeberht, who gave him a place on which to build a monastery, near the sea inside a fort known as Cnobheresburg.[5] It is generally considered that this is identical with Burgh Castle, the Saxon Shore fort Garannonum. Excavations on the site have revealed what are probably the cells and little church of a monastic settlement, apparently Fursa's foundation. It is likely that Fursa was one of the Scottish monks sent by Oswald and Aidan to spread the Christian faith among the pagan East Angles and it is apparent from this that Sigeberht had accepted Oswald as Bretwalda. The site of Burgh Castle, like Lindisfarne,

Representation of St. Aidan at Lindisfarne.

illustrates the Celtic preference for locations in remote and desolate places near the sea, where the ascetic style of devotion could be practised by the monks. The evidence set out above shows that during Sigeberht's reign his kingdom was being introduced to Christianity from two sources: during the time when Edwin was Bretwalda the episcopal centre was established in the south under Roman influence from Canterbury; during the time when Oswald was Bretwalda the northern part was being converted under Celtic influence from Ireland. Two different religious traditions arose, contributing to the division of the East Angles into the North Folk and the South Folk.

Bede also reported the existence of a Celtic monastery in Sussex at Bosham (SU 8004), another desolate site by the sea.[6] Bede did not know

---

[5] Bede, *Historia Ecclesiastica.* part III ch. 19
[6] Bede, *Historia Ecclesiastica.* part IV ch. 13.

when the monastery was founded, but it had been in existence for some time when he reported it in about 680. At that time it consisted of only five or six monks under Abbot Dicul. One of Fursa's companions had this name and could have been the same man. The possibility, therefore, arises that the monastery at Bosham was also founded as a result of Aidan's initiative and that the South Saxon kings had accepted Oswald as Bretwalda.

In East Anglia, Sigeberht's allegiance to Oswald would have been opposed by Penda and, indeed, his reign ended soon after the arrival of Fursa. Bede reported that Sigeberht abdicated in favour of his kinsman, Ecgric, who had already been ruling part of the kingdom, and he entered a monastery which he himself had founded. According to William of Malmesbury, Sigeberht entered the monastery at Bury St Edmund's in 634. (This date appears to be too early.) In the political rivalries of the time, Sigeberht abdicated probably under pressure from Penda. Ecgric replaced Sigeberht on the throne, but when he failed to submit to Penda, the latter sought a military solution. Bede tells that Penda attacked East Anglia with his army and when the East Angles saw that they were no match for the Mercian army they turned to Sigeberht and implored him to come to their aid. At first he refused, but they dragged him forcibly from the monastery to join the soldiers. But in view of his monastic vows he refused to wield a weapon and held only a rod. Not surprisingly, Sigeberht and Ecgric were both slain and the East Anglian army was scattered. Anna, son of Eni, a brother of Raedwald, succeeded to the throne.[7] William of Malmesbury gives a date of 635 for this campaign.[8] It will be noted that Mercia does not have a common frontier with East Anglia. When he invaded East Anglia in 635 Penda would have led his army across Middle Anglian territory, which would have been left severely weakened militarily as a result of Aethelberht's successive victories, and by 635 had apparently been brought under Mercian protection.

King Anna would have had to give satisfactory assurances and probably hostages to Penda. A marriage was arranged between Anna's

---

[7] Bede, *Historia Ecclesiastica.* part III ch. 18.

[8] Malmesbury, *The Kings before the Norman Conquest.* para. 97.

daughter Aetheldreda and Tonberht, prince of the South Gyrwe, a Middle Anglian folk occupying the Fen District.[9] As the Middle Angles, like the Mercians, were still entirely pagan, it appears that King Anna had had to agree to the marriage of his Christian daughter to a pagan, a dynastic union probably sponsored by the pagan Penda.

The conquest of East Anglia by Penda would have been a matter of great concern to Oswald. His power base in Northumbria had become separated from his southern allies, the West Saxons and the Hwicce, by a hostile block of kingdoms stretching from west to east (Mercia, Middle Anglia and East Anglia). The same year (635) Oswald travelled south to Dorchester-on-Thames for important discussions with the West Saxon kings. In view of the rival claims of Talorcen, son and heir of Eanfrith, Oswald would have needed to ensure that the West Saxons recognised him as *de facto* leader of the Bernicians. The extension of Mercian power was a strong inducement for the West Saxons to recognise Oswald's position, to accept him as Bretwalda and to confirm with him the Bernician-West Saxon military alliance. To seal this alliance it was agreed that Oswald should marry the daughter of King Cynegils. According to Reginald of Durham she was called Cyneburh.

It so happened that Oswald's presence in Dorchester coincided with the arrival there of Bishop Birinus, who had been sent by Pope Honorius to convert the pagan Saxons. Bede reported how King Oswald acted as godfather at the baptism of King Cynegils. The two kings gave Birinus the city of Dorchester for his episcopal see.[10] The Chronicle reported that Cwichelm, son and joint king of Cynegils, was baptised by Birinus at Dorchester in 636 (he died later in the same year) and that Cuthred, Cwichelm's son, was likewise baptised in 639. It is accepted that the nave of the present Abbey church (built about 1120) stands on the site on the bank of the river Thame, where Birinus built his cathedral church and may contain portions of it in its fabric. A shrine recently rebuilt and rededicated to St Birinus may be seen in the present Abbey church. Bede's account confirms that Dorchester was being used as the capital city of the West Saxons. It is of interest that Bede should report

---

[9] Bede, *Historia Ecclesiastica.* part IV ch. 17.

[10] Bede, *Historia Ecclesiastica.* part III ch. 7.

that the two kings gave Birinus the site at Dorchester, showing that Oswald exercised authority in Wessex by virtue of his position as Bretwalda.

As in East Anglia, the Christian faith was brought to the West Saxons not only by a Roman bishop, but also by monks from the Celtic church. William of Malmesbury reported the arrival of an Irish monk called Meildulf in Wiltshire, but did not give a date, so it cannot be confirmed that he had been sent by Aidan. He founded a monastery suitable for the ascetic life on a former hill fort surrounded on three sides by the river Avon. His monastery became known as Meildulfesburh, modern Malmesbury. It received royal support at an early stage, when Aldhelm, a member of the royal family, became a monk there, and eventually was appointed abbot in 672.

Abbey Church at Dorchester-on-Thames.

Among the peoples who would have welcomed Cadwallon's invasion of Northumbria in 633 were the Votadini. By this time the southern Votadini had been absorbed by the Bernicians, but the northern Votadini had maintained their independence with their capital probably on the rock fortress of Caer Eidyn (or Dun Eidyn). It is not known to what extent (if at all) the Votadini gave active support to Cadwallon after Hatfield, but it is apparent that soon after Oswald had returned from Dorchester he decided that the continued independence of the northern Votadini constituted an unacceptable threat to his kingdom: a military linkage with Mercia was a possibility that he could not ignore. The Annals of Ulster indicate that action against the northern Votadini was taken about 638 by the Scots and Bernicians, probably acting together as allies. The Scots under their king, Domnall Brecc, advanced from the west but were defeated at Glen Mureson, probably Murieston Water twelve miles southwest of Edinburgh. Oswald besieged and succeeded in capturing Eten, a version of Eidyn, and its name was anglicised to Edinburgh. This action completed the final conquest of the Votadini, who disappeared as a separate political entity. Northumbrian power now stretched to the southern shore of the Firth of Forth, and the northern frontier now impinged on the territory of the Picts and the Strathclyde Britons. It is likely that both of these peoples were sufficiently overawed by Northumbrian power to accept Oswald as overlord. Bede reported that he had under his dominion all the nations and provinces of Britain, speaking four languages, the Britons, the Picts, the Scots and the English.[11]

Another province which Oswald brought under his control as Bretwalda was the kingdom of Lindsey, but the people of Lindsey were not pleased to have him as overlord. Bede told how the monks of Bardney (TF 1169) in Lindsey were opposed to him, because he came from another province and had obtained dominion over them.[12] It is apparent that when Oswald brought Lindsey under his rule the monastery at Bardney was already in existence and therefore must have been founded during the episcopacy of Bishop Paulinus (626-633). It would have been one of the earliest churches within Lindsey, after Lincoln itself, and would have practised the rites of the Roman church.

During the year 641 the situation in the Midlands moved to a major crisis. Cynegils, king of the West Saxons, died and was succeeded by his son Cenwealh. The change of ruler revealed a curious situation about the status of the Christian religion at the West Saxon court. The old king had embraced the Christian faith and his example was followed by

---

[11] Bede, *Historia Ecclesiastica*. part III ch. 6.
[12] Bede, *Historia Ecclesiastica*. part III ch. 11.

other members of the royal family, including his son Cwichelm, who appears to have been the chosen favourite to succeed his father. But Cwichelm met an untimely death in 636. It may be significant that the new king in 641 had decided to remain a pagan, and it is also noteworthy that Cenwealh had married Penda's sister. There is, therefore, evidence that he had come under Penda's influence and had become a Mercian puppet either at the time of his accession or soon after. The result was a change in the political alignment of the West Saxons from the Northumbrian to the Mercian camp. The military alliance with Oswald was abandoned and Oswald's entire situation in the south came under threat. The Bernician regime of the Hwicce became isolated and was in urgent need of military support if it was to resist pressure from Penda. Oswald was left with no option but to intervene militarily to restore the situation in Wessex and to bring support to the Hwiccian regime.

During the summer of 641 he marched his army from York across the Pennines and turned in a southerly direction towards the territory of the Cornovii, a still independent British people occupying roughly the area of modern Shropshire and allied to Penda. Oswald's route would have taken him near to the city of Chester, which he may have re-possessed. There is no specific information on this, but it would have been tactically unsound for Oswald to leave Chester in Welsh hands as his army moved further south. Penda led the Mercian army north to support of his ally, Cyndyllan, king of the Cornovii, (son of Cyndrwyn), whose territory was about to be invaded. Their combined forces took up a defensive position in the Cornovian frontier area in the hill fort at Old Oswestry (SJ 2931) to block Oswald's southerly advance. A major battle ensued on 5th August 641, reported in the Anglo-Saxon Chronicle as the battle of Maserfeld and in the Welsh Annals as the battle of Maes Cogwy.

The Welsh bard Llywarch Hen recorded:

> I saw the Field of Maes Cogwy
> Armies, and the cry of men hard pressed.
> Cynddylan brought them aid[13]

---

[13] Morris, *The Age of Arthur.* p. 242.

The Northumbrian army was defeated and Oswald killed at the age of thirty-eight. A Mercian prince, Eoba, a brother of Penda, was also slain. The death of Oswald at the hands of the pagan Penda caused him to be regarded and venerated as a martyr. Some years later his younger brother Oswy retrieved his head, hands and arms, which had been severed, and preserved the head at Lindisfarne, the hands and arms at Bamburgh. The remaining relics were removed by Queen Osthryth of Mercia to the monastery at Bardney in or soon after 679.

The Annals of Ulster show that the armed struggle in the Midlands was accompanied by an outbreak of hostilities in the north. The British kingdom of Strathclyde, presumably an ally of Penda, was attacked from two directions. In December, Domnall Brecc, king of the Scots, marched against Owain, king of Strathclyde, son of Beli, from the northwest in support of his Bernician allies. A battle took place at Strath Carron (NS 1585), where the Scottish army was defeated and Domnall Brecc was slain. At about the same time, Oswy advanced against the Britons from the east; fortunately, he fared better than his brother and his Scottish ally and survived the encounter. It will be noted that in both the Midlands and the north it was the Bernicians who took the military initiative.

THE RIVALRY OF PENDA AND OSWY

The battle of Maserfeld resulted in another reversal of the political balance, with Penda now the most powerful ruler in Britain. The British kings continued to give him their support, while none of the Anglian or Saxon kings south of Hadrian's Wall was strong enough to oppose him actively. In Northumbria the shock of defeat caused the kingdom to split again into its two constituent parts and it ceased to be the dominant power. The Deiran throne went to Oswine, a son of King Osric. In Bernicia the death of Oswald posed the problem of the rightful succession to the throne. He had a son Aethelwald, but as he had married only in 635, the boy was still very young when his father was killed. There can, however, be little doubt that on the principle of primogeniture it was Talorcen, son of Eanfrith, who had the legal right to be head of the Bernician royal dynasty and to succeed to the Bernician throne. In 641 he would have been about twenty-three years of age, but probably without an effective power base. When the question of the succession arose, Oswald's younger brother Oswy was in a strong position: he had an army already mobilised, which had survived its encounter with the Britons of Strathclyde. He ignored the rights of his nephew, Talorcen, and was able to seize the Bernician throne for himself at the age of about thirty. At this time he had already contracted a marriage which linked him to the former Regedian royal family. His first wife was Rieinmellt, daughter of Royth, son of Rhun,[1] who had officiated at the baptism of Edwin. She was probably the mother of his son Alhfrith and daughter Alhflaed.

Of the two Northumbrian kingdoms Deira was the weaker militarily. From Bede's description, Oswine appears to have been an unwarlike king. Oswy, on the other hand, remained defiant of Penda and refused to submit to his demands. For the next thirteen years hostility persisted between Mercia and Bernicia and erupted three

---

[1] Nennius, *Historia Brittonum*. para. 57.

times into open warfare. But Oswy was powerless to help the Bernician regime established in the land of the Hwicce. Although there is no direct evidence about the situation of the Hwicce at this time, it appears that after the death of Eanfrith in 634 his brother Eanhere continued to rule the Hwicce and, indeed, raised a family there. At first he would have been dependent upon Oswald for the protection of his kingdom and may have had support from the West Saxon kings, but after Oswald's death in 641 he was left with no choice but to bow to the will of Penda.

For four years there was no challenge to Penda's rule, but in 645 King Cenwealh deserted from the Mercian camp. Bede reported: 'He put away the sister of Penda, king of the Mercians, whom he had married and took another wife; and thus, attacked in war and deprived of his kingdom by him, he withdrew to the king of the East Angles, whose name was Anna.'[2] William of Malmesbury made it clear that Cenwealh was 'attacked and defeated by Penda, king of Mercia, whose sister he had repudiated.'[3] It appears that Penda had led his army across Middle Anglia into Wessex and occupied the capital at Dorchester. All the Gewissian territory north of the Thames, which had been seized by the Middle Angles in 592, was detached from Wessex and once more incorporated into Middle Anglia. After Cenwealh had fled, Cuthred, son of Cwichelm, was placed as a Mercian puppet on the vacant throne. The West Saxons had to seek a new capital and they chose Venta, modern Winchester, which had been unused as a political centre since the collapse of the kingdom of the Belgae.

Although King Anna of the East Angles may at first have given assurances of loyalty to Penda, it later became apparent that Bernician influences were being exerted in East Anglia, when, as reported by Bede, the King and certain of his nobles endowed the Celtic monastic foundation at Burgh Castle with finer buildings and gifts.[4] Their action suggests that East Anglia had become aligned with Oswy against Penda, thus explaining why Cenwealh found a refuge there when he was expelled from his own kingdom. Soon after his arrival he renounced his

---

[2] Bede, *Historia Ecclesiastica*. part III ch. 7.

[3] Malmesbury, *The Kings before the Norman Conquest*. para. 19.

[4] Bede, *Historia Ecclesiastica*. part III ch. 19.

paganism and in 646 was baptised by Bishop Felix.

As a result of these developments, Penda accepted the necessity of undertaking direct military action against the Bernicians. At some date before 651 he carried out an invasion of Bernicia and attacked the very gates of Bamburgh, but he failed to capture the fortress as a result of what Bede regarded as a miracle wrought by Bishop Aidan. He tells how Penda instructed his army to gather planks, beams, wattle and thatch from the neighbouring villages and pile it up against the defences of the fortress on the landward side. When the wind was in the right direction he set fire to it. At this time Bishop Aidan was on one of the Farne islands, two miles distant from Bamburgh. When he saw the flames and smoke he raised his hands and called out to the Lord, exclaiming against Penda. As soon as he had spoken, the wind changed direction and blew the fire and smoke back against the attackers, who called off their assault, because they saw that the fortress was under divine protection.[5] It is apparent that Penda's campaign failed to bring the Bernicians to subjection and he withdrew without achieving his purpose.

In 648 Cenwealh returned to Wessex and retrieved his throne, compensating his nephew, Cuthred, by a large grant of land on Ashdown amounting to three thousand hides − a hide is the amount of land needed to support one household. The name Ashdown denoted the line of the Berkshire Downs. Cenwealh may have timed his return to Wessex to take advantage of Penda's absence in the far north, which would indicate that Penda's invasion of Bernicia took place in 648. The revolt against his rule in Wessex would have threatened the security of Mercia and Middle Anglia and this could explain why Penda withdrew from Bernicia before his objective had been achieved. The interplay of events in the north and south was probably more than fortuitous and may be attributed to Oswy's skilful diplomacy.

The removal of the West Saxon capital to Venta would have required the episcopal see to move there, but Bishop Birinus remained at Dorchester until his death. Upon Cenwealh's return to his kingdom in 648 he lost little time in founding a new cathedral church at Winchester

---

[5] Bede, *Historia Ecclesiastica*. part III ch. 16.

dedicated to St Peter the same year. Cenwealh's Minster, of which nothing remains above ground, was erected on the site now occupied by its successor, the present Cathedral church.

The events of 648 had moved to Penda's disadvantage. The West Saxons had regained their independence and the West Saxon-Bernician alignment was re-established. The armies of the main participants were still intact and capable of further combat. A renewal of hostilities seemed inevitable, so both sides reviewed their situation in preparation for the next encounter. Penda decided that it was necessary to summon his British allies to his aid. Oswy perceived that the political status of Deira was a major factor in the security of Bernicia. To reach Bernicia in 648 Penda must have marched his army across Deiran territory. Oswine appears to have been unable to prevent this use of his territory, because of the weakness of his forces. It is likely, in fact, that Deira had become politically subservient to Mercia, a situation which had become unacceptable to Oswy. By 651 he had come to the decision that the security and independence of Bernicia could be ensured against a Mercian assault only by his annexation of Deira. Some time earlier he had strengthened his claim to rule Deira by contracting a dynastic marriage with Eanflaed, daughter of King Edwin, who had been living in Kent. Relations between the two Northumbrian regimes deteriorated and by the year 651 had reached a point where they were preparing for war with one another. Bede described the climax of their dispute. When the two armies had been mobilised Oswine realised that his army was no match for Oswy's and that he could not go into battle with it. The Deiran army had been assembled at Wilfaresdun, ten miles northwest of Catterick, when Oswine gave the order for it to be disbanded. He then went into hiding with a nobleman he thought he could trust. But the nobleman betrayed him to Oswy, who sent his reeve, Aethelwine, to put him to death; this was carried out on 20 August at Gilling (NZ 1805), two miles north of Richmond. Some time later a monastery was erected on the spot to atone for the crime.[6]

The elimination of Oswine left the Deiran throne vacant. Oswy himself had a strong claim to it through his mother Acha, daughter of

---

[6] Bede, *Historia Ecclesiastica*. part III ch. 14.

Aelle, but his responsibility for the murder of Oswine made him unacceptable to the Deiran Witangemot. To fill the vacant throne, the Deirans appointed Aethelwald, son of Oswald. He would now have been about fifteen years of age and would have had hopes of recovering his rightful patrimony as king of Northumbria. He was now half way to this goal, but his uncle, Oswy, was firmly established on the Bernician throne, and their aims were diametrically opposed. The relationship between Aethelwald and Penda is not clear, although they had a common political goal to remove Oswy from the Bernician throne. There is a distinct possibility that Aethelwald gained the Deiran throne with Penda's support and became politically subservient to him. Bede tells how Aethelwald as king of the Deirans gave land at Lastingham (SE 7920) near Pickering to Cedd for the foundation of a monastery,[7] showing that Oswy had withdrawn from Deira, leaving Aethelwald in possession.

By the year 652 Penda was ready to mount a further assault on Bernicia, but this time re-inforced by the armies of his British allies. But he had learned an important lesson from the campaign of 648: before he left his own kingdom he must first ensure that it was secure against intervention by Cenwealh. In this connection he was able to invoke his friendly relations with the Britons in the west (known as the West Welsh), for whom he had a special role: to neutralise the West Saxons and the Hwicce. For the year 652 the Chronicle reported briefly that Cenwealh fought at Bradford-on-Avon. This town has historically formed part of the county of Wiltshire and it is likely that in 652 it lay in the northwest corner of Wessex, adjacent to the frontier with the Hwicce and the West Welsh. It will be noted that the chronicler does not specify the identity of Cenwealh's opponents, but William of Malmesbury confirms that they were Britons, who according to him were trying to regain their lost lands. This was a major invasion of West Saxon territory by the West Welsh and Cenwealh considered it sufficiently serious to justify him taking personal charge, so that he could deploy levies from other shires if necessary. The chronicler does not actually report the outcome of the fighting, but William of Malmesbury

---

[7] Bede, *Historia Ecclesiastica*. part III ch. 23.

considered it a victory for Cenwealh. It is likely, therefore, that the invaders were repelled and failed in their attempt to recover their lost lands. But they served Penda's purpose well by tying down West Saxon troops and preventing them from being deployed against Mercian or Middle Anglian territory.

Penda was now able to leave Mercia and march north with his Welsh allies to Bernicia. He would have needed to cross Deiran territory again and this was presumably carried out without opposition from Aethelwald. There is, however, no evidence that the Deirans joined in the invasion of Bernicia. It is likely that a further attempt was made to capture Bamburgh, as Bede reported that Penda burned the royal residence near the capital together with the associated church and village. It was at this church that Bishop Aidan had died on 31 August 651. Bede told how the wooden beam in the church upon which the bishop was leaning when he died was miraculously spared from the flames. A similar miracle occurred when the church was burnt a second time accidentally.[8] It is likely that these events took place at the royal estate at Yeavering, which archeologists report was twice destroyed by fire. It is clear that the Bernician army was completely outnumbered by Penda's huge allied force. Oswy's tactics were to avoid a direct confrontation and he gradually withdrew his army until it reached Iudeu, probably the rock fortress at Stirling. This location was in the immediate vicinity of the land of the Picts. There is no evidence that they intervened militarily, but their natural sympathies would have inclined them against Penda's British allies.

Oswy was clearly in an extremely desperate situation – he was in the most northerly part of his kingdom and could retreat no further. On the other hand, his army was intact and protected behind the defences of the rock of Stirling. Penda's allied force was a great distance from home and he was probably reluctant to carry out a protracted siege. Oswy had brought the Bernician royal treasury with him and he used this to induce Penda to leave his kingdom. The proceeds were shared out among Penda's Welsh allies.[9] Soon after Iudeu, perhaps as part of the

---

[8] Bede, *Historia Ecclesiastica*. part III ch. 17.

[9] Nennius, *Historia Brittonum*. para. 65.

agreement there, the Mercian and Bernician royal families were linked in reciprocal dynastic marriages by the eldest son of the two kings. Alhfrith, Oswy's eldest legitimate son, was married to Penda's daughter Cyneburh, and soon afterwards Peada, Penda's eldest son, was married to Oswy's daughter, Alhflaed.

The agreement at Iudeu brought the fighting in the north to an end, but it was not a comprehensive peace settlement and both Penda and Oswy continued their intrigues to strengthen and extend their area of influence. It was apparent from Penda's campaigns against Wessex and East Anglia that he was treating Middle Anglia as an extension of Mercian territory. In 653 he strengthened his hold by arranging for Peada to become king of the Middle Angles. At the same time King Oswy arranged that his new son-in-law should be accepted into the Christian faith and Peada was baptised together with his retinue by Bishop Finan, the successor of Aedan, at the royal estate of At-the-Wall.[10] The location of At-the-Wall is probably modern Wallbottle near Newcastle. Penda's action provides firm evidence that Middle Anglia was considered to be a kingdom and the appointment of Peada as king has some important implications. First, it follows that the Middle Anglian throne was vacant at the time. It is not known for how long it had been vacant or who was the previous occupant, but there was no sign of a Middle Anglian ruler when Penda was marching his army across Middle Anglian territory. Constitutionally Peada could have been appointed king only with the approval of the Middle Anglian Witangemot. It is significant that, although Penda was acting as if he had authority over this area, he did not attempt to gain the throne for himself, and therefore it may be accepted that he had no legal claim to it. Peada is unlikely to have been appointed king without a claim of some kind: his right to the Middle Anglian throne could have derived from his mother. In that case Queen Cynewise would have been a princess of the Middle Anglian royal house. Her children (sons Peada, Wulfhere, Merewalh, Aethelred, daughters Cyneburh, Cyneswith) would be half Mercian, half Middle Anglian. The proposition that Penda's consort was Middle Anglian provides a consistent explanation for his

---

[10] Bede, *Historia Ecclesiastica*. part III ch. 21.

behaviour as lord of the Middle Angles.

During 653 the Picts (or at least the southern Pictish kingdom of Fortriu, lying north of the river Forth) became directly involved in the power struggle between Oswy and Penda, when the Pictish king Talorc was succeeded by Talorcen, son of his sister (name unknown) and her husband Eanfrith. Talorcen ascended the Pictish throne by matrilineal succession. By the rule of primogeniture Talorcen could also claim to be the rightful head of the Bernician royal dynasty. He would have considered that his uncle Oswy was illegally occupying the Bernician throne, which was his by birthright. When he became king of the Picts he acquired a power base from which he could pursue his claim to the Bernician throne. This turn of events among the Picts was so favourable to Penda's cause that the possibility has to be considered that it was not entirely a normal succession, but resulted from intrigues initiated by Penda the previous year, when he was present at the siege of Iudeu.

Bede's account of the conversion of the East Saxons shows how King Oswy was extending his influence as far south as Essex. In about 653 the East Saxons were being ruled by Sigeberht surnamed the Good, who had succeeded Sigeberht surnamed the Little. King Oswy had established good relations with the former, who used to visit him in Northumbria. As the East Saxons were still pagan, Oswy used these occasions to try to persuade Sigeberht to accept the Christian faith. He finally succeeded and Sigeberht was baptised, like Peada, by Bishop Finan in the royal estate of At-the-Wall. When Sigeberht returned to Essex he asked Oswy to give him teachers to start the work of converting his kingdom. Oswy summoned the monk Cedd to undertake this task and Bishop Finan ordained him as bishop of the East Saxons. It is of interest that after the attempt to convert the East Saxons into the Roman church had failed they were finally converted into the Celtic church as a result of pressure from King Oswy. Bishop Cedd established two centres of Christian worship at Tilbury and Ythancaestir.[11] The latter was the former Roman fort of the Saxon Shore Othona, now known as Bradwell-on-Sea. The Saxon stone-built chapel of St Peter

---

[11] Bede, *Historia Ecclesiastica*. part III ch. 22.

may still be seen there, standing presumably on the site of Cedd's foundation. The location was similar to that of the earlier foundation of Fursa at Burgh Castle and is another illustration of the preference of Celtic churchmen for remote waterside locations.

Having absorbed the Middle Saxons and expanded towards the Chiltern Hills, Essex was the immediate neighbour of the Middle Angles. Bernician penetration of Essex would have been anathema to Penda, who would have seen it as a threat to his heart-land. It, therefore, comes as no surprise that Bede goes on to report that King Sigeberht was murdered by two of his relatives. As in the case of the East Angles and the West Saxons, Penda had succeeded in suborning disaffected members of the royal house.

In East Anglia King Anna was still successfully withstanding Mercian pressure, but Penda had found an ally in the king's brother, Aethelhere. He had married Hereswith, a daughter of Hereric, the Deiran prince who had fled from Aethelfrith to Elmet in 605 and had been poisoned there. Because of his marriage Aethelhere would have opposed Bernician influence in East Anglia. In 654 Penda decided to seek a military solution and led his army into East Anglia. King Anna's army was forced to retreat and according to the Ely Chronicle (Liber Eliensis), the king and his son were slain at the battle of Bulcamp Hill near Blythburg (TM 4575). This place is only three miles from the east coast and Anna's army had had to make a choice between being driven into the sea or making a last-ditch stand on Bulcamp Hill. Upon the death of Anna his brother Aethelhere ascended the East Anglian throne as a Mercian puppet. Another result of the renewed pagan attack on East Anglia was that the Irish monk Fursa left his monastery at Burgh Castle and went to Gaul.[12]

Penda's success in gaining control of Essex and East Anglia appears to have disturbed the accord he had reached with Oswy in 652 and the latter again came to the decision that it was essential for him to take possession of Deira to ensure the security of Bernicia. With his son Alhfrith he led his army into Deira, but Aethelwald, like Oswine, realised that his army was no match for Oswy's. He withdrew it to the

---

[12] Bede, *Historia Ecclesiastica.* part III ch. 19.

south and sent an appeal to Penda for the protection which Deira as a subordinate kingdom could claim from its overlord. Penda assessed that he needed the help of his British and East Anglian allies and sent out a call for their mobilisation. The *Historia Brittonum* stated that the British kings who accompanied him on the campaign to Iudeu rejoined him, but Cadafael, king of Gwynedd, withdrew his army on the eve of the battle. According to Bede, Penda's allied army, when assembled, amounted to thirty legions under thirty royal leaders and considerably exceeded the size of Oswy's small army. The two sides met on 15 November 655 near the river Winwaed (modern river Went), where the Roman road crosses the river near the modern village of Wentbridge (SE 4917). This was in the former British kingdom of Elmet. The conditions were difficult as the river was in flood and had overflowed its channel. Aethelwald of Deira withdrew his army before the battle started and awaited the outcome in a safe place. Penda's large force was put to flight and more men perished in the flood waters than fell in the battle. Penda was killed as were several of the allied leaders, including Aethelhere, king of the East Angles.[13]

Winwaed was an epic battle, which produced a complete reversal in the political and military balance in Britain. It brought to an end the reign of one of the most dynamic of early Anglo-Saxon kings. Throughout his reign Penda had striven to assert Mercian dominion over the other kingdoms. His aim appears to have been to restore the right, which his dynasty possessed before the migration, to govern all the Angles. On the eve of the battle of Winwaed he was overlord of Mercia, Middle Anglia, East Anglia, Lindsey and Deira and had almost achieved his goal. A striking feature of his reign is the remarkable rapport he enjoyed with the British kings. Their readiness to accept the leadership in battle of an Anglian king who was also a pagan suggests that he had a special quality, which strengthened their trust in him. A possible explanation could be that Penda's mother was British and that he was therefore half-British and perhaps bilingual.

The position of Aethelwald at Winwaed is noteworthy. During the battle he refused to commit his forces; there was certainly some logic in

---

[13] Bede, *Historia Ecclesiastica.* part III ch. 24.

this, as, with his aim of regaining his full patrimony, he supported neither side. His best hope was that Penda and Oswy would both fall in the battle or at least emerge so weakened that they could no longer prevent him from realising his aims.

THE CONQUEST OF THE WEST

For Penda's British allies the battle of Winwaed was a major disaster. After the battle each of the British kings would have led his shattered army back to their home area. Subsequent evidence shows that Oswy was determined to follow up his victory by the pursuit and destruction of those British forces which had been deployed against him. From the verse of the bard Llywarch Hen it is possible to discern the outline of the events in the land of the Cornovii after the battle. Some stanzas described a Welsh victory at Caer Luitcoet:

> My heart is aflame like a firebrand . . .
> Brothers I had, better it was when they were alive,
> Heirs of great Arthur, our strong fortress.
> Before Caer Luitcoet they triumphed;
> There was blood beneath the ravens, and fierce attack;
> They shattered shields the sons of Cyndrwyn . . .
> Glory in battle, great plunder,
> Before Caer Luitcoet, Morfael took it.

Caer Luitcoet is the Roman Letocetum, a station on Watling Street at its junction with the Ryknield Way. Its modern name is Wall-by-Lichfield (SK 0906). Archaeologists report that pagan Anglo-Saxons burials do not extend further west than the area of Lichfield, an indication of the limit of early Mercian settlement. Caer Luitcoet would, therefore, have been in the frontier area separating Mercia from the Cornovii. These people were still ruled by Cynddylan, who had fought with Penda at Maserfeld. Although not specifically mentioned, Cynddylan and his army may well have been one of the legions, who fought under Penda's command at Winwaed. The location of Caer Luitcoat suggests that after the battle a Bernician contingent advanced south from Winwaed along Ryknield Way until it was checked and defeated by Cynddylan's army. The Bernicians were prevented from entering the land of the Cornovii only

163

temporarily, for the bard goes on to lament the seizure of the land by the English:

> Cynddylan, hold thou the hillside
> Where the English come today . . .
> Cynddylan, hold thou the ford
> Where the English come through Tren . . .

But Cynddylan's hall was destroyed and he was slain:

> Cynddylan's hall is dark tonight.
> No fire is lit, no candle burns.
> God will keep me sane.
> Cynddylan's hall, it pierces me
> To see it roofless, fireless.
> Dead is my lord, and I am yet alive.
> Cynddylan's hall is desolate tonight
> Where once I sat in honour.
> Gone are the men who held it, gone are the women.
> Cynddylan's hall. Dark is its roof
> Since the English destroyed
> Cynddylan and Elvan of Powys.[1]

Cynddylan was the last of the kings of the Cornovii. The location of his hall is not known, but the bard tells that Cynddylan's body was taken for burial to Eglwysau Basa, the church of Basa, presumably modern Baschurch (SJ 4221). There can be no doubt that the English referred to were the Bernicians. A brief entry in the Welsh Annals recorded that in 656 Oswy came and raided, and the result was the destruction of Cynddylan's regime. With the land of the Cornovii in his possession, he was able to go to Maserfeld, as reported by Bede, and recover the head, arms and hands of his brother Oswald and remove them for enshrinement to Bamburgh and Lindisfarne.

After their campaign against the Cornovii the Bernician troops

---

[1] Morris, *The Age of Arthur.* pp 241- 4.

crossed the river Severn and invaded the adjoining British kingdom of Erging. It occupied a large area to the west of the Cornovii and Dobunni, and had been named by the Britons after the name of the Roman town of Ariconium (near modern Weston-under-Penyard SO 6326). During Roman times this town had grown up as a centre of an important area where iron ore was mined and smelted (now the Forest of Dean). The Llandaff charters record the names of the ruling king of Erging prior to the battle of Winwaed in a dynastic succession Gurcant, son of Cinvin, son of Peipiau, son of Erb.[2] From an early date the Anglo-Saxons referred to the people of Erging as the Magonsaetan, i.e. the people of Magnis. This town was located near modern Kenchester (SO 4343) and had been built by the Romans soon after the conquest as an oppidum to house the Britons, who at that time were occupying the nearby hill-fort of Credenhill (SO 4544). It appears that during the Roman period Ariconium was the Roman administrative centre, while Magnis was the centre of the British tribal chiefs. When the Romans withdrew, Ariconium probably went into a decline, while Magnis became the capital of the British kingdom, which continued to use the name Ariconium, absorbed into Old Welsh as Erging. The Bernicians in 656 knew that the centre of military and political power was at Magnis and that from here a hostile force had been deployed against Oswy at Winwaed. Their aim, therefore, was to eliminate Magnis as a centre of opposition. Oswy's troops would probably have advanced along the Roman road from Viroconium; after the capture of the town, they continued further along the same road, but when they reached the river Wye they found the crossing blocked by a British army deployed on the southern bank. A battle took place, in which the Bernicians were defeated. The evidence for this is provided by one of the Llandaff charters in which Gurvodius, king of Erging, granted three uncias of land at Bolgros on the Wye to the church at Llandaff for the foundation of a church in thanksgiving for a victory over the Saxons.[3] It was customary that before a battle kings made a vow to make a donation to the church if they were able to gain a victory. The donation was usually

---

[2] Finberg, *Early Charters of the West Midlands.* items 388-96.

[3] Finberg, *Early Charters of the West Midlands.* item 397.

relevant to the situation at the time and it is likely that the land donated was at or near the site of the battle. Bolgros is identical with modern Bellamore (SO 3940), situated about a mile from the south bank of the Wye. The charter contains no date, but is considered to have been issued in the period 630-660. There can be little doubt that the Saxons defeated near Bolgros were Oswy's troops whose advance was halted on the line of the river Wye. But the territory north and east of the Wye remained in their possession and, like the land of the Cornovii, became part of England. The area south and west of the river remained under the rule of the Welsh king, who retained the name Erging for the kingdom, although it no longer included the town of Ariconium, now within the northern and eastern part conquered by Oswy's army. Since the battle of Bolgros the name Erging, its Anglo-Saxon equivalent Ircingafeld and its modern English version Archenfield have come to designate only the area lying between the river Wye and its tributary the Monnow. The battle had resulted in the division of the original British kingdom of Erging. This partition was never accepted by either side and, as will be shown in later chapters, attempts to re-unite the kingdom by one side or the other led to conflict between them. It will be noted that Magnis would have occupied a central position in a kingdom consisting of territory on both sides of the river Wye, but after 656 it was in the southern extremity of the land seized by the Bernicians.

The location of the three uncias of land granted for the foundation of a church is not known. There is no trace of a religious establishment ever having been built at Bellamore itself. The actual site of the battle was not stated, but the key place in dispute between the Bernicians and the Britons of Erging would have been the spot, presumably a ford, where the Roman road crossed the river Wye (SO 4441), near modern Canon Bridge. The nearest known religious establishment to this location is the parish church of Madley at a distance of two miles to the south. The existence of a church at this spot has been traced back to at least the early or mid-twelfth century.

From subsequent events it may be inferred that in addition to the troops sent to pursue the Cornovii and the Magonsaetan, Oswy also despatched a contingent to pursue the army of Cadafael of Gwynedd, who had withdrawn from Penda's alliance on the eve of the battle.

166

Oswy's troops would have seized Chester and then continued their western advance until they were halted at the river Vyrnwy and along a line of hill forts stretching north from Maserfeld (Old Oswestry) towards the Dee estuary. It will be explained below that this line of forts formed part of what became known as Wat's Dyke.

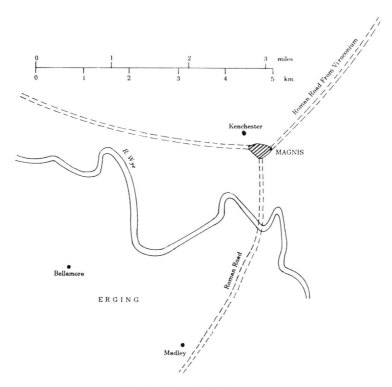

The battle on the River Wye 656.

OSWY, KING OF THE BERNICIANS AND BRETWALDA

From 655 until his death in 670 Oswy was the most powerful ruler in Britain. During the period of rivalry between Penda and Oswy it is likely that the post of Bretwalda had remained unfilled, but after Winwaed Oswy was clearly the most suitable ruler to have the supreme authority of Bretwalda, and he became the seventh holder of the post. Yet he cannot have felt secure on his throne while two challengers to his position as head of the Bernician royal dynasty were still alive. There is no further mention of Aethelwald after Winwaed. His ultimate fate is unknown, but it may be supposed that he fled from the scene of his uncle's triumph and found refuge among his mother's family in Wessex. With the Deiran throne vacated by the departure of Aethelwald, Oswy did not press his own claims against the wishes of the Deiran Witangemot, but persuaded it to accept his son, Alhfrith. He was the son of Rieinmellt, Oswy's first wife, and hence a descendant of Urien of Reged. His accession to the throne would have facilitated the integration of British elements into Deiran society. Constitutionally Northumbria remained divided, but Oswy was able to control Deira as Bretwalda through his son. It is likely that King Cenwealh of Wessex supported the claims of his nephew and would have refused to recognise Oswy as Bretwalda.

In the far north Oswy's position was under threat from his nephew, Talorcen, son of Eanfrith, who had acquired a power base as king of the Picts. The changed alignment of the Picts was shown by the entry for 654 in the Annals of Ulster, which reported that hostilities had broken out between the Picts and the Scots. Talorcen inflicted defeat on his uncle's Scottish allies at Strath Ethairt (unlocated). This led to war between the Picts and Bernicians, as Bede stated that Oswy conquered the greater part of the Picts, presumably those in the southern half of the Pictish kingdom. The Annals of Ulster report the death of Talorcen in 657, but it is not clear if he fell in battle. He was succeeded by Gartnait, who may have been the son of Domnall Brecc and a Pictish princess. Under his rule the Picts apparently rejoined the alignment with Oswy. Gartnait continued to rule the Picts as a tributary king of Oswy until his death in 663.

The military power of Mercia and of the Welsh kings had been destroyed at Winwaed and a power vacuum existed in the heart of the country. Despite the hostility, which Penda had displayed towards him, Oswy showed restraint in his treatment of Penda's family. In the difficult political situation after Winwaed, reconciliation with Penda's successors would have been to his advantage. Bede reported that for three years king Oswy ruled Mercia and the other southern provinces. But as Peada was his son-in-law he allowed him to rule the kingdom of the southern Mercians, which amounted to 5,000 hides and was separated from the kingdom of the northern Mercians, amounting to 7,000 hides, by the river Trent.[1] In addition to South Mercia, Peada would also have continued to rule his other kingdom, Middle Anglia. Peada is best known as the founder of the monastery of Medeshamsted, modern Peterborough, in Middle Anglia on the north bank of the river Nene.

After Winwaed, Oswy devoted much of his attention to spreading and strengthening the Christian faith in his domains. Bede reported that before the battle he had vowed that if he were victorious he would give twelve estates, each of ten hides, six in Deira and six in Bernicia, for the foundation of monasteries. He also dedicated his daughter, Aelfflaed, who was barely one year old, to a life-time of religious devotion. She first entered a monastery at Hartlepool, where the abbess was Hilda, daughter of the Deiran prince Hereric poisoned in Elmet and sister of Hereswith, widow of Aethelhere, former king of the East Angles. Two years later Hilda founded a monastery at Streanaeshalch (modern Whitby) and dedicated it to St Peter. The location was typical of religious sites favoured by the Celtic church, on the bleak cliff-top overlooking the North Sea. The site is now occupied by the ruins of the Benedictine Abbey. Aelfflaed served here under Hilda as a novice and eventually became abbess. Another monastery dating from this period was founded by Aebbe, half-sister of Oswy, at

---

[1] Bede, *Historia Ecclesiastica.* part III ch. 24.

Coldingham (NT 9065) also near the cliff edge. Her name is preserved in nearby St Abb's head.

Oswy became increasingly conscious of the difficulties caused by the differing practices of the Celtic church and the Roman. The most serious difference concerned the calculation of the date of Easter, but there were other differences, such as the tonsure. These differences were causing problems in his own family, as his wife, Eanflaed, continued the Roman practices, in which she had been brought up in Kent, and his son Alhfrith was instructed by Wilfrid, who had studied in Rome. Oswy decided that this situation must be resolved and in 664 he summoned a special synod at Hilda's monastery at Streanaeshalch/Whitby. A full discussion was carried out. Colman, bishop of Lindisfarne, a Scot from Iona, presented the case for the Celtic practices and Wilfrid the case for the Roman. Oswy's ruling in favour of the Roman church was based on the role of St Peter as keeper of the keys of the kingdom of heaven: 'I will not oppose him; but, as far as I know and am able, I wish to obey his decrees in all things; lest perchance, when I come to the gates of the kingdom of heaven there should be none to unlock them, he being my enemy who is proved to hold the keys.'[2] After this historic ruling, Roman practices became general throughout England and the cult of St Peter became widespread.

Soon after the Synod of Whitby, Alhfrith decided to go on a pilgrimage to Rome, but Oswy overruled him and ordered him to remain in Deira. Oswy had another son called Ecgfrith, for whom he had arranged a marriage in about 660 with Aetheldreda, one of the daughters of Anna, king of the East Angles. The purpose of the marriage was presumably to strengthen East Anglian subordination to Oswy's rule. Aetheldreda had already been married to the pagan Middle Anglian prince, Tonberht, in about 635, but he had died soon after the marriage, which was not consummated. For about fifteen years she had remained a widow, probably in her dead husband's land of the South Gyrwas in the Fen District. During this period she probably devoted herself to the religious way of life. By the time she came to marry Ecgfrith she would clearly have become middle-aged. Bede tells how

---

[2] Bede, *Historia Ecclesiastica.* part III ch. 25.

relations between Oswy and Alhfrith deteriorated until Oswy was attacked by Alhfrith. The reasons for this are not explained, but at an unknown date Alhfrith was replaced as king of the Deirans by Ecgfrith and Aetheldreda became queen.

ULFHERE, KING OF THE MERCIANS

As reported above, immediately after the battle of Winwaed southern Mercia and Middle Anglia were being ruled by Peada, son of Penda, as a tributary king of Oswy, but Peada only survived his father by a few months. Bede tells how Peada was murdered in the following spring, allegedly betrayed by his wife. She was Alhflaed, daughter of Oswy, and her alleged complicity in his murder points to Bernician involvement. The ravaging of Bernicia by Penda during his two invasions would have aroused strong feelings against Mercia and many Bernicians would be satisfied with nothing less than the total suppression of Penda's dynasty. They would have opposed Oswy's leniency towards his son-in-law, Peada, and could have taken the law into their own hands with Alhflaed's connivance. Peada's death meant a break in the ancient Anglian dynasty and for two years the Mercian and Middle Anglian thrones stood vacant. North Mercia had already been annexed by Oswy. After Peada's death Oswy would have needed to appoint ealdormen to govern South Mercia and Middle Anglia. In this situation Oswy may well have founded his military resources overstretched to give protection to Mercia and Middle Anglia and at the same time to provide troops to deal with the military situation in the north, south and west.

If the assassination of Peada had been an attempt against the Mercian royal dynasty it proved to be counter-productive. Bede reported that three years after the death of Penda (i.e. in 658) three Mercian ealdormen, Immin, Eafa and Eadberht, rebelled against Oswy, expelled his ealdormen and appointed Penda's son Wulfhere to be king of the Mercians.[1] It might be expected that following the eviction of his ealdormen Oswy would oppose the accession of Wulfhere to the Mercian throne, but he chose not to do so. In the political balance of 658 Oswy decided to continue his policy of reconciliation with Penda's family. In a passage about Medeshamsted the chronicler described Oswy as the

---

[1] Bede, *Historia Ecclesiastica.* part III ch. 24.

sworn brother of Wulfhere, which means that they had been bound together by a solemn oath as brothers. Wulfhere would have given firm assurances to Oswy that he acknowledged him as Bretwalda. Oswy may well have needed a subordinate king to whom he could delegate the government of Mercia and Middle Anglia. He may also have perceived that he could make good use of Wulfhere in dealing with the West Saxons and the Britons. The latter would have welcomed the appearance of a son of Penda on the Mercian throne and would have given him their co-operation. Wulfhere made full use of his accord with Oswy to make a start on rebuilding the fortunes of his crippled kingdom.

THE POLITICAL SETTLEMENT IN THE WEST

With the death of Cynddylan, the kingdom of the Wreocensaetan (the Anglo-Saxon name for the Cornovii) came into the possession of Oswy. This occurred in or soon after 656, when, according to the Welsh Annals, Oswy came and raided. When the fighting came to an end Oswy would have discovered that the collapse of Cynddylan's regime had left his kingdom with no form of orderly government, and arrangements needed to be made for the permanent government of the area and for its integration into the rest of his realm. The following evidence shows that it was Wulfhere, who became the ruler of the area. A charter, composed probably on the basis of tradition and ancient records, shows that in 664 Wulfhere confirmed the rights and privileges held at a number of places by St Peter's monastery at Medeshamstede (modern Peterborough). Among these places were Shifnal (SJ 7407), Cosford in Albrighton (SJ 7905) and Lizard Hill (SJ 8010), all in the land of the Wreocensaetan.[1] This action was taken at the time of the consecration of the monastery. There is also evidence that Wulfhere's rule extended as far north as Chester; the Benedictine Abbey of St Werburgh, now Chester Cathedral, is reported to have been founded about 660 by him, and built on the site of an earlier church within the limits of the Roman city.

There is no direct evidence to explain how he came to rule the kingdom of the Wreocensaetan and the Chester area, but it is quite certain that it was not as a result of armed conflict with Oswy. The friendly relationship which existed between the two kings was illustrated in 664 at a great ceremony at Peterborough for the consecration of the monastery, which was founded jointly by Oswy and Wulfhere's brother, Peada, when he was king of the Middle Angles. Besides Wulfhere, those present at the ceremony as reported in the Anglo-Saxon Chronicle included King Oswy, King Sighere and King

---

[1] Ed. Birch, *Cartularium Saxonicum* item. 22. Finberg, *Early Charters of the West Midlands.* item 426.

Sebbi of the East Saxons, Wulfhere's brother Aethelred and his sisters, Cyneburh and Cyneswith, Deusdedit, the Archbishop of Canterbury and the bishops of Mercia, Lindisfarne, Rochester and London. It is apparent that Oswy as Bretwalda had appointed Wulfhere to rule the Wreocensaetan and the Chester area on his behalf as a subject king. This arrangement was advantageous to both of them. Oswy retained his sovereignty over the areas he had conquered, without the onerous task of maintaining order and extracting tribute. Wulfhere received an extensive addition to his realm and would have taken his share of the tribute. The subject Britons remaining in the area would already have been acquainted with Wulfhere as a son of Penda and would have found it easier to accept him as their immediate lord than a Bernician prince or ealdorman. This political dispensation made in about 658-660 facilitated the integration of these areas into the governmental framework of England.

A reference in the Domesday Book to Wulfhere's Ford in the area of Melverley (SJ 3316) is taken to refer to a ford on the river Vyrnwy, where a supposed treaty was signed by Wulfhere and the kings of Powys and Gwynedd. This river still forms part of the border between England and Wales. It is relevant that just north of Melverley at Maesbury (SJ 3026) the earthwork known as Wat's Dyke stretches north towards the Dee estuary. It is a more modest earthwork than Offa's Dyke, occupies lower land to the east and covers only the area north of the river Severn. Although the date of its construction is not known, it is generally considered to have preceded the construction of Offa's Dyke in 787. A significant feature is that it incorporates within its line some hill forts, including the multi-ramparted fort of Old Oswestry and further to the north the fort at Caer Estyn (SJ 3257) and another on the outskirts of Wrexham (SJ 3353). It is possible that these and perhaps other strong points were manned and defended in 656, when Oswy's army invaded and that the line connecting them formed the dividing line separating his troops pushing from the east and the Welsh troops of Gwynedd and Powys defending from the west. When the fighting ceased the military front became the political boundary, which was demarcated by Wat's Dyke. South of Maesbury the political frontier probably continued along the Morda river and the river Vyrnwy, as agreed in the supposed treaty between Wulfhere and the Welsh kings.

In the adjoining kingdom of the Magonsaetan a similar situation had arisen after the battle of Bolgros. The Welsh king had been driven from his capital at Magnis and the area north and east of the river Wye was left without orderly government. Oswy had to find someone suitable to rule the kingdom under his sovereignty. His solution was similar to that for the Wreocensaetan. By 660 the Magonsaetan was being ruled by a king called Merewalh. There is little doubt that he was a son of Penda, according to Goscelin, Penda's third son and hence the younger brother of Wulfhere. As a son of Penda, Merewalh was known to the Magonsaetan and acceptable to them as their immediate ruler. The earliest date giving Merewalh as king of the Magonsaetan is 660, when he is reported to have founded an abbey at Leominster. It was more than coincidence that Wulfhere founded his abbey at Chester at this time. The first abbot of Leominster was a Northumbrian, Ealfred, a sign of Oswy's influence. Local historians at Leominster record that the first Christian community on the site, then known as Llanllieni, was founded by St David in the sixth century.

Wulfhere and Merewalh contracted marriages which were linked with one another. Wulfhere married Eormenhild, daughter of Eorcenberht, king of Kent, while Merewalh married Eormenburgh, daughter of the king's brother Eormenred. It was more than chance that the two Mercian athelings married two Kentish princesses, who were cousins. The significance of the marriage was that the two Kentish princesses were related to Oswy's queen Eanflaed, who was a cousin of their fathers. Because of the family relationship Eormenhild and Eormenburgh could be depended upon to encourage their husbands to remain loyal to Oswy. The course of events in the lands of the Wreocensaetan and Magonsaetan when the fighting came to an end present a striking dichotomy and appear to have been stages in a master-plan devised by Oswy and his Kentish queen. The two Mercian princes were offered a remarkable deal after the defeat and death of their father. They were given the opportunity of ruling territory previously governed by allies of their father on condition that they recognised the suzerainty of Oswy. To guarantee this, they would have had to swear oaths of allegiance, to accept marriages arranged by Oswy and Eanflaed and to strengthen the Christian faith in their new kingdoms by founding a new abbey. For Oswy the advantage of this deal was that it brought peace to his new provinces and maintained his sovereignty over them at a time, when he still had unresolved problems in the north and south.

The land of the Magonsaetan and Archenfield

Wulfhere had a son, Coenred, and a daughter, Werburgh, who both became strong supporters of the church. Wulfhere's foundation at Chester later became the resting place of Werburgh's relics and was dedicated to her as its patron saint; her shrine may still be seen within Chester Cathedral. When Merewalh became king he already had two sons, Merchelm and Mildfrith. He had further children by Eormenburg, three daughters, Mildburg, Mildthryth and Mildgith and a son Merefin, who died in infancy. It is not known when Merewalh died, but Goscelin stated that he was not buried in his own kingdom, but at Repton, which became a favourite burial place for the Mercian royal family. Queen Eormenburgh later returned to her native Kent and became abbess at Minster on the Isle of Thanet. Merewalh was succeeded as king by his son Merchelm. Merewalh's daughter Mildburg founded a monastery at Much Wenlock (SO 6199) within her father's kingdom in about 680; the ruins of the Cluniac Priory erected on the site of St Mildburg's foundation are still to be seen there.

177

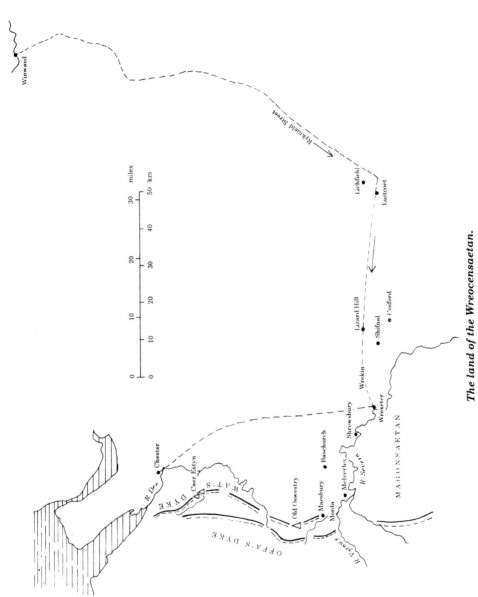

The land of the Wreocensaetan.

THE WAR AGAINST THE WEST WELSH

It became apparent that after the battle of Winwaed Oswy and King Cenwealh had become estranged. The events after 655 indicate that Cenwealh did not recognise Oswy as Bretwalda. The reason for this is not explained, but is probably connected with Aethelwald, Cenwealh's nephew, who had a strong claim to the Northumbrian throne. It was suggested that after the battle he may have been given a secure refuge in Wessex, and in these circumstances Wulfhere and Oswy would have had a bond in their antipathy to King Cenwealh. Oswy took no direct action, but he appears to have given Wulfhere a free hand in his dealings with him. A matter which demanded the immediate attention of Wulfhere was the situation in Middle Anglia – William of Malmesbury describes how in the early years of his reign he was heavily oppressed by the king of the West Saxons.[1] One effect of Winwaed was that the Middle Angles had lost Mercian protection and it is likely that Cenwealh took advantage of the changed situation by repossessing the Gewissian ancestral lands north of the Thames, including the former capital at Dorchester. He may even have aimed to retake the lands in the Chiltern Hills, which were first seized in 571, including the towns of Aylesbury and Limbury. Wulfhere would have regarded these lands as properly belonging to the Middle Anglian kingdom of his brother Peada, which he had inherited. He lost little time in making plans to wrest these lands back from the West Saxons and to subjugate Wessex. But he realised that in Mercia's weakened condition, action against a strong martial kingdom like Wessex could not be carried out in isolation, but would need the collaboration of allies. In view of his father's friendship with the Welsh kings he knew that he could count on their support. He would have been aware of the strained relations between the West Saxons and the South Saxons, which had erupted into hostilities in 607 and he decided to encourage South Saxon aspirations. Soon after his accession

---

[1] Malmesbury, *The Kings before the Norman Conquest.* para. 76.

Wulfhere invited King Aethelwalh of the South Saxons to the Mercian court. Bede stated that while he was in Mercia, Aethelwalh was persuaded by Wulfhere to accept baptism into the Christian faith.[2] It may be safely concluded that Aethelwalh left the Mercian court a firm ally of Wulfhere. A source of West Saxon weakness, which had not escaped Wulfhere's notice and which he thought he could exploit, was the servile condition of the people of the former Jutish lands within Wessex. All the above factors were taken into account in his strategy which was ready to go into operation soon after his accession. Correct timing was essential so that the Mercian forces should not have to do battle against the West Saxons on their own. The first blow was to be struck by the West Welsh.

In 658 fighting broke out. The Anglo-Saxon Chronicle reported that Cenwealh fought the Welsh at Peonnan and drove them in flight to the river Parret. William of Malmesbury placed the battle in the same category as the battle of Bradford-on-Avon: 'He totally defeated in two actions the Britons, furious with the recollection of their ancient liberty and in consequence perpetually meditating resistance; first at a place called Witgeornesburg (Bradford-on-Avon) and then at a mountain named Pene.'[3] Peonnan or Pene are early forms of the name of the Pen ridge, a high finger of land situated in southeast Somerset, just west of the border with Wiltshire. This border probably dates back to Saxon times and in 658 the Pen ridge probably lay just within the territory of the British tribe of the Durotriges. It consists of heights overlooking the Roman road from Old Sarum (Sorviodunum) to Ilchester (Lindinis). This road was one of a few highways providing communication between Wessex and the British lands to the west. Today the line of this road is followed by the A303 (T), a modern trunk road carrying a heavy volume of traffic between east and west.

The heights of the Pen ridge are not known to have been fortified with defensive positions like the hill forts in the area. The fact that a battle took place on unprepared hill-top positions just within the British border suggests that the Britons were forced to occupy improvised

---

[2] Bede, *Historia Ecclesiastica*. part IV ch. 13.

[3] Malmesbury, *The Kings before the Norman Conquest*. para. 19.

defences, having been thrown back from a thrust into West Saxon territory. In contrast with the raid on Bradford-on-Avon, the West Saxons seem to have had good warning of an impending attack. They apparently had sufficient time to call up and deploy their forces to block the British army when it marched along the highway into their territory. On the basis of the available evidence, the course of the battle may be reconstructed along the following lines. The West Welsh assembled an army and marched it along the Roman road from Ilchester towards Old Sarum in Wessex. The West Saxons learned of the British preparations and called up their forces in strength. When the British army crossed into the West Saxon frontier area they were confronted by the West Saxon forces, which completely routed them and forced them to take up improvised defensive positions on the nearby Pen ridge. Here the main battle took place. The British defences proved of no avail and their army was decimated.

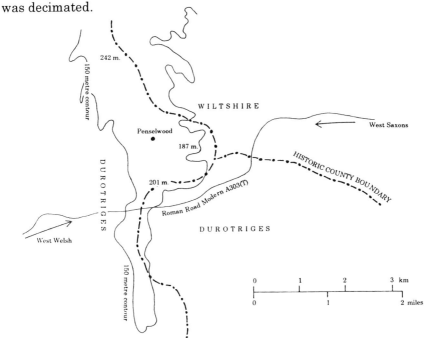

The battle of the Pen Ridge 658.

The West Saxon kings had never sought to acquire territory west of the Forest of Selwood. Their main concern was to maintain the territorial integrity of the ancestral lands of the Gewissi around Dorchester-on-

Thames. They had been content to live in peace with their Welsh neighbours to the west, but by 658 the situation had changed. Twice the West Welsh had shown their hostility towards the West Saxons and there was no assurance that they would not carry out further hostile acts. For the safety of his realm, Cenwealh decided that he had to destroy the military power of his neighbours in the west. To do this he would have to invade Durotrigan territory. It is likely that the land of the Durotriges consisted of two kingdoms, which were the successor states of two corresponding Roman *civitates*. The principal Roman city had been Durnovaria, modern Dorchester, with Lindinis, modern Ilchester, second in importance. Two stones from Hadrian's Wall bear an inscription 'C(ivitatas) Durotrigum Lindiniesis', apparently a reference to construction teams of the Durotriges from Lindinis. This evidence is taken to indicate that during the second century the Romans had divided the land of the Durotriges and placed the northern half under the separate administration of Lindinis, leaving the southern half to be ruled from Durnovaria.

After the British defeat on the Pen ridge, the road to the west lay open and the West Saxons marched along it to Ilchester, then along the Fosse Way until they reached the river Parret. Here they halted. The Parret itself would not have formed an insurmountable obstacle at this point, but the military situation was that the West Saxons now occupied a salient twenty-two miles in length projecting into hostile territory. Military prudence demanded a pause to consolidate. Another consideration was that beyond the Parret the West Saxons would have been approaching, if not entering, Dumnonian territory, where they could expect to encounter the main Dumnonian resistance. During their march from the Pen ridge to the Parret the West Saxons could have continued to meet opposition from the Britons. Indeed, three military installations lay along the route of their advance: the town of Ilchester and the hill forts at South Cadbury and Ham Hill. Ilchester was a fort during Roman times and had been built where the Fosse Way crosses the river Yeo (or Ivel). Its defences may well have fallen into disrepair since the withdrawal of the Romans and it is doubtful that the Durotriges could have put up serious resistance here. The hill fort at South Cadbury lies a half a mile south of the military highway, and it had been re-activated and strengthened when the southern Jutes had invaded Durotrigan territory. It is most likely that it would have been manned again when the West Saxons advanced along the highway towards the Parret. The hill fort at Ham Hill (ST 485166) lies one mile south of the Fosse Way and one and a half miles east of the river Parret. It has an enclosed area of about 200 acres and is considered to be the largest hill fort in Britain. But when the Saxons first encountered it, it had ceased to be a fort; to them it was a hill and they named it accordingly.

For three years after their arrival at the Parret in 658 the West Saxons were engaged in consolidating and extending their hold along the military highway. The long sliver of Saxon-held territory had bisected the Durotrigan land and separated the southern from the northern Durotriges. The next major military engagement after the battle of the Pen ridge took place in 661. It is reported in the Anglo-Saxon Chronicle as follows: 'In this year at Easter Cenwealh fought at Posentesbyrig.' This place has not been definitely identified, but it is most likely that it is identical with Poundbury (ST 682912), the modern name for the hill fort half a mile from Dorchester on the northwest side. Poundbury extends to about fifteen acres. Originally it was an Iron Age fort, which was refortified in about 25 BC to meet the threatened Roman invasion. When the Romans built a road from Ilchester to Dorchester they laid a course, which skirted Poundbury on its south-western side. Poundbury, therefore, occupied a key position which commanded access to Dorchester from the northwest. At the start of the campaigning season in 661 Cenwealh marched his troops south from Ilchester along the Roman road towards Dorchester. He probably appreciated that the resistance of the southern Durotriges was being directed from there and, as Ceawlin had advanced against the capital of the Dobunni at Cirencester in 577, Cenwealh advanced against the Durotrigan capital. The course of the road is now followed along much of its length by the modern A37, except that the modern road passes Poundbury on its eastern side. It is to be expected that the southern Durotriges would mount an all-out effort for the defence of their capital city and it is likely that a major battle developed at Poundbury a half a mile from the gates of Dorchester.

Wulfhere can hardly have expected that his West Welsh allies would suffer such a devastating defeat at the Pen ridge, with the West Saxon army triumphant and still in good fighting condition. But Cenwealh's decision to pursue the West Welsh into their own territory served Wulfhere's purpose well. By the beginning of the campaigning season in 661 the West Saxon army had become locked in battle with the West Welsh. It was far from its home base and the defences of the West Saxon homeland had been left depleted. Now was the time for Wulfhere to make his next move. He led a force of Mercian troops south across Middle Anglia, first into the disputed territory north of the Thames and then across the Thames. The Anglo-Saxon Chronicle reported: 'Wulfhere, son of Penda, harried on Ashdown . . . and Wulfhere, son of Penda, harried in the Isle of Wight, and gave the people of the Isle of Wight to Aethelwold, king of the South Saxons, because Wulfhere had stood sponsor to him at baptism.' By Ashdown was meant the Berkshire Downs. Bede added that Wulfhere 'as a sign of his adoption gave him two provinces, namely the Isle of Wight and the province of the Meonware (the Meon valley) among the nation of the West Saxons.' William of Malmesbury provided a piece of crucial evidence, that the Isle of Wight had rebelled in confederacy with the Mercians.[4] Wulfhere's military intervention freed the former Jutish people of the Isle of Wight and those on the mainland adjoining Sussex from West Saxon rule, but instead of giving them back their lost freedom, he handed them over to the rule of his South Saxon ally. It is apparent that he did not attempt a permanent Mercian occupation of the two areas, but marched his army back to Middle Anglia. The news of his sudden strike into the West Saxon heartland appears to have reached Cenwealh after the battle of Poundbury and the situation demanded his immediate return home. There is no evidence that he personally took any further part in the war in the west.

There is little evidence about the course of the war in the west after Cenwealh's departure, but it is apparent that the West Saxons were unable or unwilling to disengage and they continued their struggle. Cenwealh would have handed over the conduct of the war to his senior

---

[4] Malmesbury, *The Kings before the Norman Conquest.* para. 34.

commanders. As the Anglo-Saxon Chronicle at this time recorded only the activities of the king, it mentions no further battles after Posentesbyrig. The Welsh Annals, however, make a valuable contribution. Under the year 665 they report the second battle of Badon, without providing any details of participants, outcome etc. It was reported above that Badon was probably the name used by Welsh writers to refer to Badbury Rings, the hill fort successfully defended by the Durotriges against the southern Jutes. By the mid-seventh century it would almost certainly still be in good defensible condition. It is necessary, however, to make a small adjustment of date. The annal for 665 also reports the Synod of Whitby, which actually took place in 664. The second battle of Badon should, therefore, be dated 664, three years after the battle of Poundbury. A Roman road, called Ackling Dyke by the Saxons, linked Dorchester with Badbury Rings and further east with Old Sarum. The West Saxon troops would have marched along this road for their assault on Badbury Rings. The battle must have been a major event, because of the sheer size of the defences, but the West Saxons triumphed where the southern Jutes failed. The battle shows that the southern Durotriges continued their resistance after the fall of Poundbury and could, indeed, have continued to hold out at a number of hill forts in their territory.

Dorchester is separated from the south coast by a distance of only five miles. The only possible obstacle to a West Saxon advance to the coast would have been Maiden Castle, one and a half miles southwest of Dorchester and a half a mile from the road leading south to the coast. Maiden Castle is a most impressive site. It embraces an area of about a hundred acres, defended by lines of deep ditches and ramparts. In 43/44 AD it was captured by the 2nd Augustan Legion under Vespasian. It is not known if the Durotriges defended Maiden Castle against the West Saxons, but in 662 or soon afterwards the West Saxons pushed past it along the Roman road until they reached the sea in the area of Weymouth. Saxon nomenclature provides an indication of which sites they regarded as fortresses. Two of the largest Durotrigan hill forts were Hod Hill (ST 857106), covering 55 acres, and Hambledon Hill (ST 845125). They were not named as forts by the Saxons and it may be concluded that by the mid-seventh century they were no longer in a defensible state. Some smaller sites were named as fortresses by the Saxons and could, therefore, have been manned and defended against Cenwealh's troops. They are Chalbury (SY 6878), Rawlesbury (ST 7806), Woodbury (SY 8595), Bulbury (SY 9694) and Spettisbury (ST 9102). Resistance by the southern Durotriges cannot have continued for long and soon after 664 all of their territory came under West Saxon control. The West Saxons established a new shire in place of the kingdom of the southern Durotriges and retained Durnovaria as the capital city, which they called Dornwarana Caester. The new shire would have been governed by an ealdorman appointed by Cenwealh. The inhabitants of the new shire took their name from the political capital and became known as the Dornsaetan, modern Dorset.

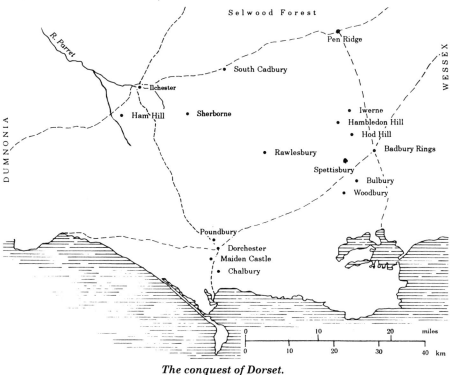

The conquest of Dorset.

The fighting against the northern Durotriges probably continued at the same time as the fighting against the southern Durotriges and the West Saxons would have advanced northwards as well as southwards from the military highway. Eventually they acquired so much territory of the northern Durotriges that they needed to establish an administrative

186

framework. So they set up a new shire in the north, but with an important difference from the new shire in the south: they decided not to use the former Roman centre at Lindinis, but instead to use a site four miles to the north at a place they called Sumurtun, modern Somerton (ST 4828). The people ruled from Sumurtun became known as the Sumorsaetan, hence modern Somerset. The reason for the decision not to use Lindinis as the political centre is not known, but it may be surmised that in 661 it was in such a ruinous state that it was unusable. The damage to the Roman town could have occurred during the fighting between the West Saxons and Durotriges, but perhaps more likely it resulted from the insurrection of the Germanic settlements. There is little information about the origins of Sumurtun. The West Saxons did not call it *caester* as in the case of Durnovaria and Lindinis, so it was probably not a Roman town. It appears to have emerged as a replacement for the damaged Lindinis, but it is not clear if it was originally founded by the Durotriges or the West Saxons.

The conquest of Somerset.

187

As the Saxon conquest progressed a number of British religious houses came under Saxon control. King Cenwealh allowed them to retain the estates with which they had been endowed and confirmed their tenure by issuing charters, the dates of which mark the progress of the Saxon conquest. In Dorset, Cenwealh confirmed in 671 the tenure of land at Lanprobi, almost certainly the original name of the British church at Sherborne.[5] During the 670s, land at Iwerne Minster (ST 8714) was granted to the Bishop of Winchester. In Somerset Cenwealh had obtained control of the Glastonbury area by 670. William of Malmesbury reveals that at this time there was an interesting situation at Glastonbury Abbey; he states that the abbot was Bertwald, the 'son of a brother of Aethelred, king of the Mercians',[6] which reflects the close relationship between Penda's family and the West Welsh. Soon after the change of political control Bertwald moved from Glastonbury and became abbot at Reculver in Kent. In 672 Cenwealh confirmed the tenure of estates by the Abbey located on the western side of Glastonbury at Meare (ST 4541), Westhay (ST 4342), Godney (ST 4842) and Beckery (ST 4838). He also granted land at Nyland (ST 4550) between Wedmore and Cheddar.[7]

After the battles of Poundbury in 661 and of Badbury Rings in 664, there is no written account of the fighting between the West Welsh and the West Saxons until 682. But there is good evidence that the West Saxons had gained control of Exeter by 670. This evidence is found in three charters dated 670 relating to the establishment of the original Saxon minster, the predecessor of Exeter Cathedral on the site of which it was erected. The original charters were destroyed by the Danes, but the versions drawn up as replacements in the eleventh century are considered to have a high degree of validity. Exeter was the Roman Isca, known to the Saxons as Escancastre, and was the capital city of the Dumnonii. It may be presumed that the military campaign which achieved the capture of Exeter was an extension of the campaign which had led to the defeat of the Durotriges. The Fosse Way and the Roman

---

[5] Finberg, *Early Charters of Wessex.* item 549.

[6] Malmesbury, *The Kings before the Norman Conquest.* para. 29.

[7] Birch, *Cartularium Saxonicum.* item 25. Finberg, *Early Charters of Wessex.* items 353, 354.

road from Dorchester to Exeter were the obvious routes for the West Saxon army to follow as it continued its advance westward into Dumnonian territory. The omission of this campaign from the Chronicle is a good indication that it was not carried out under the command of the king. The capture of Exeter would have been accompanied by the occupation of the intervening area lying east of Exeter as far as the western limits of the Dornsaetan. The newly acquired territory formed the nucleus of a third new shire, which took its name from the Welsh word for Dumnonia, Defnas or Dyvnaint, modified through the centuries to modern Devon. The city of Exeter was acceptable to the West Saxons as the capital of their new shire. The record of the Life of St Boniface confirms the Saxon seizure of Exeter by 670 and shows that Saxon control had been extended northwest of Exeter as far as the Crediton area by 680. Boniface was a Saxon, originally called Winfrith, who was born at Crediton (SS 8300) in about the year 680. He received his early education and training as a monk at the minster in Exeter.

Despite the loss of their chief city the Dumnonians preserved their political and military cohesion. Their royal line displayed a remarkable capacity for survival and led the resistance to Saxon encroachment for another three centuries. Of the three new shires, Devon and Somerset were left with frontier areas facing the undefeated Dumnonians. There must have been considerable uncertainty and instability about the dividing line between West Saxon and Dumnonian territories. The ealdormen of Devon and Somerset had the responsibility for defending the areas taken over by the Saxons and for extending Saxon control as opportunity allowed. The two centres of Saxon political power at Somerton and Exeter were the points from which control was exercised over further Saxon advances into Dumnonian territory.

There is no record of any military activity undertaken by Cenwealh to regain the former Jutish lands and it appears that with a major component of his army engaged against the West Welsh he was unable to overcome the South Saxon defence of their newly acquired territory.

THE PROBLEM OF ESSEX

It was reported above that before the battle of Winwaed Sigeberht the Good, king of the East Saxons, received the support and protection of King Oswy, showing that Essex had become a Bernician fiefdom. Bede stated that after the assassination of Sigeberht in 654 he was succeeded as king by Swidhelm, son of Sexbald. As he was a pagan it was essential for him to be baptised as soon as possible. Oswy was too far away in Northumbria to arrange this himself, so he turned for help to the adjoining kingdom of East Anglia. Bede tells that Swidhelm was baptised by Cedd, bishop of the East Saxons, at Rendlesham, the country seat of Aethelwald, king of the East Angles, who acted as his godfather.[1] Aethelwald had been placed on the East Anglian throne by Oswy after the death of his brother Aethelhere at Winwaed and was therefore his subject.

Swidhelm continued subordinate to Oswy until his death in 664. Unfortunately, he had no direct heir to continue the work of spreading the Christian faith among his people. He was succeeded by two kings, Sighere, son of Sigeberht and Sebbi, son of Sexred, and it appears that because of the break in the direct succession it was necessary to place them under close supervision to ensure that the work to eradicate paganism should continue. This time Oswy did not turn to the East Anglians for help. In 664 Aethelwald also had died and was succeeded by Aldwulf, son of his brother Aethelhere. As the last-named had been Oswy's enemy at Winwaed he may have been reluctant to enlist the help of his son. Instead, he turned for help to the adjoining kingdoms of Kent and Middle Anglia (ruled by Mercia). It was decided to partition Essex with Sighere taking responsibility for the North and West (nearest to Middle Anglia) and Sebbi taking responsibility for the south and east (nearest to Kent). The city of London probably continued as the capital city of both Sebbi and Sighere. The latter was placed under the tutelage

---

[1] Bede, *Historia Ecclesiastica*. part III ch. 23.

of Wulfhere and the former under the tutelage of Ecgberht, king of Kent. They were both devoted Christians and their task under Oswy's direction was to pursue energetically the spread of Christianity among the East and Middle Saxons (including the people of Surrey). Oswy's decision to delegate to Wulfhere and Ecgberht authority over Essex may have been intended as a temporary arrangement and probably limited to ecclesiastical matters. Both overlords remained subject to Oswy as Bretwalda and answerable to him for their activity within Essex. The evidence for these developments is partly indirect and is set out below.

The unreliability of the East Saxon kings with regard to their religious faith and the need to keep them under close supervision was illustrated by an incident soon after Sighere ascended the throne. During the same year (664), a serious outbreak of the plague occurred. Bede reported that under the stress of this problem Sighere and the people in his part of the kingdom abandoned their Christian faith and turned for succour to the traditional pagan gods. But Sebbi and the people in his part of the kingdom remained true to their Christian faith. When Wulfhere heard of the apostasy of Sighere he sent Jaruman, bishop of the Mercians, to correct the error and restore the Christian faith, because Bishop Cedd had recently died from the plague at Lastingham in Northumbria and there was no bishop in London.[2] Soon afterwards Bishop Wine was expelled by King Cenwealh from the see of Winchester and he applied to Wulfhere for appointment to the see of London. As bishop of London, Wine was present with Kings Oswy, Wulfhere, Sighere and Sebbi at the consecration of the monastery of Medeshamstede in 664.

Kent had been under the rule of King Eorcenberht, who was a cousin of Eanflaed, Oswy's queen, and because of this family connection Oswy's relations with Kent were good. When he died in 664, he was succeeded by his son, Ecgberht. Until this time there is no evidence of any Christian churches in Surrey, but a charter dated 672-4 stated that the abbey at Chertsey was built under the orders of this King,[3] agreeing with the tradition of the abbey that it was founded in 666. From this

---

[2] Bede, *Historia Ecclesiastica.* part III ch. 30.

[3] Birch, *Cartularium Saxonicum.* item 34. Whitelock, *English Historical Documents.* item 54.

evidence it is apparent that Surrey had come under the authority of King Ecgberht. Bede also knew about Chertsey Abbey and he wrote that before he became bishop of London, Eorcenwald founded two monasteries, one for himself at Chertsey, where he became the first abbot, the other for his sister Aethelburga, at Barking in southern Essex.[4] The identity of Eorcenwald and Aethelburga is not stated, but their names indicate strongly that they were members of the Kentish royal family. The linkage of Chertsey with Barking shows that southern Essex, held by King Sebbi, had also come under Ecgberht's authority. The foundation of the monasteries may be seen as one of the acts carried out by King Ecgberht in fulfilment of his responsibility to Oswy to advance the Christian religion in these areas.

The relationship between Kent and southern Essex at this time was illustrated by an incident told by Simeon of Durham. King Ecgberht had two young cousins, Aethelred and Aethelberht, sons of his uncle Eormenred. They had been left orphans while still children and were being brought up in the royal court. But a servant of Ecgberht's called Thunor, or Thunder, probably a pagan, urged that they represented a threat to the royal family and that they should be eliminated. Hoping to gain Ecgberht's favour, he took it upon himself to murder the two young princes in the royal residence at Eastry (TR 3155). They were removed for burial to a monastery at Wakering (TQ 9487) in southern Essex, indicating that this area was part of the King's domain. Simeon tells how Thunor himself was subsequently buried as a pagan under a large mound of stones at a place known as Thunerhleow, literally Thunder's mound. This name probably survives at modern Thundersley (TR 3155) also in southern Essex. The young princes had a sister Eormenburg, who had married Merewalh, king of the Magonsaetan, and she demanded compensation (*wergild*) for the murder of her brothers. This was granted in the form of estates on the Isle of Thanet, which she used to found a monastery at Minster (TR 3164). Attempts were made to declare the murdered princes martyrs, with the cult presumably centred on the new monastery at Minster, but King Hlothhere, brother of Ecgberht, whom he succeeded on his death in 673, refused to permit this. Eormenburg

---

[4] Bede, *Historia Ecclesiastica.* part IV ch. 6.

became the first abbess at Minster, using the name Aebbe or Eafe (retaining the customary initial alliteration). This name is now preserved in the place-name Ebbsfleet, two miles southeast of Minster.

Another monastery was founded in 669, when King Ecgberht granted land for this purpose to a priest Bassa at the Saxon Shore Fort at Reculver. His monastery became an important abbey, which was repeatedly extended until the fifteenth century. It was dismantled in the nineteenth century except for the twin west towers, which are still a prominent landmark. The site now stands on the cliff edge and part of the fort has fallen into the sea. However, when founded it stood a short distance inland, but on the west bank of the river Wantsum, which separates the Isle of Thanet from the Kentish mainland.

Towers of former abbey at Reculver.

The authority over northwestern Essex given by Oswy to Wulfhere represented a further gain in his power in southern England. A small kingdom which was also brought under his control was Lindsey. When Chad was transferred from Lastingham monastery by Oswy in about 667 Bede explained that he was appointed bishop of Mercia and Lindsey, where he was given fifty hides of land for the foundation of a monastery. When Chad died in March 672 his successor, Wynfrith, was ordained as bishop of Mercia, Middle Anglia and Lindsey, all of which were ruled by

Wulfhere.[5] The transformation in Mercian fortunes after the disaster at Winwaed was a remarkable achievement, but it could have been carried out only with the agreement of Oswy; throughout Oswy's reign Wulfhere never challenged or clashed with him. He would have had to agree to the payment of tribute as demanded by Oswy not only in respect of Mercia, but also in respect of the other territories which he ruled.

---

[5] Bede, *Historia Ecclesiastica.* part IV ch. 3.

AFTER OSWY

In the year 670 Oswy died at the age of fifty-eight. He was buried in the monastery on the cliff top at Whitby, which was founded in 657 after the battle of Winwaed. It was dedicated to St Peter and became the mausoleum of Oswy's family, as his wife Eanflaed, their daughter Aelfflaed (abbess of the monastery), the former King Edwin (Eanflaed's father) and other eminent people were buried there. Important constitutional changes followed as a result of Oswy's death. His son, Ecgfrith, had been king of Deira for some years and when Oswy died two vacancies ensued: the throne of Bernicia and the post of Bretwalda. Ecgfrith was able to secure the Bernician throne, thereby re-uniting Northumbria under a single crown; he may have hoped to become Bretwalda, but this appointment was not in the gift of the Northumbrian Witangemot and it was denied him.

Wulfhere's constitutional position changed completely when Oswy died; he no longer had an overlord and was now a free agent. The territories which he had obtained from Oswy were now entirely under his own control and all tribute could be diverted into the Mercian treasury. He became the most powerful ruler south of the Humber, and only the West Saxons were strong enough to continue their opposition to him. The changed situation would have been most unwelcome to Ecgfrith, whose relations with Wulfhere must have become severely strained. In the situation in which he found himself in 670 Wulfhere may have had visions of realising the ambitions manifested by his father of restoring the ancient Anglian royal dynasty to its historic role as paramount ruler of all the Angles.

Early in Ecgfrith's reign he encountered serious problems with the Picts. After the death of Talorcen in 657 they had been ruled first by Gartnait and then in 663 by his brother Drest, who continued to rule as a subject king of Oswy and Ecgfrith. But the Annals of Tigernach reported that in 672 Drest was expelled from his kingdom and his place on the throne taken by Brude (or Bredei), son of Bile (or Beli), king of the British kingdom of Strathclyde. According to the *Historia Brittonum* Brude was a cousin of Ecgfrith's,[1] in which case they would have had a common grandfather, Aethelfrith of Bernicia. It may be inferred that an unrecorded daughter of Aethelfrith (a sister of Eanfrith and Oswy), having been brought up in the land of the Picts and Scots after 617, had married Bile, king of Strathclyde, and became the mother of Brude. An Irish annal, erroneously entered for a subsequent date, provided a clue to Brude's motives, when it stated that Brude was fighting for the inheritance from his grandfather.[2]

The change of regime among the Picts was a serious matter for Ecgfrith and his response was described by Eddi Stephanus in his *Life of St Wilfrid*,[3] where he stated that early in his reign the Picts started to rebel against English rule and Ecgfrith called up his cavalry. With the help of the sub-king Beornhaeth (probably his prefect) he completely suppressed the rebellion. These events must raise the suspicion that Mercian diplomacy had been active again; circumstances suggest that Wulfhere had used his influence with the British king of Strathclyde and had persuaded him to send his son Brude to lead the Picts in an insurrection against Bernician rule, as he had earlier incited the West Welsh against Wessex. The ultimate objective was that Brude should supplant Ecgfrith as head of the Bernician royal dynasty and king of Northumbria. His legal right to do so devolved from his grandfather, King Aethelfrith, through his mother. Although defeated in 671, Brude survived the battle and withdrew further north beyond the reach of Ecgfrith.

The political changes following the death of Oswy had a major impact in the kingdom of Essex. They were reflected in a charter dated 672-4 confirming the grant of 300 hides of land along the river Thames to the abbey at Chertsey. The donor was Frithuwald of the province of Surrey, who was described as a sub-king of Wulfhere, king of the Mercians. The charter was signed by Frithuwald and three other sub-kings and was confirmed by Wulfhere in his residence at Thame in Middle Anglia.[4] The

---

[1] Nennius, *Historia Brittonum*. para. 57.

[2] Anderson, *Kings and Kingship in Early Scotland*. pp. 170-5.

[3] Stephanus, *Life of St. Wilfrid*. ch. XIX.

[4] Birch, *Cartularium Saxonicum*. 34. Whitelock, *English Historical Documents*. item 54.

grant was probably not a fresh donation, but confirmation of the existing estates following a change of political control. It was reported above that Surrey and southern Essex formed that part of the kingdom ruled by King Sebbi under the tutelage of King Ecgberht. Wulfhere already exercised authority in the northwestern half of the kingdom, but probably limited only to ecclesiastical matters. As soon as he was free of his obligations to Oswy he extended his authority to full political control not only of the northwestern half, but also of the southeastern half. The king of Kent was evicted from his half of Essex and the sub-kings of Surrey became directly subordinate to Wulfhere with no mention of Sebbi. This *coup-d'etat* by Wulfhere was the first move in the long-running rivalry between Kent and Mercia for dominion over Essex and the southeast. It is likely that the Kentish king was also brought under Wulfhere's control. It was in or soon after 670 that Bertwald, described by William of Malmesbury as the son of a brother of Aethelred, king of the Mercians, and hence a close relative of Wulfhere's, transferred from Glastonbury Abbey to become abbot of Reculver (TR 2269) in Kent.[5]

There is good evidence that Wulfhere established his dominion over the Hwicce. In an undated charter (the original of which has been lost), he approved a grant of land at Hanbury (SO 9663), seven miles east of Droitwich.[6] Using his authority over the Hwicce he arranged a diplomatic marriage between his ally, Aethelwalh, king of the South Saxons, and Eabae, daughter of Eanfrith and niece of Eanhere.[7] The purpose of this link-up was to strengthen the ring of hostile states, which Wulfhere was forging round the West Saxons: the Hwicce, Mercians and Middle Angles in the north, the South Saxons (still in possession of the Isle of Wight and southeast Hampshire) in the south and the West Welsh in the west. It is not stated when Wulfhere took the Hwicce under his protection, but he could not have done so while still bound by his allegiance to Oswy.

Ecgfrith had been experiencing difficulties with his marriage to Queen Aetheldreda. Already middle-aged when she married him in about 660, she had become strongly attached to the religious way of life

---

[5] Malmesbury, *The Kings before the Norman Conquest.* para. 29.

[6] Finberg, *Early Charters of the West Midlands.* item 195.

[7] Bede, *Historia Ecclesiastica.* part IV ch. 13.

after the death of Tonberht, her first husband. Through twelve years of marriage to Ecgfrith she had steadfastly refused to consummate the union. In this attitude she was strongly supported by Bishop Wilfrid. In about 672 Ecgfrith agreed to divorce her and she took the veil in the abbey at Coldingham (NT 9065), where the abbess was her husband's aunt, Eabba. She remained at Coldingham for a year and in 673 returned to the Fen District, where she founded a double monastic house on the Isle of Ely and became the first abbess.[8] This was the predecessor of Ely Cathedral, which still holds her relics. Her name is preserved in St Etheldreda's church in Ely Place off Holborn Circus in London, once the location of the palace of the bishop of Ely.

In 672 King Cenwealh died and appears to have left no direct heir, with the consequence that a period of political instability ensued. According to Bede the government of the West Saxons was divided among sub-kings (sub-reguli) and it continued so for about ten years.[9] There may well have been dissension within the royal house concerning the succession. There appears to have been no obvious successor and the Chronicle reported that Cenwealh's queen Seaxburh occupied the throne for a year. Cenwealh had a younger brother, Centwine, but for an unknown reason he was not appointed to succeed: perhaps he was still a minor. Cenberht, who had been joint king with Cenwealh until his death in 661, had a son Caedwalla, born in 658 and hence only fourteen years of age when his father died. In 673 Aescwine was appointed king. He was the son of Cenfus, descended from Cuthgils, brother of Cynegils. His name was the first to break the succession of K sounding names, reminiscent of Cerdic. The earliest record of the name Aescwine was the founder of the East Saxon royal dynasty. This raises the possibility that Eascwine's mother was an East Saxon princess. This period of political instability presented a golden opportunity for Wulfhere to use his diplomatic skills to obtain a pliant occupant of the West Saxon throne, but there is no evidence that he was able to do so.

In 674 the tension between Mercia and Northumbria came to a head over the question of tribute and war broke out between them. Eddius

[8] Bede, *Historia Ecclesiastica.* part IV ch. 17.
[9] Bede, *Historia Ecclesiastica.* part IV ch. 12.

Stephanus reported that Wulfhere mobilised the southern nations against Northumbria and demanded tribute from Ecgfrith.[10] This amounted to a challenge that Ecgfrith should acknowledge Wulfhere's supremacy and was an essential step if Wulfhere was to realise the ambition of becoming paramount king of the Angles. Ecgfrith refused to submit and led his army against Wulfhere's force, which was defeated. The location of this important battle is not reported. The sons of the victor and vanquished at Winwaed were the victor and vanquished in 674. For a second time victory had eluded Mercia as she was poised to take over Northumbria; she had to continue to pay tribute and Wulfhere became subordinate to Ecgfrith. All the gains he had made since his accession were lost, but he was allowed to retain the Mercian throne and to continue Mercian rule of Middle Anglia. This is consistent with the proposition advanced above that Wulfhere's mother was a princess of the Middle Anglian royal house. Despite his victory, Ecgfrith was still unable to obtain appointment as Bretwalda, probably because of the opposition of the southern kings, notably Wessex. The territories gained by Oswy after Winwaed, which Wulfhere had ruled on his behalf, were returned to Northumbrian rule. Bede explained that after Ecgfrith had defeated Wulfhere in battle, he acquired the province of Lindsey. Hitherto Lindsey had been combined with Mercia and Middle Anglia to form one large diocese, but in 674 the incumbent bishop Seaxwulf had to withdraw from Lindsey and for the first time Ecgfrith gave the people of Lindsey their own diocese under Eadhead, a Northumbrian.[10] Evidence set out in the following chapter will show that the land of the Wreocensaetan and the Chester area were also transferred back to Northumbria as a consequence of Ecgfrith's victory in 674. Similarly Ecgfrith would have been able to re-assert Northumbrian sovereignty over the Magonsaetan. The Hwicce were able to regain their independence under Northumbrian protection.

Wulfhere's defeat led to a reversal of the situation in the southeast. His power in Essex collapsed and the East Saxon kings were left without protection. They were ineffective and unable to withstand the military power of the Kentish kings. In 673 King Ecgberht had died and was

---

[10] Stephanus, *Life of St Wilfred*. Ch. XX.

succeeded by his brother Hlothhere and his son Eadric, acting as joint kings. Their response to the new situation was revealed in the code of laws which they issued containing special provisions relating to London, such as the king's hall in the town and the king's town reeve.[11] This document shows that they had moved in and taken over the city of London. King Sighere and King Sebbi would have had to accept them as the new overlords of Essex, including Surrey and Middlesex. While they were in control of London, Archbishop Theodore appointed Eorcenwald, abbot at Chertsey, to the see of London in 675.[12] The East and Middle Saxons now came under the rule of Kentish kings and a Kentish bishop.

The name of Hlothhere is of significance. He is the first of only two kings descended from Hengist who did not have a name with an initial Eh or Ea sound. His was the name of two Frankish kings, Chlothar I, the youngest son of Clovis, and his grandson Chlothar II (ruled 613-629). Hlothhere was probably named after one or both of these Frankish kings: he was descended from the former through the marriage of King Aethelberht to Berhta; the latter ruled a re-united Frankish kingdom at about the time of Hlothhere's birth. His name is the last sign of the influence of the Merovingian dynasty at the Kentish court. (The power of this dynasty was already in decline by the 670s).

Wulfhere's set-back gave the West Saxons an opportunity to regain the disputed territory north of the Thames. In its annal for 675 the Chronicle reported that Wulfhere and Aescwine had been in combat at Biedanheafde. This place cannot be identified, but it is possible that it is the same place as Biedcanford, where the West Saxons defeated the Britons in 571. Although unlocated the latter was definitely north of the Thames. Such an identity would indicate that Aescwine had led the West Saxons across the Thames and re-occupied the Gewissian lands, thereby leading to a clash with Wulfhere, who in response marched his army across Middle Anglia towards Dorchester. The Chronicle does not report the outcome of this battle, but it stated that later in 675 Wulfhere died.

---

[11] Whitelock, *English Historical Documents*. item 30.

[12] Bede, *Historia Ecclesiastica*. part IV ch. 6.

PART 5

THE MERCIAN
PERIOD

AETHELRED, KING OF THE MERCIANS

When Wulfhere died in 675 he had a son Coenred, but it was Wulfhere's younger brother Aethelred, who succeeded to the throne, presumably because Coenred was still a minor. The kingdom inherited by Aethelred consisted only of Mercia and Middle Anglia and was still subject to the payment of tribute to Northumbria. In 676 Aethelred decided to intervene in the situation caused by the establishment of Kentish dominion over Essex. Bede, who knew nothing of the situation in London, reported that in that year King Aethelred took his army into Kent, which he ravaged. Churches and monasteries were attacked and in particular the city of Rochester was destroyed.[1] It is possible that this action was taken at the request of the East Saxon kings. Aethelred led his army from Middle Anglia across Middlesex to London, from which the Kentish army was driven and pursued back into Kent. Despite the defeat of their army, Hlothhere and Eadric were allowed to continue their reign as kings of Kent, but now under Mercian suzerainty. The East Saxon kings presumably continued to rule the two halves of their kingdom, but now under the protection of Aethelred as their overlord.

Aethelred's main quarrel was with Ecgfrith of Northumbria, but it was not until 679 that the dispute between them came to a head. Bede stated that in the ninth year of Ecgfrith's reign he and King Aethelred fought in a great battle by the river Trent. But the battle did not proceed to a decisive conclusion, because Archbishop Theodore intervened to halt the slaughter. Subsequent events indicate, however, that before the hostilities ceased Aethelred had established his military superiority.[2] This is supported by the fact that Ealfwine, Ecgfrith's brother, a young man of eighteen years, lost his life in the fighting. The exact location of the battle is not stated, but as it took place somewhere along the river Trent it appears that it was Ecgfrith who first took military action by

---

[1] Bede, *Historia Ecclesiastica.* part IV ch. 12.

[2] Bede, *Historia Ecclesiastica.* part IV ch. 19.

leading his army south towards or into Mercia. The most likely reason is that Aethelred was withholding tribute due to Northumbria and thereby virtually declaring Mercian independence of Northumbria. The battle of the river Trent is another important turning point in early English history. It marked the end of the period dominated by the great Northumbrian kings and marks the beginning of the period in which Mercia became the major Anglo-Saxon power. The intervention of Theodore was crucial and the peace negotiated by him was reinforced by the full spiritual authority of the church. No record of the treaty has survived, but its provisions became apparent as the events of Aethelred's reign unfolded, as explained below. They may be summarised as follows:

1. Peace was imposed upon Mercia and Northumbria. It may be supposed that in a treaty drawn up under the auspices of the church neither side was made tributary to the other.
2. Aethelred regained control of the territories which were ruled by Wulfhere until his defeat in 674.

The return of the land of the Wreocensaetan to Mercian rule was shown by a charter signed by Aethelred in 680 confirming the holding of lands at Shifnal, Cosford and Lizard Hill by the monastery at Peterborough.[3] These were the estates for which Wulfhere had issued a charter in the year 664. There would have been no need to re-confirm the tenure of land so soon after Wulfhere's charter, if there had not been a change of political control in the intervening period. The date of Aethelred's charter within a year of the battle of the river Trent places it beyond reasonable doubt that it was issued as a consequence of the peace negotiated by Archbishop Theodore. There is also evidence that Aethelred had regained control of the Chester area. In about 679 he founded the church of St John just outside the city walls of Chester, overlooking the river Dee; a portrayal of this event is provided in the stained glass window. The kingdom of Lindsey was also returned to Mercian control and the Northumbrian bishop Eadhaed was transferred

---

[3] Birch, *Cartularium Saxonicum*. item 49. Finberg, *Early Charters of the West Midlands*. item 427.

from Lindsey to become bishop of Ripon. When the Oswestry area returned to Mercian rule in 679 it became possible for Queen Osthryth to go there to seek out the remaining relics of St Oswald. When she found them they were translated to the monastery at Bardney in Lindsey.[4]

Theodore was a strong personality, who exerted a major influence as Archbishop of Canterbury. A native of Tarsus in Asia Minor, he had been appointed by Pope Vitalian to fill the vacant chair at Canterbury when he had reached the advanced age of sixty-six. He arrived in England in May 669. (Bede's principal source of information about him was Abbot Albinus, who had been educated at Canterbury by Theodore and his close collaborator, Hadrian, Abbot of the monastery of St Peter and St Paul, Canterbury, later known as St Augustine's.) The see at Canterbury had been vacant since the death of Archbishop Deusdedit in 664.[5] Theodore was, therefore, the first archbishop to preside over the entire English church following the Synod of Whitby in 664, and he set about the task of consolidating the merger of the two components of English Christendom with skill and vigour. In 673 he summoned a synod of clergy to assemble at Hertford, where important decisions were taken to regulate the life of the church according to canon law. Bede's record of the proceedings showed that one item on the agenda was a proposal that additional bishops should be ordained as the size of the church increased. However, no decision was taken on this matter.[6] Theodore had been aiming to strengthen the church by reducing the size of the dioceses, but the bishops were clearly opposed to any diminution of their power. Theodore had to wait for suitable opportunities to create new dioceses.

Such an opportunity soon occurred in East Anglia. One of the bishops present at the synod was Bisi, bishop of the East Angles, successor to Boniface (the third East Anglian bishop). Soon after the synod Bisi became so infirm that he could no longer carry out his duties. In his place two new bishops were ordained, Aecci and Baduwine. East Anglia was divided into two dioceses, one in the south with the original see at

---

[4] Bede, *Historia Ecclesiastica*. part III ch. 11.

[5] Bede, *Historia Ecclesiastica*. part IV ch. 1.

[6] Bede, *Historia Ecclesiastica*. part IV ch. 5.

Dunwich, the other in the north with a new see at North Elmham (TF 9820). This location was within a mile of Spong Hill, where a large pagan cemetery has been excavated, from which we can deduce that there must have been an extensive settlement in the area. Christianity had been introduced in the northern half of East Anglia by the Irish monk Fursey and the teachings and practices of the Celtic church would have spread among the North Folk from his monastery at Burgh Castle. Theodore would have seen the need for a bishop to wean them away from their Celtic practices and therefore Baduwine was appointed to carry out this mission. A fresh start was made by abandoning the original remote Celtic foundation at Burgh Castle and, in accordance with Roman practice, establishing the new see in one of the main settlement areas of the North Folk. No trace of Bishop Baduwine's original cathedral church may be seen at North Elmham; it may well have been destroyed by the Danes, but the remains of a late Anglian church may still be seen there.

Aethelred continued Mercian rule of the former Gewissian lands north of the Thames, but now annexed as part of Middle Anglia. Although the Middle Anglian throne had been vacant since the death of his brother, Peada, in 656, Aethelred, like Wulfhere, did not formally claim it for himself, although there can be little doubt that he had the strongest claim to it. In his charters, Aethelred was content to describe himself simply as king of the Mercians. In 681 he signed a charter concerning land along the river Cherwell in Middle Anglia.[7] Theodore succeeded in establishing a separate diocese for Middle Anglia, with the see at Dorchester-on-Thames in the extreme south of the kingdom;[8] this choice appears to have been determined by the availability of a suitable cathedral church and is consistent with the analysis given above that the Middle Angles had no political leadership of their own. Had there been a Middle Anglian political capital in existence at the time, Archbishop Theodore would have established the new episcopal see at or near the political capital in accordance with normal Roman practice.

The Hwicce had been free of Mercian rule from 674 to 679.

---

[7] Birch, *Cartularium Saxonicum.* item 57. Whitelock, *English Historical Documents.* item 57.

[8] Bede, *Historia Ecclesiastica.* part IV ch. 21.

Documents show that by 675 they were being ruled by the brothers Osric and Oshere as joint kings. The name of the latter shows that they were the sons of Eanhere, who may have continued to rule the Hwicce into the early 670s. In 676 Osric issued an important charter which he signed as king. In it he stated that 'we' decided to erect an episcopal see in accordance with synodal decrees, a reference apparently to the synod of Hertford in 673.[9] This is the earliest reference to the new diocese of the Hwicce. Osric then stated that he wished to establish monasteries and nunneries and to this end he granted 100 hides of land adjoining the city of Bath for the Abbess Bertana. Osric's charter was attested by King Aethelred, Archbishop Theodore and four bishops from outside the Hwicce, as a bishop of the Hwicce had not yet been appointed. The new abbey at Bath was the first of the series of monastic houses founded as a result of the introduction of Roman practices among the Hwicce.

Documents in and after 679, the year of the battle of the river Trent, illustrate how the political situation had changed completely and that King Aethelred had established his suzerainty over the Hwiccian kings, who were no longer able to look for protection to their Northumbrian kinsmen. This year the Hwicce lost their independence, never to regain it, and their kings were down-graded to sub-kings – *reguli* or *subreguli*. In a document of the fifth year of his reign (679) King Aethelred granted 300 hides of land for the foundation of a monastery at Gloucester and the same amount of land for a monastery at Pershore (SO 9446) to Osric and his brother Oswald, who were described as ministers of King Aethelred.[10] These were the original abbeys at Gloucester and Pershore. In an undated charter, Aethelred confirmed a grant of land at Withington (SP 0315) made by Oshere, who was described as sub-king of the Hwicce and companion of King Aethelred.[11] The use of the expression companion shows that Oshere had become a military companion of Aethelred and as such in the event of hostilities would be present in the field in the immediate vicinity of Aethelred and under his command. Oshere would have the Hwiccian armed forces under his

---

[9] Finberg, *Early Charters of the West Midlands*. pp. 172-4.

[10] Finberg, *Early Charters of the West Midlands*. p 158.

[11] Birch, *Cartularium Saxonicum*. item 156. Whitelock, *English Historical Documents*. item 68.

command, which automatically became integrated into the Mercian army.

Statue of King Osric at South Door Gloucester Cathedral.

According to Florence of Worcester, it was Oshere who founded the cathedral church of the diocese of the Hwicce at Worcester in 679. Like the abbeys at Bath and Gloucester it was dedicated to St Peter. The documented history of this church shows that it was a foundation of the royal house, and that its purpose was to serve as the royal mausoleum. This accords with the dedication to St Peter. Its siting followed the contemporary practices of the Celtic church: on an elevation overlooking water at an abandoned military site (like the abbeys at Burgh Castle, Bradwell-on-Sea and Reculver). It had the convenience of being situated only six miles from the Hwiccian capital at Wic. It appears to have been the Hwiccian counterpart of St Peter's at Whitby and could have been founded at about the same time (657). From 679 it served a second function as the cathedral church of the new diocese. Its association with Whitby was shown when the first bishops (Tatfrid, Bosel and Oftfor) were chosen from the monks of Whitby Abbey. The area of the diocese was identical with that of the kingdom. The status of Worcester was given explicitly in a charter issued during the period 718-745, which described the city as the 'metropolis' (i.e. the see) of the Hwicce.

Osric and his brothers had a sister, Osgith, who married King Sighere of Essex. As Essex was a Mercian dependency this marriage had probably been arranged by King Wulfhere during the period when he had gained control of the Hwicce 670-674. Osgith founded the priory, which perpetuates her name as St Osyth (TM 1215). It was located within her husband's part of the kingdom close to the Essex coast near Clacton.

Oshere left four sons, Aethilheard (the eldest), Aethilric, Aethilweard and Aethilberht, who were recorded in the periods 692-709, 692-736, 692-717 and 692-709 respectively. The first three appear in documents as sub-kings (*subreguli*).

King Merchelm of the Magonsaetan had a half-sister Mildburg, who founded an abbey within his kingdom at Much Wenlock. Her biography written by Goscelin provides evidence that King Aethelred became overlord of the Magonsaetan. Charters recording grants of land to the abbey at Much Wenlock stated explicitly that the grants were made with the consent of King Aethelred.[12] The sovereignty over the Magonsaetan, originally vested in King Oswy, was presumably transferred to King Aethelred under the terms of Theodore's peace treaty of 679. It is to be noted that Merchelm, who was Aethelred's nephew, used the full title of king, whereas Osric and Oshere had been down-graded to sub-king. It is not known what difference this made in practice.

After the synod of Hertford, Archbishop Theodore created a diocese for the Magonsaetan in 676, the same year in which he established the diocese of the Hwicce. His action showed that he considered the Magonsaetan to be a separate and distinct political entity, which required its own ecclesiastical organisation. From an early date, perhaps from the outset, the see of the Magonsaetan was established at Hereford, indicating that the political centre was also there. Merewalh seems to have decided to abandon Magnis, only five miles distant, which may have been wrecked by Oswy's troops. Hereford's situation in the extreme south of the kingdom seems an unsuitable location for a political centre, but may suggest an expectation that the Welsh area south of the river would soon be re-united with the area north of the river. In a memorial tablet set up in the cathedral church at Hereford in 736-40 Mildfrith, brother of King Merchelm, was described as *regulus* – sub-king – and given credit for founding the cathedral church.

The new dioceses established by Archbishop Theodore throughout England reflected closely the existing political structure and it is

---

[12] Finberg, *Early Charters of the West Midlands.* item 204-7.

significant that the Wreocensaetan and the Chester area were not accorded, either separately or jointly, their own diocese and bishop, but were presumably placed under the pastoral care of the bishop of the Mercians at Lichfield. This would signify that they were not considered to be self-contained political areas under their own ruler, but had been absorbed into the kingdom of Mercia.

After the peace treaty of 679 Northumbria retained its unity under King Ecgfrith, but never again exerted power or influence south of the Humber. Ecgfrith continued to exercise suzerainty over the southern Picts and in 681 appointed Trumwine to be bishop of the Picts.[13] Bede reported disapprovingly that in 684 Ecgfrith sent an army to Ireland under the command of Ealdorman Berht, his prefect and son of Beornheath, who had fought with Ecgfrith against the Picts in 672. His army ravaged this unoffending people, who were most friendly to the English.[14] The purpose of this Northumbrian venture across the Irish Sea was not explained.

The next year a serious situation developed, when Brude moved further south towards the Pictish territory ruled by Ecgfrith. Brude's claim to the inheritance of his grandfather (King Aethelfrith), as reported by an Irish source, amounted to a claim to be head of the Northumbrian royal dynasty. It was a challenge, which Ecgfrith could not ignore, as he marched his army north across Strathmore. The Picts pretended to retreat, drawing Ecgfrith's army into a narrow pass in the mountains, where it was decimated and Ecgfrith was slain. This was the battle of Nechtansmere, also known as Dunnichen Moss (NO 4848), southeast of Forfar. The significance of this battle is that it marked the turning point of English power in the north. The Picts regained their independence and even Bishop Trumwine was withdrawn from the monastery at Abercorn, which was located south of the river Forth and hence not in Pictish but Northumbrian territory. Bede's evidence shows that the Scots in Argyll and the Strathclyde Britons took advantage of the Northumbrian reverse to throw off the domination which Oswy had established. Never again would English power extend so far to the north.

---

[13] Bede, *Historia Ecclesiastica.* part IV ch. 12.

[14] Bede, *Historia Ecclesiastica.* part IV ch. 26.

Bede in his *Life of Cuthbert* tells how Cuthbert, who had recently been ordained bishop of Lindisfarne, had advised against the campaign. At the time of the battle he and Ecgfrith's queen, Iurminburh, were visiting a convent at Carlisle, when Cuthbert had a prophetic vision about the outcome of the battle.[15] The incident confirms that by 685 Carlisle formed part of the Northumbrian kingdom.

Upon the death of Ecgfrith there was a problem of the succession, as he had left no heir. Only one of Oswy's sons was still alive, Aldfrith, who was illegitimate, the child of Fina, a princess of the Irish royal family Ui Neill. During Ecgfrith's reign he had remained in exile in Ireland and Iona and had gained a wide reputation as a scholar. In 685 he returned to Northumbria and succeeded Ecgfrith on the throne.

The annal for 698 showed that war with the Picts had broken out again and in the course of it Ealdorman Berht was killed, suggesting that the Northumbrians had suffered defeat. This is supported by William of Malmesbury, who summarised Aldfrith's reign thus: 'During the space of nineteen years, he presided over the kingdom in the utmost tranquillity and joy; doing nothing that greedy calumny itself could justly carp at, except the persecution for the great man Wilfrid. However, he held not the same extent of territory as his father and brother, because the Picts, proudly profiting by their recent victory, and attacking the Angles, who had become indolent through a lengthened peace, had curtailed his boundaries on the north.'[16] Subsequent evidence, set out below, shows that the Picts had crossed the river Forth and penetrated into Northumbrian territory to a depth of about ten miles.

Aldfrith died in 705 and immediately a problem of the succession arose. He had left a son, Osred, who was only eight years old. At first the throne was occupied by one Eadwulf, whose claim to occupy it is not known, but he was opposed by Aldfrith's prefect, Berhtfrith, who was the son of Berht. He championed Osred's right to succeed his father although he was still a minor. Fighting broke out between the two parties and after two months Eadwulf was driven out. These events

---

[15] Bede, *The Life of Cuthbert.* ch. 27.

[16] Malmesbury, *The Kings before the Norman Conquest.* para. 52.

were described during the proceedings of the Synod on the Nidd, which was held the following year to decide the position of Bishop Wilfrid. According to the account provided by Eddius Stephanus, a crucial stage in the struggle for the succession was reached, when Osred and Berhtfrith were besieged in the fortress at Bamburgh and surrounded by the hostile army. They then took a vow that if Osred succeeded to his father's kingdom, they would carry out the Pope's command concerning Wilfrid. As soon as this vow was taken they were able to put the besiegers to flight.[17] Osred secured his father's throne and Wilfrid was restored to the bishopric of York.

In 704 King Aethelred abdicated in favour of his nephew Coenred, son of Wulfhere, and took holy orders as a monk in the monastery at Bardney in Lindsey, which was growing in importance as the cult of St Oswald became more widespread. Aethelred became abbot and upon his death was buried there. He had a son Ceolred, but he was passed over possibly because he was still a minor and/or because he was illegitimate. King Coenred continued to observe the provisions of Theodore's treaty of 679 and there was no return to the aggressive policies of his father and grandfather. During his reign there appear the first signs of friction between the Mercians and Welsh, who were apparently trying to regain the territory they had lost in 656. In the *Life of St Guthlac* written by Felix in about 740 it was stated that during Coenred's reign the Britons carried out attacks against the English and pillaged them.[18]

During Coenred's reign the kingdom of Essex continued to be divided into two parts: the southeastern now ruled jointly by Sigeheard and Swaefred, sons of Sebbi, and the northwestern ruled by Offa, son of King Sigehere and his Hwiccian queen, Osgith. Both parts remained subject to Mercian suzerainty. The transfer of land at Fulham in Middlesex required the approval of Sigeheard, king of the East Saxons, and also of Coenred.[19] Offa was the only East Saxon king since Sleda with a name which did not begin with the S sound. Offa was well known as the name of the famous king of continental Angulus, but it is also recorded as the name of the father of Erchenwin/Aescwini, founder of the East Saxon

---

[17] Stephanus, *Life of Wilfrid*. ch. IX.

[18] Stephanus, *Life of Wilfrid*. ch. XXXIV

[19] Whitelock, *English Historical Documents*. item 62.

royal line. For the latter reason Offa would have been an acceptable name to the East Saxon royal family and for the former reason it would have been acceptable to Queen Osgith and her retinue. (Offa was also the name of a younger brother of King Oswy, who was probably an uncle of Queen Osgith.) King Offa appears to have compensated for his father's lack of faith by strong support of the church. He made a gift of land at Hemel Hempstead to the bishop of London,[20] showing that at this time the kingdom of Essex included areas now forming part of Hertfordshire. He inherited land in the Hwicce from his mother and his name survives in modern Offenham (SP 0546), two miles northeast of Evesham. He donated estates in the vicinity of Evesham to the abbey, which was founded there in 701.[21]

After five years on the throne Coenred decided to abdicate in favour of his cousin Ceolred, son of Aethelred. Together with King Offa, who also abdicated, he went to Rome, where they both lived out their lives as monks.[22]

---

[20] Whitelock, *English Historical Documents*. item 63.

[21] Finberg, *Early Charters of the West Midlands*. part VIII.

[22] Bede, *Historia Ecclesiastica*. part V ch. 19.

THE SOUTHERN KINGDOMS
676 - 709

In its annal for 676 the Chronicle announced that Centwine had succeeded to the West Saxon throne upon the death of Aescwine. He continued to prosecute the war in the west and had a break-through in 682 when the Chronicle reported that his army had reached the sea, without specifying which sea was meant. As the West Saxons were already in control of the south coast as far west as the estuary of the Exe, this statement is taken to refer to the Bristol Channel. In that case, it shows that the West Saxons had advanced north from the Glastonbury area and were in control of the coast between the mouths of the Parret and the Bristol Avon. Any remaining British resistance in the Mendip Hills must have ended soon after 682. The wording of the entry indicates that Centwine took personal responsibility for this campaign. He issued a charter for land at Wedmore (ST 4347) in 680-5.[1] During his reign the West Saxons were able to advance across the river Parret into the area south of the Quantock Hills. Church records show that at an unknown date he granted lands at West Monkton (ST 2628), four miles northeast of Taunton, to the Abbot of Glastonbury.[2] This grant was probably confirmation of an existing holding. To take control of this area the West Saxon forces appear to have advanced along the southeastern slopes of the Quantock Hills.

About the year 685 a monastery was founded at Frome (ST 7747) and Aldhelm, a relative of the king, was appointed abbot. He had previously been abbot of Malmesbury since 672. Aldhelm described Centwine as a powerful king, who won three great battles, the locations of which were not stated, but were presumably in the west and connected with his advance to the sea.

The South Saxons continued to hold the Isle of Wight and southeast Hampshire and Centwine, intent upon prosecuting the war in the west,

---

[1] Finberg, *Early Charters of Wessex*. 362.

[2] Birch, *Cartularium Saxonicum*. item 62. Finberg, *Early Charters of Wessex*. item 361.

gave no sign of attempting to regain the lost territories. At this time most of the South Saxons were still pagan, but in about 680 Bishop Wilfrid arrived in Sussex. Bede reported that King Aethelwealh gave Bishop Wilfrid 87 hides of land at Selsey, a name which means 'Seal Island'.[3] It was surrounded on three sides by the sea and was joined to the mainland by a narrow piece of land to the west. Wilfrid founded a monastic settlement there. The Celtic style of settlement has a striking similarity with the foundation made about the same time close to the sea on the Essex coast by Queen Osgith, cousin of Queen Eabae, which would suggest that the latter may have been involved in the donation of Selsey to Wilfrid. In the year 685 two important changes in the situation took place. Caedwalla, son of King Cenberht, became active in Wessex and laid claim to the throne. His claim was as strong as Centwine's and he probably considered that he should at least be joint king. But his claim was rejected and he was banished from the kingdom. He found refuge in the wild areas of the Chiltern Hills and the Anderida Forest (the Sussex Weald). In the former he was in the frontier area between the Middle Angles and the East and Middle Saxons; in the latter in the no-man's land between Kent and Sussex. He appears to have decided that the growth of South Saxon power at the expense of Wessex had to be resisted. Bede reported that while in exile Caedwalla attacked Sussex with his army, killed King Aethelwealh and ravaged the province until he was expelled by two ealdormen, Brihthun and Andhun, who afterwards ruled the kingdom.[4] It appears that Caedwalla mounted his attack on Sussex from his hide-out in the Anderida Forest. According to Eddius Stephanus, the biographer of Bishop Wilfrid, it was while Caedwalla was in exile in the Weald that he formed a close friendship with Wilfrid and the two men made a compact to help one another.[5]

At about this time a proposal was made for a military alliance between Kent and Sussex, but the proposal did not receive the united support of the Kentish kings: King Hlothhere opposed the suggested military alliance, while his nephew, Eadric, supported it. The latter received armed support from the South Saxons and fighting erupted.

---

[3] Bede, *Historia Ecclesiastica.* part IV ch. 13.

[4] Bede, *Historia Ecclesiastica.* part IV ch. 15.

[5] Stephanus, *Life of Wilfrid.* ch. 42.

Bede reported that Hlothhere was wounded in a battle against a South Saxon army, which was supporting Eadric against him. The wound was so serious that he died on 6 February 685, while it was being dressed.[6] Upon the death of Hlothhere the military alliance came into effect. Its purpose was not spelt out, but the co-incidence with Caedwalla's activity suggests that it represented a combined response by Kent and Sussex against Caedwalla.

Caedwalla's next step was to make his bid for the West Saxon throne and in doing so he was given help and support by Bishop Wilfrid. Centwine was deposed and Caedwalla ascended the throne, appointing Wilfrid to be his supreme counsellor over the kingdom. Caedwalla gave an entirely new direction to West Saxon policy: the over-riding priority was to regain the lost territories and to remove the threat posed by the South Saxon-Kentish alliance. The acquisition of more British territory in the west was of less importance and could be temporarily abandoned, and so the war in the west was brought to a halt. No battles are reported against the West Welsh after 685 until 710. With the cessation of hostilities Aldhelm, while still abbot at Frome (685-705), was able to write to Geraint, king of Dumnonia, about the error of the Celtic church in calculating the date of Easter and addressed him most respectfully as *"Dominus gloriosissimus, occidentalis regni sceptre gubernator* – the most glorious lord, holder of the sceptre of the western kingdom."[7] The actual date of the cease-fire is not known, but it enabled the West Saxons to concentrate on the armed struggle in the east.

Bede reported that after Caedwalla had obtained the throne he invaded the Isle of Wight, the population of which was still entirely pagan. The island was under the rule of King Arwald, who is otherwise unknown. He was presumably one of the kings of the South Saxons, who practised multi-kingship like other Saxon kingdoms. He had two young brothers, who escaped from Caedwalla's army and found hiding on the mainland at a place called Stone, modern Stoneham (SU 4315). But their hiding place was betrayed, they were captured and condemned to death. Bede tells how Caedwalla agreed that they should be baptised

---

[6] Bede, *Historia Ecclesiastica*. part IV ch. 24.

[7] Major, *The Early Wars of Wessex*. p. 77.

into the Christian faith before they were put to death.[8] Caedwalla tried
to exterminate all the islanders and replace them with West Saxons,
presumably as retribution for their rebellion against West Saxon rule in
661. Before embarking on the invasion, Caedwalla, although not a
Christian himself, had made a vow that if he was successful in
conquering the island, he would give a quarter of the land to the church.
The island was assessed as consisting of 1,200 hides. When the conquest
was complete Caedwalla was ready to fulfil his vow and he handed over
300 hides to Bishop Wilfrid. Local historians report that the first
Christian church on the Isle of Wight was founded at Brading (SZ 6286)
by Wilfrid. Brading, although now completely inland, was an important
port with a large harbour on the eastern side of the island in Roman and
Saxon times, and was only about sixteen miles by boat from Wilfrid's
monastery at Selsey. It seems likely that some of the land granted by
Caedwalla was at Brading.

William of Malmesbury's account of Caedwalla's activity at this time
was as follows: 'Hostile towards the South Saxons with inextinguishable
hatred, he totally destroyed Eadric, the successor of Aethelwalh, who
opposed him with renewed boldness.'[9] It appears that following the
death of Aethelwalh, Eadric became king of Sussex as well as of Kent,
but soon afterwards he fell in the fighting against Caedwalla's army.
Bede stated that Eadric reigned for one and half years after the death of
Hlothhere. On this evidence he would have fallen in about August 686.
The result was the collapse of the Kentish-South Saxon military alliance
and Caedwalla became the most powerful figure in the southeast. Eadric
appears not to have left a direct heir, with the result that both the
Kentish and the South Saxon thrones became vacant. Caedwalla
planned to fill them with his own nominees. A member of the West
Saxon royal family called Nunna became king of the South Saxons and
Caedwalla's brother Mul was apparently intended to become king of
Kent. At about this time Bishop Wilfrid returned to the north, leaving
the South Saxon see vacant. No fresh appointment was made; instead
the South Saxons became dependent on the bishop of the Gewissae (i.e.

---

[8] Bede, *Historia Ecclesiastica.* part IV ch. 14.

[9] Malmesbury, *The Kings before the Norman Conquest.* para. 34.

the West Saxons) at Winchester.

A charter dated 688 showed that Caedwalla had taken possession of Surrey by this year. It recorded the grant of 60 hides of land for the foundation of a monastery at Farnham (SU 8446). Among the signatories were Bishop Wilfrid, Eorcenwald, Bishop of London, and Haedde, Bishop of Winchester. In the charter Caedwalla used the title King of the Saxons; he was certainly ruler of the West Saxons and the South Saxons. By taking possession of Surrey Caedwalla had established himself as overlord of the militarily impotent kings of the East Saxons. Caedwalla also granted 70 hides of land at Battersea to the abbey at Barking in Essex in a charter also signed by bishops Wilfrid, Eorcenwald and Haedde.[10] A charter probably dated March, 687 relating to the land held by Barking Abbey was signed by the same bishops, by Sebbi as king of the East Saxons and by his sons Sigeheard and Swaefred, also designated as kings.[11] (Bede reported that King Sebbi was a man of deep religious faith and that he reigned for thirty years.)

From Surrey, Caedwalla and Mul were able to advance into Kent. Their occupation of northwest Kent was shown by Caedwalla's signature on a charter granting land at St Mary Hoo (TQ 7977), four miles southwest of Allhallows, to the monastery at Peterborough.[12] This act was probably confirmation of an existing tenure following a change of political control of the St Mary Hoo area. But Caedwalla and Mul encountered opposition by the men of Kent and the attempt to establish Mul on the Kentish throne was prevented in 687 when he was burned to death with twelve supporters in a house, an incident which provoked great anger in Wessex.

In 688 Caedwalla signed a charter granting lands at Ewen (SU 0097) and Somerford Keynes (SU 0195) in the frontier area between the Hwicce and Wiltshire to Aldhelm,[13] confirming that all of Wiltshire was under West Saxon control.

Caedwalla had never been baptised as a Christian, but had shown

---

[10] Birch, *Cartularium Saxonicum. item* 72. Whitelock, *English Historical Documents.* item 58.

[11] Hart, *The Early Charters of the Eastern England.* item 123.

[12] Birch, *Cartularium Saxonicum.* item 89.

[13] Birch, *Cartularium Saxonicum.* item 70. Finberg, *Early Charters of Wessex.* item 185.

himself to be a strong supporter of the Christian faith. The Chronicle reported that in 688 he went to Rome, where he was baptised in the name of Peter by Pope Sergius at Easter 689. But seven days later he died and was buried wearing his baptismal robes in St Peter's church. The epitaph on his tomb (quoted by Bede) gave his age as thirty and his title as Peter, King of the Saxons.[14]

Throughout this period there is no evidence that King Aethelred undertook any action to intervene in the fighting between the southern kingdoms or to extend Mercian influence beyond Kent. The explanation for this may be that he was restrained by the terms of the peace treaty of 679 and/or by Archbishop Theodore. The last-named died in 690 and was succeeded by Berhtwald, abbot of Reculver. According to William of Malmesbury Berhtwald was a nephew of King Aethelred, who presumably used his influence to obtain the appointment for him. He was the first Mercian to become archbishop of Canterbury and as head of the church would have been able to support Aethelred's political plans.

In 688 Ine succeeded to the West Saxon throne, which he occupied for thirty-seven years. He was the son of Cenred, who was descended from Ceawlin. Although Cenred's ancestors had shown their descent from Cerdic by names with an initial K sound, Cenred had given his sons names which were not of the typical West Saxon style, Ine and Ingeld. By contrast, his daughters had typical West Saxon names, Cwenburh and Cuthburh. The significance of the names Ine and Ingeld is not known, except that their mother was presumably not West Saxon. The main problem confronting Ine upon his accession was West Saxon policy towards Kent. In general he continued Caedwalla's aims, but using diplomatic rather than military means. Two external powers, Mercia and Wessex, were endeavouring to assert their suzerainty over Kent and to install puppet rulers. Their aims were diametrically opposed and could have led to a clash between the two kingdoms. Bede stated that after the death of Eadric 'kings of doubtful title and foreigners wasted that kingdom for some time until the legitimate king, Wihtred, the son of Egbert, becoming secure in his kingdom, delivered his people from

---

[14] Bede, *Historia Ecclesiastica.* part V ch. 7.

foreign invasion by his piety and zeal.' The foreigners who wasted the kingdom included Caedwalla, Mul and Ine. Another foreigner was the East Saxon, Swaefred, son of King Sebbi, who was not driven out and was reported explicitly by Bede to have been king of Kent with Wihtred on 1st July, 692.[15] The presence of an East Saxon prince side by side with the legitimate Kentish king certainly seems remarkable. He can hardly have been acceptable to the Kentish Witangemot and must have depended upon Mercian support. Indeed, King Aethelred continued to demonstrate his authority over Kent by confirming charters drawn up by other kings. In supporting Swaefred's presence in Kent, Aethelred was giving approval to East Saxon aspirations in Kent, but more practically from the Mercian point of view he could depend upon Swaefred to inhibit any action taken within Kent to restore full Kentish independence. A king of doubtful title could have been Oswine, who appeared in three charters in 689-90. William of Malmesbury's version of event was as follows: 'In this desperate state of the affairs of Kent, there was a void of about six years in the royal succession. In the seventh, Wihtred, son of Egbert, having repressed the malevolence of his countrymen by his activity, and purchased a peace from his enemies by money, was chosen king by the inhabitants, who entertained great and well founded hopes of him.'[16] This account sounds as if Wihtred's claim to the throne was not clear-cut and that there were doubts about his right to succeed. It took six years for him to gain acceptance as king by the people of Kent. Although Bede and Malmesbury agree that Wihtred was the son of Egbert, it may be significant that he had not been given a typical Kentish style name with an initial Eh sound. These facts may suggest that his right to succeed was impaired by illegitimacy.

In 694 Ine negotiated a peace treaty with King Wihtred. The annal for this year stated: 'The people of Kent made terms with Ine and paid him thirty thousand (pence), because they had burnt Mul. And Wihtred succeeded to the kingdom of the people of Kent and held it for thirty-three years. Wihtred was the son of Egbert, the son of Eorcenberht, the son of Eadbald, the son of Ethelbert.' Mul was given an honourable

---

[15] Bede, *Historia Ecclesiastica*. part V ch. 8.

[16] Malmesbury, *The Kings before the Norman Conquest*. para. 15.

burial at Canterbury alongside the tombs of the kings of Kent, presumably as agreed in the treaty. Ine aimed to retain as much influence within Kent as possible and to this end he used his brother Ingeld, who appears to have replaced Caedwalla's brother Mul in West Saxon plans for Kent. With Wihtred firmly established on the Kentish throne, it was not possible to instal a West Saxon puppet king, so Ine sought to marry his brother into the Kentish royal family. The genealogical table shows that Ingeld founded a dynastic line, all with Kentish style names beginning with the Eh sound, indicating that Ingeld had indeed, married a princess of the Kentish royal house. Her name was not reported, but convention demanded a blood relationship as close as that of Ine and Ingeld. Hence, she would have been either a daughter or sister of Wihtred. Ine's aim was presumably that the marriage should produce a future line of Kentish kings with strong West Saxon ties. The names of Ingeld's descendants, son Eoppa and grandson Eafa, were appropriate for a king of Kent and could signify that the maternal family name Aesc had been retained to strengthen their claim to the throne.

Another measure, which either formed part of the peace treaty or was associated with it, was the modification of the laws of the two kingdoms. Wihtred drew up a code of laws for Kent, which was promulgated in 695.[17] Ine drew up a code of laws for Wessex, not later than 694.[18] They gave recognition to the legal rights of his British as well as his Saxon subjects. The two codes have strong similarities and contain one clause with almost identical wording, and so it is likely that collaboration between the two kings took place. These two sets of laws became so well thought of that King Alfred included Ine's laws as a supplement to his laws and King Canute used Wihtred's code in the compilation of his own laws. In 694 Ine and Wihtred had agreed not only to forge a link between their dynasties, but also to bring their legal systems closer together.

Apart from the immediate aims of Ine and Wihtred, their agreement in 694 had a major historical impact, because Ingeld's marriage to a

---

[17] Whitelock, *English Historical Document.* item 31.

[18] Whitelock, *English Historical Document.* item 32.

Kentish princess produced a line which united the West Saxon royal dynasty dating back to Cerdic with the Kentish royal dynasty back to Hengist. It was this line, which in the course of time produced the historic succession of English monarchs, whose descent can therefore be traced back not only to Cerdic, but also to:

1. Hengist.
2. Through the Frankish marriages of Aethelberht and Eadbald to Clovis, king of the Franks;
3. Through the East Anglian marriage of Eorcenberht, to Wuffa, founder of the East Anglian royal dynasty.

Another provision of Ine's treaty with Wihtred concerned the status of Surrey. The West Saxons were still in possession of this province and Ine was under no compulsion to surrender it. Documents confirm that he retained suzerainty over Surrey. His code of laws was published with the advice not only of Haedde, bishop of Winchester, but also of Eorcenwald, bishop of London, whose diocese covered the lands of the East and Middle Saxons. He would have been consulted by Ine in connection with the people of Surrey, who were under his political control, but came under the pastoral care of Bishop Eorcenwald. This situation was also reflected in a letter of 704-5 from Waldhere, bishop of London in succession to Eorcenwald, to Archbishop Berhtwald concerning the settlement of disputes between the kings of Essex and the kings of Wessex with regard to ecclesiastical persons. Apparently the kings had agreed to accept any agreement devised by Waldhere and the West Saxon bishop and to meet at Brentford on the frontier between their two kingdoms.[19] Although Surrey is not explicitly mentioned, this was the area of common concern to the West Saxon king and the bishop of London. There can be little doubt that King Wihtred had to concede the West Saxon annexation of Surrey, when he agreed the treaty with Ine in 694.

King Ine continued the West Saxon control of Sussex. Confirmation of this is given in a charter dated 692 and signed by Nunna, king of the

---

[19] Birch, *Cartularium Saxonicum.* item 115. Whitelock, *English Historical Documents.* item 164.

South Saxons, and Cenred, king of the West Saxons and Ine.[20] Cenred was Ine's father, who appears to have been joint king with him. (Cenred had also given advice about the preparation of Ine's code of laws.) In several of his charters Ine continued to use the title King of the Saxons, originally used by Caedwalla.

An urgent problem was the need to strengthen the religious organisation in Wessex to implement the provisions of the Synod of Whitby. The British people of the three new shires had been members of the Celtic church and needed to be assimilated into the English church. Upon the death of Bishop Haedde in 705, Ine created a second diocese within his kingdom with the see at Sherborne in Dorset. It was to have responsibility for the spiritual care of the new shires. Geographically the divide between the old and the new parts of Wessex was formed by the forest of Selwood. The original diocese controlled from Winchester was described as 'east of Selwood', while the new diocese was described as 'west of Selwood'. Aldhelm was appointed to be the first bishop of Sherborne. This was a very suitable appointment, since he had been brought up in the Celtic monastery at Malmesbury and also had experience of the areas west of Selwood as abbot of Frome in Somerset. Moreover he had written a treatise on the errors of the Britons in following the teachings of the Celtic church.

---

[20] Birch, *Cartularium Saxonicum*. item 78. Whitelock, *English Historical Documents*. item 59.

CEOLRED, KING OF THE MERCIANS

Ceolred, son of King Aethelred, succeeded his cousin Coenred in 709. His full parentage is not known. Aethelred's consort, Queen Osthryth, had died without a direct heir in 697 and there is no evidence that Aethelred had remarried. It is, therefore, likely that Ceolred was illegitimate. It is apparent that he soon decided to abandon the moderate policies of his father and cousin and return to the aggressive and ruthless policies of his grandfather, King Penda. It is probably more than co-incidence that within a year of Ceolred's accession, the two neighbouring kingdoms Wessex and Northumbria again became involved in hostilities.

The annal for 710 in the Anglo-Saxon Chronicle reported that Ine and his kinsman Nunna fought Geraint, king of the Britons. Nunna was the West Saxon prince, who had been appointed King of the South Saxons. From evidence set out below it is apparent that he led a contingent of South Saxons to support the West Saxons in the fighting against the West Welsh in the frontier area west of the river Parret. The West Saxon command centre was situated at Somerton, but it was separated from the fighting area by the watery wilderness of the Somerset wetlands. A need arose for a forward headquarters and Ine responded to this need by building a fortress on the south bank of the river Tone on the site now occupied by Taunton Castle. At first the fortress would have consisted only of a ditch with earthen ramparts surmounted by a wooden palisade on three sides, with the river protecting the northern side. The actual date for the foundation of the fortress is not known, but it is likely to have been in or soon after 710.

There is evidence that Nunna lost his life while fighting the Dumnonians. About seven miles southwest of Taunton a huge mound called Noon's barrow used to stand on the northern slope of Buckland Hill (ST 165176), at 916 feet one of the highest spots on the range of the Blackdown Hills. In this area the county boundary between Devon and Somerset runs from east to west along the crest of the Blackdown Hills. The first edition of the Ordnance Survey map shows Noon's barrow lying about a half a mile on the Somerset side of the county boundary. The barrow was presumably erected to mark the spot where Noon or Nunna fell in battle. It may be deduced that Buckland Hill was the site of a crucial battle in 710 or soon afterwards. It was reported that the barrow was high enough to be seen from Taunton, but unfortunately it has been removed since the publication of the first Ordnance Survey map and is no longer to be seen.

Local tradition reports that the leader of the Britons on Exmoor was a man called Simon. It was he who gave his name to Simonsbath. He was engaged in battles, presumably against the Saxons, until he was killed at Simonsbarrow (SY 1416), which also preserves his memory. A large cairn of stones was erected there, surrounded by four smaller cairns, but these stones were removed by a contractor in the 1870s for road-making. Although the traditions surrounding Simon are confused and in some respects clearly untrue, there may be a degree of truth that a battle between Saxons and Britons took place at and around Simonsbarrow, which lies in the Blackdown Hills, a half a mile on the Devon side of the county border and only two miles from the spot on Buckland Hill, where Noon's barrow stood. This evidence, together with the lay-out of the terrain, suggests that in the course of the campaign which began in 710 the West Saxon troops advanced from Taunton in a westerly direction into the Vale of Taunton Deane. The West Welsh fell back and took up positions in the wooded Blackdown Hills. The West Saxons sought to capture these hills and gain access to the Culm valley, which led into the Exe valley and the areas of southeast Devonshire already under Saxon control. But the West Welsh positions held firm and a breakthrough by the troops under command from Taunton was prevented. In the intense fighting for these hills each side lost a senior war-leader, and each side marked the spot where he fell by a cairn of stones, and in Simon's case by four smaller cairns for subordinate leaders. The West Welsh did not hold the crest of the Blackdown Hills for long after Simon's death. The troops commanded from Exeter advanced from the south and the West Welsh were forced to withdraw to the west. The county boundary along the top of the Blackdown Hills remains a permanent marker of the division of the land conquered by the men of Devon from that conquered by the men of Somerset. The two

West Saxon armies continued to advance to the west, as the West Welsh were forced to withdraw. Eventually the men of Devon reached the north coast and the river Tamar. The men of Somerset ceased to be in contact with the West Welsh and drew their western boundary where they encountered the men of Devon. The latter continued their advance and crossed the river Tamar in the north and south.

The Conquest of Devonshire.

In its annal for 710 the Chronicle also reported that Ealdorman Berhtfrith fought the Picts between the Avon and Carron rivers. He was prefect and next in rank to the king and appears to have been acting as regent during King Osred's minority. In 710 Osred would have been only about thirteen years of age, so Berhtfrith led the Northumbrian army in battle against the Picts. The fighting took place south of the river Forth in an area traversed by the Antonine Wall. The purpose of the activity

226

appears to have been to evict the Picts from the Northumbrian territory, which they had occupied since 698. According to an Irish source, the fighting resulted in an English victory. Berhtfrith was able to avenge the defeat and death of his father in 698 and the Pictish frontier was re-established along the river Forth.

The activities of Ealdormen Beornhaeth, Berht and Berhtfrith during this period clarify the role of prefect within the Northumbrian political system and indicate a continuity from the time in 369, when Theodosius appointed *praefecti* to help the British tribal leaders north of the Wall to resist Pictish infiltrations. Their duties were identical with those of Cunedag before he was transferred from Manau Guotodin to North Wales. Throughout the political changes since 369 the Picts had remained a threat to their neighbours in the south and the need for a military commander responsible for guarding the frontier against their incursions had remained unchanged. The retention of the Latin word *praefectus* indicates that the post continued to function after the Roman withdrawal and that when king Oswald took over power from the northern Votadini at Caer Eidyn in 638 he retained the post and incorporated it in his administration.

Any designs by Ceolred against Wessex and Northumbria were failing to bear fruit. The war between the West Welsh and the West Saxons was going so badly that in 715 Ceolred decided to intervene directly by opening a second front against the West Saxons. The Chronicle announced that Ine and Ceolred fought at Woden's barrow. It may be supposed that Ceolred used the same route as in 592 from Middle Anglia along the Ridgeway. The eastern section of the Wansdyke may have served well to hold back the invaders from the north. The Chronicle does not report the outcome of the encounter, but it became clear that Ine's warriors were not defeated and he was able to continue the war in the west.

Ceolred's external policies were matched by his internal policies, which showed total disrespect for the church and disregard for its rights. Unfortunately, similar policies were being carried out in Northumbria by King Osred, who had grown up to become a dissolute young man. In a letter of 746-7 sent to King Aethelbald, Bishop Boniface bracketed Ceolred and Osred in their personal behaviour and treatment of the church. He recalled that since the time of Augustine the privileges of the church had been respected by all kings until the reigns of Ceolred, king of the Mercians, and Osred, king of the Deirans and Bernicians. 'These two kings, by the prompting of the devil, showed by their wicked example and open display of these two greatest sins in the provinces of the English, in defiance of the evangelical and apostolic commands of our Saviour. And lingering in these sins, that is, debauchery and adultery with nuns and violation of monasteries, condemned by the just judgment of God, thrown down from the regal summit of this life and overtaken by an early and terrible death, they were deprived of the light eternal and plunged into the depths of hell and the abyss of Tartarus. For Ceolred . . . feasting in splendour amid his companions, was – as those who were present have testified – suddenly in his sin sent mad by a malign spirit, who had enticed him by his persuasion to the audacity of breaking the law of God; so that without repentance and confession . . . he departed from this light without doubt to the torments of hell. Osred also was driven by the spirit of wantonness, fornicating, and in his frenzy debauching throughout the nunneries virgins consecrated to God; until with a contemptible and despicable death he lost his glorious kingdom, his young life and his lascivious soul.'[1]

---

[1] Whitelock, *English Historical Documents*. item 177.

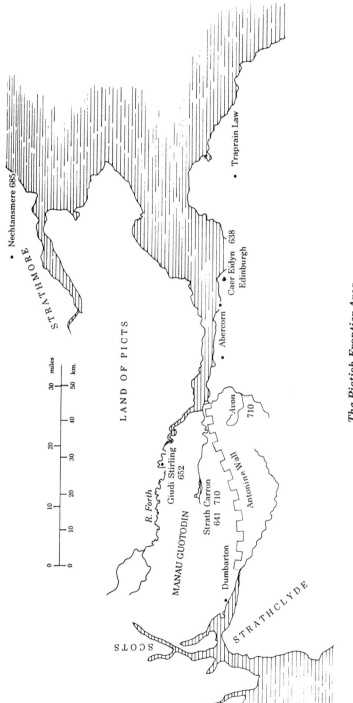

The Pictish Frontier Area.

AETHELBALD, KING OF THE SOUTHERN ENGLISH

Ceolred was succeeded by Aethelbald, a grandson of Eowa, the brother of Penda, who was slain in the battle of Maserfeld in 641. Felix, the biographer of St Guthlac, tells that before his accession Aethelbald had been banished from the kingdom by Ceolred, who pursued him from province to province, apparently in fear of an attempt by Aethelbald to seize the throne.[1] It soon became apparent after Aethelbald's accession that he had adopted and was continuing the aggressive external policies of his predecessor.

The killing of Osred south of the border may be taken to signify that he was abducted to Mercia, where he was murdered, with the object of replacing him on the throne by a Mercian puppet. His murder introduced great instability into Northumbrian politics, from which it never recovered. Osred was succeeded by Coenred, who was descended from Ocga, one of the illegitimate sons of Ida. This succession is truly remarkable, as it indicates that in 716 there was no descendant from the six legitimate sons of Ida. There is no explanation for such a high mortality, but it could have resulted from the political instability of the period, including Mercian machinations. Coenred reigned for only two years and was succeeded by Osric, who occupied the throne for eleven years. According to Simeon of Durham he was a son of Aldfrith. This has a certain plausibility: it is known that besides Osred King Aldfrith also had a son Offa, indicating an alliterative O for the names of his children. It is possible that when Osred was killed his brother Osric was too young to ascend the throne and the succession, therefore, went to Coenred. When he died the succession returned to Aldfrith's line. Summarising the events between 716 and 729 William of Malmesbury stated that Osred was 'taken off by the hostility of his relations. Yet he poured out to them a draught from the same cup; for Kenred, after reigning two, and Osric eleven years left only this to be recorded of them: that they

---

[1] Whitelock, *English Historical Documents*. item 156 ch. XLIX.

expiated by a violent death the blood of their master, whom they supposed they had rightfully slain.'[2] Bede reported that Osric nominated Ceolwulf, brother of Coenred, to succeed him.[3] This action by Osric indicates that there was no hostility between these two branches of the Northumbrian royal house, as is suggested by William of Malmesbury.

Bede and Ceolwulf were contemporaries and Bede dedicated his *History of the English Church and People* to Ceolwulf. Bede stated that the disturbances at the beginning of Ceolwulf's reign and during it were such that he did not know what should be written about them or what their outcome would be. One disturbance took place in 731, when King Ceolwulf was forcibly removed from his kingdom, tonsured and sent back to his kingdom. The purpose of this amazing incident was presumably to make him a member of a monastic order. As a monk he would be prohibited from bearing arms and so fulfilling the basic function of a king, leadership in battle. Bede did not state where Ceolwulf was forcibly removed to, but the circumstances suggest that this action like the violent deaths of Osred, Coenred, Osric and perhaps other unnamed members of the Northumbrian royal family may be attributed to Mercian attempts to subvert the Northumbrian regime.

Bede gave a report on the state of Northumbria in 731. There were four bishops, Wilfrid at York, Aethelwold at Lindisfarne, Acca at Hexham and Pehthelm at the recently created diocese of Candida Casa at the monastery of Whithorn (NX 4440), originally founded by St Ninian. The Picts were keeping their treaty of peace with the English and were following the teachings of the Roman church. The Scots (in Argyll) intend no attacks against the English. The Britons were partly subordinate to the English, partly still independent. The creation of the new diocese of Whithorn showed that the area north of the Solway Firth was under Northumbrian rule in 731.

When Aethelbald acceded to the throne, the war between the West Welsh and the West Saxons was still in progress, but in 721-2 a major internal crisis developed in Wessex. The first sign was a bald announcement in the Chronicle that in 721 Ine had slain the atheling

---

[2] Malmesbury. *The Kings before the Norman Conquest.* para. 53.

[3] Bede, *Historia Ecclesiastica.* part V ch. 23.

(royal prince) Cynewulf. This drastic action suggests that a *coup d'etat* had been attempted by a rival member of the royal house. The annal for 722 showed that a serious and widespread rebellion had broken out simultaneously in Surrey, Sussex and at Taunton. Ine exiled an atheling called Ealdberht, who went to Surrey and Sussex. His name indicates that he could have been a member of the Kentish royal family. The most serious situation was in Sussex and Ine took personal charge of activity to suppress the revolt there. At Taunton the rebellion may well have been carried out by South Saxon elements led there by Nunna in 710. Ine sent Queen Aethelburh to put down the revolt at Taunton, with the result that the fortress built by Ine was destroyed. This appears to have been a well planned attempt against West Saxon rule in Sussex, Surrey and Somerset led by a Kentish prince, probably sponsored by Aethelbald. The annal for 725 reported that the fighting in Sussex was continuing and that Ine slew Ealdberht there, which presumably means that Ine had finally put down the rebellion in Sussex. There is no information about the situation in Surrey.

At about this time there was evidence that the West Welsh had been able to halt the West Saxon advance in the area west of the river Tamar. The Welsh Annals report that the Welsh gained a victory at Hehil in Cornwall in 721 or 722. Hehil has the sense of a salt river or estuary and is identical with the modern river Hayle and the port of Hayle (SW 5637). The name Hayle is also the old name of the Camel estuary. The word survives in Egloshayle (SX 0172), signifying the church on the Hayle, adjoining Wadebridge, where the modern road A39 crosses the River Camel at its lowest point. The former place is too far west to be convincing. It seems more likely that the battle at Hehil in 721-2 took place at or near the spot where the fifteenth century bridge at Wadebridge crosses the Camel. In that case Ine's warriors were advancing from the northeast, perhaps along the route of the modern A39 road, but were thrown back by the Dumnonians as they tried to cross the Camel. It is not known if the West Welsh activity at Hehil was co-ordinated at all with the South Saxon revolt, but there can be no doubt that Ine was hard pressed.

Ine made a number of grants of land in Somerset to the church: at Isle Abbots (ST 3421) and Ilminster (ST 3514) west of the Parret; and in the area of the Mendip Hills at Croscombe (ST 5745), Priddy (ST 5251), Congresbury (ST 4363), Brent Knoll (ST 3352).[4] By the end of Ine's reign the shire of Somerset had completed the occupation of its historic territory. But the Dumnonian army was still intact and Geraint and his successors controlled most of the land west of the Tamar. It fell to the men of Devon to hold the frontier with the West Welsh for the next two hundred years.

In 726 Ine abdicated and went to Rome, where, like his predecessor, he died. His departure would have afforded an opportunity to Aethelbald to secure a co-operative successor on the West Saxon throne, because Ine had left no adult heir and his brother Ingeld had predeceased him in 718. The succession went to Aethelheard, about whom the only direct evidence concerning his place in the royal family was that he was a kinsman of Ine's. His name was a further break in the West Saxon tradition of names with an initial K sound and followed the Kentish style of names with an initial Eh sound. This points to a Kentish association and raises the possibility that he was the son of Ingeld and his Kentish wife. In this connection it is relevant that the annal for 722 revealed that Ine's queen was called Aethelburh. This is a name known to have been used by Kentish princesses: by the daughter of King Aethelberht and by the sister of Eorcenwald, the Kentish bishop of London. It seems unlikely that Ine and Ingeld had made separate marriages to a Kentish princess and this suggests the possibility that it was Aethelburh, who married Ingeld in about 694 and that upon his death in 718 she married Ine. Such close remarriages within a royal family are not unknown, an earlier case being the marriage of King Eadbald of Kent to his father's second wife. From her name Aethelburh it could be inferred that she was the daughter of Wihtred and sister of Aethelberht, Eadberht and Elric. If Ine had, indeed, married his brother's widow, Aethelheard would have been not only Ine's nephew, but also his step-son. He would also have been a close relative of the Kentish kings. When Ine decided to abdicate and depart for Rome there would have been a need for a strong and secure succession, because of the threat of Mercian subversion. Aethelheard, as step-son and nephew

---

[4] Finberg, *Early Charters of Wessex.* items 364, 365, 371, 372, 380.

of Ine would have provided such a succession. Another feature of the West Saxon royal family at this time supports the thesis that Queen Aethelburh had previously been married to Ingeld. It was stated that Aethelheard had a brother called Cuthred, who succeeded him in 740 and was, therefore, a younger brother. He is distinguished from Aethelheard by his West Saxon style of name, which may suggest that he was in fact the son of Ine and not a full brother but only a half-brother of Aethelheard. He would have been only a child, when Ine abdicated in 726. This analysis based upon name patterns presents a tentative, but consistent reconstruction of the West Saxon succession after Ine. It may also be significant that in his charters from 688 until 706 Ine made grants on his sole authority, but in 725 two charters made grants in the names of "Ine, King of the West Saxons and Aethelburg, his consort".[5]

In the event Aethelheard's succession was disputed by the atheling Oswald, who was descended from Ceawlin by another branch. The two parties came to blows, from which Aethelheard emerged the victor. It is not known if Oswald had been sponsored by the Mercians, but Aethelheard continued the West Saxon opposition to Mercian ambitions. Matters came to a head in 733, when Aethelbald led the Mercian army into Somerset and captured Somerton. The route taken could well have been along the Fosse Way through Bath. If so, this would have been an occasion when the West Saxons could have manned the western section of the Wansdyke south of Bath in an attempt to block the Mercian incursion. Somerton was not only the chief town of Somerset, but also the location of a royal estate. The Mercian aim may have been to capture Aethelheard and his court. In any case, Wessex became subject to Mercian hegemony. This was confirmed by a charter in which King Aethelbald approved the sale of land in Somerset to Glastonbury Abbey.[6]

No battles against the West Welsh are reported during Aethelheard's reign. Indeed, with the establishment of Mercian authority over Wessex the fighting in the west may have come to a halt. But West Saxon

---

[5] Finberg, *Early Charters of Wessex.* items 379, 380.

[6] Birch, *Cartularium Saxonicum.* item 168. Finberg, *Early Charters of Wessex.* item 384.

administration of the three western shires continued. In Devon minsters were founded at Yealhampton (SX 5852), eight miles east of Plymouth, and at Tavistock (SX 4874) during the 720-730s. About 729 ten hides of land in the valley of the river Torridge were granted by Aethelheard to the abbey of Glastonbury, perhaps in the parishes of Hatherleigh (SS 5404) and Jacobstowe (SS 5802). Aethelheard died in 740 and was succeeded by his brother, Cuthred, who reigned for sixteen years. He inherited a kingdom already subject to Mercian suzerainty.

Church records confirm Aethelbald's control of London and Essex;[7] and of Berkshire, where the monks of Abingdon regarded him as their protector and where he granted the monastery of Cookham (SU 8885) to the Archbishop of Canterbury.[8] Bede stated that in 731 the provinces south of the Humber and their kings were subject to him. The style of title used by Aethelbald proclaimed his supremacy. At first he was simply king of the Mercians, but in a charter of 736 (three years after his invasion of Somerset) he describes himself as king not only of the Mercians, but also of the provinces which are called by the general name South English (SUTANGLI). He signed it as *rex Britanniae* and in an addendum as king of the South English.[9] It is to be noted that sovereignty over the kingdoms south of the Humber entitled Aethelbald to use the title of Bretwalda, but he chose not to do so: his dynasty had a claim to the title King of the Angles, used by his ancestors before the migration to Britain. This title could not be used until the Northumbrians, as well as the Southumbrians, accepted his supremacy.

In 737 Ceolwulf abdicated in favour of Eadberht, a son of his uncle, took clerical vows and ended his days at Lindisfarne. The same year King Aethelbald ravaged Northumbria. The Continuation of Bede records for the year 740 that Aethelbald deceitfully harried part of Northumbria and that King Eadberht was active with his army against the Picts. This suggests that the Mercians and the Picts had agreed on

---

[7] Birch, *Cartularium Saxonicum*. item 152. Whitelock, *English Historical Documents*. item 66.

[8] Birch, *Cartularium Saxonicum*. item 291. Whitelock, *English Historical Documents*. item 79.

[9] Birch, *Cartularium Saxonicum*. item 154. Whitelock, *English Historical Documents*. item 67.

joint action against Northumbria, which could be the explanation of the deceit. It appears that Aethelbald had come to the decision that Northumbria could be brought to subjection only by a military intervention, which was carried out when Eadberht had been tricked into deploying his army against the Picts in the north. Simeon of Durham in his *Historia Regum* recorded that the monastery at York was burnt on 23 April 741. With Eadberht's army absent in the north, the city of York was apparently left defenceless against the invading Mercian army. There is no evidence that the Mercian military intervention had the desired effect.

Aethelbald's use of the title *rex Britanniae* indicates a claim to be overlord of the Welsh kings, but they refused to accept Mercian supremacy. During his reign he was engaged in at least three major campaigns against the Welsh. The Welsh Annals report that in 722 the southern Britons, meaning the Welsh, won two victories at Pencon and Garth Maelog; the former cannot be identified, but the latter is probably identical with Garthmyl (SO 1999) near a crossing of the river Severn. The Welsh would have gained or retained control of the river crossing at this point, and it is of interest that Garthmyl still lies on the Welsh side of the frontier between England and Wales. This campaign took place in the same year in which the Cornish defeated the West Saxons at Hehil, but there is no evidence to indicate a connection between the two events. Aethelbald's activity against the Welsh assumed such proportions that he found it necessary to enlist the aid of subject kings, at least the West Saxon kings. At an unknown date King Aethelheard attested a charter concerning the abbey at Abingdon while he was on an expedition beyond the Severn against the Welsh. Later in 743 the Anglo-Saxon Chronicle reported that King Aethelbald and King Cuthred were fighting the Britons. During one of his campaigns (date not known) Aethelbald crossed the river Wye and invaded Erging. The evidence is contained in one of the Llandaff charters, in which Judhail, king of the Welsh kingdom of Glywyssing, made grants of land for the restoration of places devastated by the Saxons in the time of King Aethelbald. The places quoted were throughout Erging/Archenfield and included Callow (SO 4934), Dorstone (SO 3142), Llandinabo (SO 5128), Mocca (SO 3542),

Llangarren (SO 5221) and Bellamore.[10] The last-named is identical with Bolgros, which may indicate that the church founded by King Gurvodius soon after 656 had suffered at the hands of Aethelbald's soldiers. It is apparent from the charter that the invaded area was now ruled by the king of Glywyssing. The aim of Aethelbald's campaign appears to have been to re-unite both parts of the territory of Ariconium under Mercian rule. It is clear that Aethelbald met with little success in his Welsh campaigns and failed to establish his rule over any of the Welsh kings.

There is evidence that by the time of King Aethelbald the post of prefect had been established at the senior level of the Mercian governmental system. A charter dated 770 signed by Uhtred, sub-king of the Hwicce, and confirmed by King Offa described an ealdorman called Ingild as the prefect of King Aethelbald.[11] Hitherto this appointment had existed only within Northumbria, where the analysis set out above showed that the main responsibility of the prefect was to guard the northern frontier against incursions by the Picts. The other duty of the prefect was to act as second in rank to the king. It is not known when a prefect was introduced into the Mercian governmental structure, but the most likely time would have been between 674 and 679, when King Ecgfrith extended his rule into the provinces of the Wreocensaetan and the Magonsaetan. There is no evidence that he appointed a sub-king to rule on his behalf, but he would have found that in these territories the Welsh were every bit as troublesome as the Picts in the northern part of Bernicia. The appointment of a prefect to guard the affected areas of the Wreocensaetan and Magonsaetan would have been a likely solution to the problem. When these areas returned to Mercian rule in 679 King Aethelred would have perceived the benefits of the post and retained it within his governmental system.

The concurrence of events in 750 suggests that Mercia's enemies in the north and south had formed an alliance to co-ordinate their military activity against her. Northumbria was apparently at war with the British kingdom of Strathclyde, a Mercian ally, as the Continuation of Bede reported that Eadberht had seized the Plain of Kyle and other

---

[10] Finberg, *Early Charters of the West Midlands.* item 409.

[11] *Birch, Cartularium Saxonicum.* item 203. Whitelock, *English Historical Documents.* item 74.

places. Simeon of Durham reported in the annal for 750 that Cuthred, king of the West Saxons rose against Aethelbald, king of the Mercians, which is supported by the Anglo-Saxon Chronicle. So ended a period of seventeen years of West Saxon subordination to Mercia lasting from 733 to 750. It may be presumed that with the outbreak of hostilities in the north Cuthred felt encouraged to end the position of subordination, which he had inherited. There is evidence that during 750 a *coup d'etat* against Eadberht's rule may have been attempted. Simeon of Durham reported in the annal for this year that 'King Eadberht led Bishop (of Lindisfarne) Cynewulf captive to the city of Bamburgh and made him abide in the church of St Peter in Lindisfarne. Also Offa, the son of Aldfrith, an innocent man, took refuge by compulsion at the relics of St Cuthbert the bishop. Almost dead with hunger, he was dragged unarmed from the church.' It appears that Offa, a younger son of King Aldfrith, was suspected of an attempt to overthrow King Eadberht, that he had taken sanctuary with the relics of St Cuthbert at Lindisfarne, but to no avail, he was forcibly seized and removed.

The main encounter between Aethelbald and Cuthred occurred in 752, when the Chronicle reported that Cuthred fought Aethelbald at Beorhford and put him to flight. Beorhford cannot be firmly identified. One possibility is that it may equate with modern Burford (SP 2412) in Oxfordshire, two miles from the county boundary with Gloucestershire. If the battle, indeed, took place at Burford, Cuthred would have made a dramatic advance from positions south of the Thames back to the original West Saxon territories north of the Thames. Cuthred was recorded in battle with the Britons again in 753. No location was given, but this time the Britons are likely to have been the West Welsh, who may have been encouraged to take action against the West Saxons, now that they no longer enjoyed Mercian protection.

By the year 756 the hostility between Northumbria and Strathclyde had resulted in an alliance between the Picts and Northumbrians. Simeon of Durham reported for this year: 'King Eadberht in the eighteenth year of his reign and Angus, King of the Picts, led an army to the city of Dumbarton and received the Britons there into alliance on the first of August.' Dumbarton, the capital of the Strathclyde Britons, had apparently capitulated. But ten days later the allied army of Eadberht and Angus was destroyed by an unidentified force, which had come to the rescue of the Britons.

In 756 Cuthred died and was succeeded by a kinsman called Sigeberht, who reigned for only one year. In 757 the councillors of Wessex deprived him of the throne for unlawful actions, which were not specified, and appointed Cynewulf in his place. The outcome of these political manoeuvres was that Aethelbald was able to resume his hold on Wessex. One of his last acts was to sign a charter granting land near Tockenham (SU 0379) in Wiltshire; witnesses included Cynewulf and the bishops of Winchester and Sherborne.[12]

King Wihtred's long reign in Kent had ended with his death in 725. He was succeeded by his two sons Eadberht and Aethelberht, who shared the throne as joint kings for twenty-four years until the death of Eadberht in 748. Aethelberht continued to reign until his death in 762.

In 731 Berhtwald, the Mercian archbishop of Canterbury, died and Tatwine, another Mercian, was appointed to succeed him, thereby ensuring the continuation of Aethelbald's hold on the church. The letter from Bishop Boniface to Aethelbald sent in 746-7 throws important light on his way of life. Boniface wrote: 'We have heard that you give very many alms and we rejoice greatly in this . . . We have heard also that you strongly prohibit theft and iniquities, perjury and rapine and that you are known to be a defender of widows and the poor, and that you maintain firm peace in your kingdom . . . But among other things there has reached our ears a report of an evil kind concerning your Excellency's way of life, and we were greatly grieved when we heard it. And we wish that it were not true. For it has been disclosed to us from the account of many persons that you have never taken in matrimony a lawful wife . . . If you have stained the fame of your glory before God and men by the sin of lasciviousness and adultery, we are extremely grieved by this. And yet, what is worse, those who tell us this, add that this shameful crime is especially committed in the monasteries with holy nuns and virgins consecrated to God . . . Moreover, it has been told us that you have violated many privileges of churches and monasteries, and have stolen from them certain revenues . . . And it is said that your

---

[12] Birch, *Cartularium Saxonicum.* item 181. Finberg, *Early Charters of Wessex.* item 189.

ealdormen and companions offer greater violence and oppression to monks and priests, than other Christian kings have done before . . .'[13] It is apparent that the Mercian archbishop was powerless to prevent these abuses and it had fallen to Bishop Boniface, writing from his diocese in Germany, to remonstrate with Aethelbald. As a result of this powerful and carefully worded letter Aethelbald and Archbishop Cuthbert summoned a synod in 749, in the course of which Aethelbald issued a charter to exempt churches and monasteries from taxation.

In 757 Aethelbald was murdered at Seckington (SK 2617) near Tamworth. This was probably the result of a dynastic dispute, as Simeon of Durham in his *History of the Kings of England* stated: 'Aethelbald, king of the Mercians, was treacherously killed by his guardians. In the same year the Mercians were involved in a civil war. Beornred being put to flight, King Offa was victor.' It was apparently Beornred who was responsible for the murder of Aethelbald. His identity and claim to the throne are unknown, but he occupied the throne for only a short while before being expelled by Offa.

[13] Whitelock, *English Historical Documents.* item 177.

KING OFFA AND THE SOUTHERN KINGDOMS

Offa was also descended from Eowa, brother of Penda. And so began a reign of thirty-nine years characterised by a ruthless intensification of Mercian diplomacy. Offa took up with unsurpassed vigour the political aim of his great predecessors, Penda, Wulfhere and Aethelbald, to restore the rule of his dynasty over all the Angles. In his efforts to this end he would have before him the example and renown of his great name-sake, Offa of Angulus. Because of the interlocking relationships between Anglian and Saxon kingdoms, Offa's political aims involved domination not only of Anglian, but of all the English kingdoms.

In Wessex King Cynewulf issued a charter with Offa's permission soon after his accession,[1] but between 758 and 778 he issued charters on his own authority and there is nothing to indicate that he owed Offa allegiance.[2] In 772 he was recorded at Offa's court. Hostilities occurred along the frontier in the southwest, as the Chronicle reported frequent battles between Cynewulf and the Britons. In a charter Cynewulf, king of the Gewissi, complained of harassment by his enemies, the Cornish.[3] They may have been encouraged by Offa to re-open hostilities against the West Saxons.

Wihtred, king of Kent, had a third son, Elric, who must have been only a small child when his father died in 725, as William of Malmesbury stated that he became king after the death of his brother Aethelberht in 762 and ruled for thirty-four years until his death in 796.[4] In and after 762 the political situation in Kent became complicated by the appearance of names in documents as king of Kent, whose identity and right to the title are not known. One such was Sigered, who signed as king of Kent in 762 and granted land with the consent of King

---

[1] Birch, *Cartularium Saxonicum.* item 327. Finberg, *Early Charters of Wessex.* item 388.

[2] Birch, *Cartularium Saxonicum.* item 186. Whitelock, *English Historical Documents.* items 55, 71.

[3] Birch, *Cartularium Saxonicum.* item 200. *English Historical Documents.* item 70.

[4] Malmesbury, *The Kings before the Norman Conquest.* para. 15.

Eadberht.[5] The following year Sigered signed as king of half Kent.[6] Nothing more is known about Sigered, but his name suggests that he was East Saxon. He could have been the successor of Swaefred, with the same mission of blocking Kentish attempts to regain their independence. By 764 Offa had clearly established his suzerainty over Kent and was present in Canterbury during this year with an unknown Heahberht, king of Kent.[7] Another king of Kent called Ecgberht signed a charter in 765, which was confirmed by Offa.[8]

In 776 the Chronicle reported a battle between the Mercians and the men of Kent at Otford (TQ 5259). This entry shows that the people of Kent had revolted against Mercian domination. Otford stands five miles within the Kentish border at the spot where the river Darenth is crossed by the ancient trackway now known as the Pilgrims' Way. It is a pre-historic route, which follows the crest of the North Downs and was used during the Middle Ages by pilgrims travelling to the shrine of St Thomas at Canterbury. The location of Otford shows that the Mercian army had advanced through Surrey along the crest of the North Downs and was heading for Canterbury, when it was halted by the men of Kent at the crossing of the river Darenth. The Chronicle did not report the result of the battle at Otford, but subsequent evidence makes clear that the Mercians lost the battle and with it control of Kent. The loss of the physical control of the city of Canterbury was to weaken Offa's hold on the church. Ecgberht continued to rule as king of Kent and after Otford was able to issue charters without ratification by Offa.

Another king who appeared after Otford was King Ealhmund, who was stated to be reigning in Kent by the Chronicle in its annal for 784. This was confirmed by a charter of the same year signed by Ealhmund as king of Kent, granting land to the abbot of Reculver without the signature of Offa.[9] The chronicler stated in his preface and in the annal for 855 that Ealhmund was the son of Eafa, the son of Eoppa, the son of Ingeld, brother of Ine, king of Wessex. The appearance of Ealhmund as

---

[5] Birch, *Cartularium Saxonicum.* item 193.

[6] Birch, *Cartularium Saxonicum.* item 194.

[7] Birch, *Cartularium Saxonicum.* item 195.

[8] Birch, *Cartularium Saxonicum.* item 196.

[9] Birch, *Cartularium Saxonicum.* item 243.

king of Kent confirms the analysis set out above that Ingeld had married a Kentish princess, possibly a daughter of King Wihtred: Ealhmund's right to occupy (or share) the Kentish throne derived from his great-grandmother, the wife of Ingeld. Ealhmund was also a West Saxon prince by descent through the direct male line and could equally claim to be in line for the West Saxon throne. This evidence confirms that Ingeld's marriage had led to the merger of the West Saxon and Kentish royal dynasties.

Three years after Otford occurred a head-on confrontation between Offa and Cynewulf. The Chronicle reported that in 779 they fought at Bensington, which was captured by Offa. Bensington is Benson (SU 6292) on the north bank of the Thames and only three miles from the ancestral capital of the Gewissi at Dorchester-on-Thames. It is apparent that the West Saxons had succeeded in re-establishing themselves on the north bank of the Thames, but as a result of this battle they were again evicted to the south bank. A church document shows that Offa took over control of Berkshire, apparently after the battle of Bensington. A charter concerning the monastery at Cookham confirmed that Cookham and many other towns were seized by Offa from Cynewulf and brought under Mercian rule.[10] Despite his defeat, Cynewulf continued his opposition to Offa and the West Saxons maintained their independence.

In the west a transaction of 781 showed that the frontier between Mercia and Wessex ran along the Bristol Avon. The bishop of the Hwicce (i.e. the bishop of Worcester) purchased from King Cynewulf thirty hides of land on the south side of the river Avon for the benefit of the monastery at Bath on the north side of the river.[11] It follows that the West Saxons had all of Somerset under their control and that the land of the Hwicce ran as far south as the Avon.

At about this time interference in church property was leading to strains in Offa's relationship with Jaenberht, archbishop of Canterbury, whose position was strengthened by Offa's lack of physical control of the

---

[10] Birch, *Cartularium Saxonicum.* item 291. Whitelock, *English Historical Documents.* item 79.

[11] Birch, *Cartularium Saxonicum.* item 241. Whitelock, *English Historical Documents.* item 77.

city of Canterbury. William of Malmesbury reported that Offa pilfered the lands of many churches, including William's own monastery at Malmesbury.[12] Another case concerned estates belonging to the diocese of the Hwicce amounting to 90 hides at various sites, including Bath and Stratford. The bishop disputed Offa's right to ownership of these estates and took his dispute to a synod at Brentford in 781 under the joint chairmanship of King Offa and Archbishop Jaenberht. By an agreed compromise Offa had to concede part of the bishop's claim. A document of 798 gives details of a further case of royal pilfering of church property at Cookham. When he had obtained suzerainty over the West Saxons, Aethelbald, king of the Mercians, gave the monastery at Cookham to the cathedral church at Canterbury and to guarantee the donation he sent the title deeds together with a sod of turf from Cookham to Archbishop Cuthbert (740-760). But after the archbishop's death two clerics stole the title deeds and delivered them to Cynewulf, king of the West Saxons, who had asserted his independence of Mercia. Cynewulf then took over the lands of the monastery for his own use. But when Berkshire was seized by King Offa after the battle of Bensington in 779 he took possession of the monastery at Cookham with its land. Having lost physical possession of Cookham monastery, King Cynewulf returned the title deeds to the archbishop of Canterbury. Archbishops Bregowine and Jaenberht complained through their synods to both King Cynewulf and King Offa, but to no effect as King Offa retained the use of the lands without title deeds for as long as he lived. When he died he left the monastery and its lands to his heirs and his widow became abbess there.

Because of difficulties with the church authorities Offa decided that he must be able to control the government of the church within his realm. He, therefore, made a formal request to Pope Hadrian for the establishment of a separate archbishopric at Lichfield. The new archbishopric would embrace greater Mercia and preside over the bishops of Lichfield (Mercia proper), Leicester (Middle Anglia), Worcester (the Hwicce), Hereford (the Magonsaetan) Sidnacaester (presumably Lindsey) together with the East Anglian bishops of Dunwich and Elmham. The bishops of Rochester (Kent), London (Essex),

---

[12] Malmesbury. *The Kings before the Norman Conquest.* para. 87.

Winchester (Wessex) and Selsey (Sussex) were to remain the responsibility of the archbishop of Canterbury. The Pope responded by sending a special mission to England, the first since that of St Augustine, with broad terms of reference to examine the organisation and work of the church in England. He nominated George, bishop of Ostia, and Theophylact, bishop of Todi, as his legates for the mission and they arrived in England in 786. Soon after their arrival they attended a council at which both Offa and Cynewulf were present. They then separated to examine more closely the ecclesiastical condition of England: the bishop of Todi took responsibility for England south of the Humber, the bishop of Ostia proceeded to Northumbria. When their work was finished they produced a report, which was accepted and signed by Eanbald, Archbishop of York, Aelfwold, King of the Northumbrians, his patrician, Sicga and other prelates and ealdormen of the north. The report was then taken to Mercia, where it was accepted and signed by Jaenberht, Archbishop of Canterbury, Offa, his patrician Brorda, all the bishops south of the Humber and three ealdormen.[13]

The report of the papal mission did not rule on the question of a Mercian archbishopric, but this matter was discussed in 787 at a 'contentious' synod at Chelsea and agreement was given to Offa's proposal. During 788 Hygeberht, bishop of Lichfield, received the pallium from Rome.

While these events were taking place the political situation in the south was changing dramatically. By 785 Kentish charters were again bearing the name and title of Offa. William of Malmesbury reported that the reign of Alred, king of Kent (764-794) was marred by an unsuccessful battle with the Mercians. On this evidence it appears that Offa carried out a successful invasion of Kent during 785. A striking reflection of the change of political control may be seen in a charter concerning a grant of land to Christ Church (the cathedral church) at Canterbury. The land had originally been bestowed by King Ecgberht, but when Offa regained control of Kent he took away the land, because the grant had not been authorised by him.[14]

[13] Whitelock, *English Historical Documents.* item 191.

[14] Birch, *Cartularium Saxonicum.* item 293. Whitelock, *English Historical Documents.* item 80.

A striking absentee from the signing of the report by the papal legates was Cynewulf of Wessex. The explanation for this is provided by the Anglo-Saxon Chronicle, which in its annal for 786 described how Cynewulf was killed by an armed band under the leadership of Cyneheard. This man, stated to be an atheling, i.e. prince of the royal line, was the brother of Sigeberht, who had briefly occupied the West Saxon throne in 757, before being deposed for 'unlawful actions'. The incident is described in considerable detail, without suggesting an involvement of external political influences, but a Mercian connection is shown by the statement by William of Malmesbury that Cyneheard was buried at Repton,[15] the favourite burial place for Mercian royalty. It is a reasonable inference that the incident was engineered by Offa, who used a dissident member of the West Saxon royal house as his agent. The reward for the successful elimination of Cynewulf would have been the West Saxon throne, but Cyneheard died during the fighting and this prize was denied him. Offa must have been plotting the violent removal of Cynewulf when, only a few weeks earlier, both kings had received the papal delegates.

The death of Cynewulf led to the collapse of West Saxon opposition to Offa and opened the way to a more pliant successor. This was Beorhtric, whose claim to the throne may not have been strong. William of Malmesbury stated: 'Bertric himself and the other kings after Ine, though glorying in the splendour of their parentage as deriving their origin from Cerdic, had considerably deviated from the direct line of the royal race.'[16] This is consistent with his actual name, which shows that his branch of the royal family had not maintained the tradition of using names with an initial K sound. William's description of Beorhtric was 'more studious of peace than of war. Skilful in conciliating friendship, affable with foreigners', presumably a reference to the Mercians.

It was during the reign of Beorhtric that a new major figure made his first appearance. He was Ecgberht, son of Ealhmund. Through his father he had a legitimate claim to occupy the Kentish throne and his name, already used by two Kentish kings, confirmed his place within the

---

[15] Malmesbury, *The Kings before the Norman Conquest*. para. 42.

[16] Malmesbury, *The Kings before the Norman Conquest*. para. 43.

Kentish royal dynasty. But as a descendant of Ingild, brother of King Ine, he also had a legitimate claim to the West Saxon throne. The union of the Kentish and West Saxon royal families carried out by Ingild, when he married into the Kentish royal family, had produced a prince, who had it in his power to unite Kent and Wessex legally under a single ruler. King Offa and King Beorhtric certainly perceived Ecgberht as a threat to their thrones and the chronicler reported that they sent him into exile, three years of which he spent in the land of the Franks.

The Welsh cleric Asser, who was a contemporary and biographer of King Alfred, wrote: 'Beorhtric, king of the West Saxons, received in marriage his (Offa's) daughter, called Eadburh. As soon as she had won the king's friendship and power throughout almost the entire kingdom, she began to behave like a tyrant after the manner of her father – to loathe every man whom Beorhtric liked, to do all things hateful to God and men, to denounce all those whom she could before the king, and thus by trickery to deprive them of either life or power; and if she could not achieve that end with the king's compliance, she killed them with poison. This is known to have happened with a certain young man very dear to the king, whom she poisoned when she could not denounce him before the king. King Beorhtric himself is said to have taken some of that poison unawares; she had intended to give it not to him, but to the young man; but the king took it first, and both of them died as a result.' Asser was confident about the validity of his information, because he had been told about it by King Alfred himself, who had obtained it from those with a direct recollection of those events.[17] With the death of Beorhtric in 802 the last period of West Saxon subordination to Mercia came to an end.

The situation of Sussex was closely linked to that of Kent. King Offa turned his attention to Sussex and decided to strengthen his position there. Two charters of about 770 testify to the presence of local kings Osmund, Ealdwulf and Aelfwald, who signed charters with the consent of Offa.[18] Soon after this Osmund and Ealdwulf had been downgraded to ealdormen subordinate to Offa. But Offa encountered armed resistance

---

[17] Asser, *Life of Alfred.* paras. 13-14.
[18] Birch, *Cartularium Saxonicum.* items. 197, 206.

in Sussex and Simeon of Durham reported that in 771 Offa subdued the men of Hastings by force of arms. The situation in Sussex would have been affected by the Kentish victory at Otford in 776. With Kent and Wessex free of Mercian rule, Sussex was entirely separated from Mercia and any Mercian agents in Sussex would have been cut off from their base. Communication by sea would have been impractical by land-locked Mercia. Therefore it appears that as a result of the battle of Otford Sussex regained freedom from Mercian control, but may have had to take account of Kentish military superiority. The situation was reversed again after Offa's return to power in Kent in 785. Offa's control of Sussex was made apparent, when he confirmed grants made by Oslac and Ealdwulf to South Saxon churches in 790-1.[19]

East Anglia was also a target of Offa's designs. At the time of the papal mission in 786 he clearly regarded it as part of his realm and accordingly included the two East Anglian dioceses within the new archbishopric of Lichfield. But East Anglian coinage showed that the East Anglians had a king of their own, Aethelberht, who apparently led the opposition to Mercia. Offa decided that Aethelberht stood in the way of his plans and would have to be removed, if necessary by force. In 794 Aethelberht was persuaded to leave East Anglia and to embark on a journey to meet Offa, who at the time was in the province of the Magonsaetan. One version of events stated that Aethelberht wished to ask for the hand of Offa's daughter in marriage, and this, indeed, could have been the bait, which enticed Aethelberht to leave the safety of his own kingdom. When he arrived he was lodged in the royal seat at Sutton Walls (SO 5346), about four miles north of Hereford. William of Malmesbury reported: ' . . . this same man (Offa) beheaded King Aethelberht, who had come to him through the allurement of great promises and was at the very time within the walls of his palace, deluded into security by his perfidious attentions; and (Offa) then unjustly seized upon the kingdom of the East Angles, which Aethelberht had held.'[20]

The tragic circumstances of the young king's murder quickly caused

---

[19] Birch, *Cartularium Saxonicum.* item 237. Whitelock, *English Historical Documents.* item 76.

[20] Malmesbury, *The Kings before the Norman Conquest.* para. 86.

him to be regarded as a martyr. His remains were removed to Hereford, where Offa, in expiation for the act, built a special shrine. The cathedral church at Hereford was dedicated to Saint Aethelberht.

KING OFFA AND THE WEST

When Offa came to the throne the Hwicce still constituted a semi-independent kingdom. Between 757 and 790 three brothers, Eanberht, Uhtred and Ealdred appear in documents as sub-kings (*subreguli*) of the Hwicce. Although the genealogical line is incomplete, they were probably direct descendants of Oshere. A charter of 757 making a grant of land stated that they shared their title and that their ancestors were buried at St Peter's, Worcester. The names appear to be given in order of age. Eanberht disappeared from records after 759, Uhtred after 775, and Ealdred continued active until 790. By about 770 Offa had decided to bring the territories dependent upon Mercia directly under his own rule. It was explained above how he achieved this in Sussex. Documents provide evidence that during the late 760s King Offa started to introduce changes in the constitutional organisation of the Hwicce. Charters dated 767 and 770 named one Aethelmund as a thegn of Uhtred, sub-king of the Hwicce. Aethelmund was not a Hwicce, but a Mercian and described explicitly as the son of Ingild, who was the prefect of King Aethelbald. It is apparent from these charters that King Offa had installed a Mercian nobleman as a thegn at the Hwiccian court to give the correct guidance and supervision to the Hwiccian sub-kings, but it is significant that the nobleman chosen to carry out this task was the son of the ealdorman, who had been responsible for guarding the Mercian frontier areas against Welsh raids. By 777 a modification had been effected in the personal status of Ealdred. Offa described him in a charter as sub-king Ealdred, ealdorman of his own people, the Hwicce.[1] This indicates that although Ealdred still held the title of sub-king, he was now regarded by Offa as an ealdorman. Ealdred was both the last sub-king and the first ealdorman of the Hwicce. The change was probably accompanied by corresponding constitutional adjustments. Ealdred's powers would have been reduced to those of an ealdorman.

---

[1] Finberg, *Early Charters of the West Midlands.* pp. 178-180.

The disappearance of the last vestiges of royal power would logically have led to the dissolution of the Hwiccian Witangemot. Without this body it would have been impossible to appoint a legal successor upon the death of Ealdred. As a Mercian ealdorman it is likely that Ealdred had the right to sit on the Mercian Witangemot, where he would have represented the interests of the Hwicce. Ealdred continued to use the title sub-king and was last recorded in 790 as sub-king of Worcester. Upon his death the kingdom of the Hwicce finally ceased to exist, and it was also the end of the Hwiccian royal dynasty, which stretched back to Eanfrith and through the female succession probably to the original British rulers. The Hwicce retained their identity as a separate people, but they became a province of the Mercian kingdom. Ealdred was succeeded as ealdorman of the Hwicce by Aethelmund, who had waited twenty years for the appointment. The Hwicce were now governed by a Mercian nobleman, but one with whom they were well acquainted. The absorption of the Hwicce had been carefully planned by Offa and was carried out peacefully, smoothly and without bloodshed.

The security of the Mercian frontier with the neighbouring Welsh kingdoms continued to give problems during Offa's reign. The Welsh Annals record a battle between Britons and Saxons at Hereford in 760, and they also record raids into Wales by Offa in 778 and the summer of 784. He was again involved in hostilities with the Welsh in 796, when he invaded Dyfed. A late version of the Welsh Annals reports in the entry for 787 that during the summer the Welsh carried out a devastating raid into Mercia. To help him withstand such incursions more easily Offa ordered a dyke to be built from the south to the north near Flint and it was known to both the English and the Welsh as Offa's Dyke. Reporting on Offa, Asser stated that he terrified the other kings and that he ordered a dyke to be built from sea to sea to separate Wales from Mercia.[2] This massive earthwork definitively marked the Welsh-Mercian frontier for its entire length, except for one important section, which was the stretch of frontier starting at Bridge Sollers (SO 4142), west of Hereford, where the earthwork met the river Wye, and proceeding along it for a distance of thirty-seven miles to Redbrook (SO 5310), south of

---

[2] Asser, *Life of Alfred*. para. 14.

Monmouth. No earthwork was raised along this section and the frontier remained unstrengthened. South of Redbrook the earthwork resumed along the river Wye to its confluence with the river Severn. The significance of this unstrengthened stretch of the Mercian frontier was that it faced the area of Erging/Archenfield. As explained above, when the troops of King Oswy were halted at Bolgros in 656, the territory of Ariconium was left divided; the northern part was brought under Anglian rule, the southern part remained Welsh. It appears that the Mercian kings did not accept the division of the territory of Ariconium and sought to bring the southern part under their rule. King Aethelbald had attempted to achieve this probably in 743, but had failed. When Offa came to build his dyke this section of frontier was still regarded as temporary; to have built the dyke along it would have recognised it as permanent.

KING OFFA AND THE NORTHUMBRIANS

As already reported, there had been ample evidence of Mercian attempts at subversion in Northumbria during the reign of Aethelbald. The campaign of subversion to bring Northumbria under Mercian control intensified considerably following the accession of Offa in 757. One of the main methods adopted by Offa was to suborn the king's patrician by offers to place him on the Northumbrian throne.

Within a year of Offa's accession, King Eadberht had been persuaded in 758 to abdicate in favour of his son, Oswulf, and to take holy orders. Oswulf occupied the throne for only a year. The Chronicle reported that he was slain by the men of his household on 24th July. Simeon of Durham likewise stated that he was wickedly killed by his household near Methel Wongtun on the same date. This location could be Middleton, of which there are several in Northumbria. Possibilities are Middleton (NU 0125) fifteen miles west of Bamburgh or Middleton (NU 1036), five miles west of Bamburgh. William of Malmesbury stated that he was slain 'without any cause on his part.'[1]

Oswulf's place on the throne was taken by a man called Aethelwald Moll. He was probably identical with the Moll, who had been described in a letter from Pope Paul to King Eadberht in 757-8 as patrician and brother of the king.[2] The use of the surname Moll, however, indicates that his father was not of the royal line. In that case he would have been a brother to Eadbald by marriage to his sister. He would have been an uncle to King Oswulf and may have continued to act as patrician i.e. second in rank to the king and the most senior in the royal household. Simeon of Durham, when writing about the year 759, confirmed that Aethelwald, who was also called Moll, began to reign on 5th August. He appears to have lost little time in mounting the throne after the death of Oswulf. All the circumstances indicate strongly that this was a *coup*

---

[1] Malmesbury, *The Kings before the Norman Conquest*. para. 72.

[2] Whitelock, *English Historical Documents*. item 184.

d'etat engineered by Offa, that Aethelwald was responsible for the murder of Oswulf and that he became a puppet of Offa.

But there was strong opposition within Northumbria to Aethelwald's usurpation of power. The leader of the opposition was Oswine, who was described as a most noble aetheling (royal prince). His name suggests that he was probably the brother of Oswulf and hence his rightful successor. On 7th August, 761 a severe battle took place in the Eildon Hills, two miles south of Melrose. Here there is a large hill fort (NT 555328), which had been an *oppidum* of the British tribe of the Selgovae. It is likely that Oswine established a defensive position in this hill fort as the rightful king of Northumbria. Fighting lasted three days until Oswine was killed and Aethelwald gained the victory. After this victory Aethelwald must have appeared more securely established on the throne, but opposition to his rule continued. The main contender for the legitimate succession was Alhred, descended from an illegitimate son of Ida, who raised an army, which defeated Aethelwald on 30th October, 765 at an unidentified location called Pencanheale. After his victory Alhred ascended the throne and re-established Northumbrian independence of Mercia. In 768 he married Osgifu, who was a sister of the deceased Oswulf and Oswine, which would have strengthened his position on the throne. He reigned for nine years until 774, when he was deposed by Aethelred, son of Aethelwold Moll. Alhred went into exile in the land of the Picts.

There was clearly a large party which continued to support the legitimate royal line. Evidence of this was provided in 778 when three ealdormen (names quoted) were put to death on the orders of King Aethelred. This act did not eliminate the opposition to Aethelred, as the following year he was driven from the throne by Aelfwold, son of Oswulf, who became king. Simeon of Durham described him as a pious and upright king. But Northumbria continued to be split by the strife between the Mercian and legitimist parties. The former continued to be led by Aethelred from his place of exile. In 780 two ealdormen raised an army and burnt Bearn, patrician of King Aelfwold. In 788 'King Aelfwold, a conspiracy being formed by his patrician, Sicga by name, was miserably slain on the 23rd September at a place called Scythlescester, near the Wall. The body of this excellent king was brought to Hexham

254

with a great company of monks and with the chanting of clergy and was honourably buried in the church of St Andrew the Apostle . . . The king being buried, his nephew, Osred, the son of Alhred, reigned in his place one year.' Scythlescester is thought to be Chester (NY 9370), the Roman station Cilurnum on the Wall. These entries show that Aelfwold's patricians had become involved in Mercian machinations. It may be surmised that, having resisted Mercian blandishments, Bearn had been violently eliminated and replaced by Sicga, who was finally persuaded to betray and murder Aelfwold.

In the year 790 Aethelred's efforts were rewarded with success. 'Aethelred was freed from banishment and again seated on the throne of the kingdom. But King Osred, overreached by the treachery of his princes, having been taken prisoner and deprived of his kingdom, assumed the tonsure in the city of York and afterwards, driven by necessity, went into exile.' Having regained the throne, Aethelred was determined to remove all centres of opposition to his rule by systematically destroying all possible claimants to the throne. In 791 'Ealdorman Eardwulf was taken prisoner and conveyed to Ripon and there ordered by the aforesaid king to be put to death without the gate of the monastery. The brethren carried his body to the church with Gregorian chanting and placed it out of doors in a tent; after midnight he was found alive in the church.' The identity of Eardwulf is not stated, but the importance attached to him suggests that he may have been the patrician of King Osred. During the same year 'the sons of King Aelfwold, having been carried from the city of York by force, and drawn from the principal church by deceitful promises, were miserably slain by King Aethelred in Wonwaldremere (unlocated); their names were Aelf and Aelfwine.' In 792 'Osred, induced by the oaths and pledges of certain nobles, came secretly from his exile in the Isle of Man, and there his soldiers deserting him, he was captured by the aforesaid king Aethelred, and put to death by his order on the 14th September.' After these deeds Aethelred was probably able to convince Offa that he was securely established on the throne, as shortly afterwards he married Aelfflaed, daughter of King Offa, at Catterick on 29th September.

But the opposition to Aethelred could not be suppressed and matters came to a climax in 796. 'King Aethelred was slain at Cobre (unlocated) on 18th April in the seventh year of his reign. Osbald the patrician was appointed to the kingdom by some chiefs of that nation, and twenty-seven days after, forsaken by the whole company of the royal family and princes, having been put to flight and expelled from the kingdom, he, with a few followers, retired to the island of Lindisfarne and thence went by ship with some of his brethren to the king of the Picts. Eardwulf, son of Eardwulf, recalled from exile, was raised to the crown and was consecrated on the 16th May in York in the church of St Peter at the altar of the blessed apostle Paul . . . Not long after on 26th July, Offa, the most potent king of the Mercians, died.' Osbald was one of the ealdormen who burnt Bearn, the patrician of King Aelfwold, in 780. It appears that he had been appointed the patrician of Aethelred and, following the murder of Aethelred, an abortive attempt was made by the Moll party to elevate him to the throne. The scholar Alcuin knew something of Osbald's activity and suspected that he was involved in Aethelred's murder. He wrote a stern letter to Osbald while he was in exile among the Picts, accused him of ravaging the land, associating with criminals and shedding blood and urged him to embrace the religious life.[3]

The long period of Mercian inspired turmoil in Northumbria had brought success during the reigns of the Mercian satraps Aethelwold (759-65) and Aethelred (774-9 and 790-6), a total of seventeen years.

The small kingdom of Lindsey could have been in a situation similar to that of the Hwicce i.e. under Mercian tutelage, but still partially independent. The last of the kings of Lindsey is recorded still active during Offa's reign, and, indeed, in Offa's company. Offa could have had a solution similar to that for Ealdred of the Hwicce: to allow him to retain his royal title, but to limit his powers to those of an ealdorman and to prevent the appointment of a successor upon his death by disbanding the Lindseyan Witangemot.

---

[3] Whitelock, *English Historical Documents.* item 200.

KING OFFA'S CLIMB TO SUPREMACY

The stages whereby Offa achieved a position of supremacy can be summarised as follows on the basis of the evidence set out in previous chapters. His reign can be divided into three periods, each described by the style of regnal title used by him. During the first period he used the simple title *rex Merciorum* – king of the Mercians. He had inherited suzerainty over the kingdoms of Kent and Essex, which had their own kings. In 759 Offa was acting as overlord of Sussex and in the same year he had established his satrap on the Northumbrian throne, but the latter was deposed in 765. In 771 Offa established his direct rule over Sussex and probably at the same time over the Hwicce and Lindsey. The last two were absorbed into Greater Mercia. During the middle part of his reign Offa's title was expanded to *rex Merciorum simulque aliarum circumquaque nationum* – king of the Mercians and the other nations around.

Offa secured control of Northumbria again in 774 and East Anglia had probably also been taken over by this time. This meant that all of the Anglian kingdoms had been brought together under the single rule of the historic Anglian royal house. Two centuries after the migration across the North Sea, Offa had re-established the continental kingdom of Angulus upon British soil. In 774 Offa was able to use the title *rex Anglorum* – king of the Angles, and, as if to make explicit the re-union of all the Anglian people, *rex totius Anglorum patriae* – king of the land of all the Angles. At this time Wessex had still not succumbed to Mercian domination.

The battle of Otford in 776 was a great set-back, whereby Offa lost control of Kent and Sussex. A further set-back occurred in 779 when he lost control of Northumbria. He reverted to the simple title king of the Mercians. But a recovery of his position was started in 785, when he regained control of Kent and Sussex, and in 786 when he installed a puppet ruler on the West Saxon throne. In 787 he built his great dyke. In 790 he regained control of Northumbria and this ushered in the period 790-796, which was the high point of Offa's reign, when he became king of all the English people. He never used the Saxon title Bretwalda, because he derived his right to rule from his dynasty as the historic Anglian royal house. In the period 790-796 Offa had not only equalled the achievement of his great namesake by uniting all the Angles under his rule and setting their frontier securely against the Welsh, but he had exceeded it by bringing the Saxons and the men of Kent under his rule. But the union of the English people, forged with such ruthlessness by Offa, was premature and did not endure. Regional loyalties were still strong and opposition to Mercian rule widespread. Northumbria had already broken away during the last weeks of Offa's life.

THE TRIBAL HIDAGE

An early Anglo-Saxon document known to historians as *The Tribal Hidage* is relevant to this period. It is an enigmatic document, because it consists essentially of only a listing, without an explanatory text, date or signature. The items listed are the names of most of the Anglo-Saxon political and communal entities and against each name a figure is given to show the related hidage. The figures are expressed as round hundreds ranging from 300 as the smallest to 100,000 as the largest. This suggests that the compiler based his figures on the territorial unit of the Hundred. The names include most of the major kingdoms, such as the East Angles, East Saxons, men of Kent, South Saxons, West Saxons. Additionally there are several communal groupings, some of which cannot be identified or located. A notable absentee is Northumbria: all identifiable names are located south of the Humber.

It is usually supposed that the document is Mercian in origin and was completed for an administrative purpose. The rounded figures show that they cannot have been compiled as the result of a census, but that they represent an assessment of the resources of each of the groupings, so that demands may be levied upon them. The nature of these demands is not explained. Possibilities are for the call-up of manpower for military or other service or for the levying of tribute or taxation.

An important clue to the purpose of the document may be found in the names which appear at the top of the listings. The first name given is Mercia and this accords with the supposed Mercian origin of the document. The hidage shown is 30,000. The second name is the Wreocensaetan, the third name is given as Westerna, which is an alternative name for the Magonsaetan. These are the two most westerly of the Anglo-Saxon provinces and their appearance before all other names apart from Mercia suggests that they had a special significance. It was not because of their size, as each is given a hidage of 7,000. They were, however, the two provinces, which were most directly affected by

259

the construction of Offa's Dyke, which stretched the full length of their territory. The Dyke would delineate their western frontier and would give them protection against Welsh incursions. This feature, therefore, points to a possible association with the construction of Offa's Dyke, which took place in 787. In that case, the document would have been compiled in the year 786 or 787. Such a date is fully consistent with the analysis presented above, showing the areas which were under Offa's rule. The absence of Northumbria from the listings accords with the evidence that Northumbria had regained its independence in 779, when King Aelfwold replaced the Mercian satrap Aethelred. All areas south of the Humber had become subject to Offa by 787, the last to do so being Kent and Sussex in 785 and Wessex in 786. In this connection, it is of interest that Kent, Sussex and Wessex appear at the end of the listing in that order, perhaps late additions. There is, therefore, consistent internal evidence, which indicates that the Tribal Hidage was compiled in 786-7 at Offa's court for the call-up of manpower from all parts of his realm for the construction of an enormous military work, which would protect the kingdom against Welsh raids.

The magnitude of the project would have required the maximum call-up of all available manpower. The grand total of resources set out in the document amounts to 2,441 Hundreds. Archeologists have concluded that the work on the Dyke was carried out by a number of separate gangs and in some places have been able to detect where one gang's stretch ended and the next gang's stretch began. The Hundred would have been a suitable unit for the organisation of manpower engaged on building the Dyke. The possibility, therefore, arises that on the basis of the analysis set out above, 2,441 gangs were engaged on the construction of Offa's Dyke, each with a theoretical strength of 100 men.

The document can be regarded as a reliable reflection of the composition of the Mercian kingdom and its dependencies, probably in 786-7. A noteworthy feature is that, whereas the East Angles appear as a single united group amounting to 30,000 hides, there is no mention of the Middle Angles as such. They appear as a number of small communal groupings. Among these the following can be given an approximate location:

South Gyrwa	600 hides	Ely area
North Gyrwa	600 hides	Peterborough area
East Wixna	300 hides	Wisbech area
West Wixna	600 hides	Wisbech area
Spalda	600 hides	Spalding area
Gifla	300 hides	River Ivel, Bedfordshire
Hicca	300 hides	Hitchen area, Hertfordshire
Ciltern saetna	4000 hides	People of the Chiltern Hills

It is apparent that when this document was compiled the Middle Angles had no central organisation, but were fragmented into 12-15 small communities. This is consistent with the analysis presented above, which showed that the Middle Angles had suffered military defeats by King Aethelberht as Bretwalda at the turn of the sixth to seventh centuries. Military leaders usually fought to the death when faced with defeat and by the second quarter of the seventh century the Middle Anglian royal dynasty had become so weakened that Penda, the Mercian king, was able to take over the government of Middle Anglia, and in 653 to secure the Middle Anglian throne for his son Peada. It was suggested that Peada's claim to the throne derived from his mother. To give Peada's title full legal validity it would have required the consent of the Middle Anglian Witangemot. After Peada none of the Mercian kings took the title king of the Middle Angles, although they continued to rule them. This suggests that the Middle Anglian Witangemot had not assembled after Peada's time and some 130 years later had virtually fallen into disuse. The Tribal Hidage confirms that at the time of its compilation the most senior authorities within Middle Anglia were the leaders of the small communal groupings such as the Gyrwas, Wixnas, etc. These groupings, or some of them, may well have originally taken shape in the earliest days of the Anglian settlement.

ECGBERHT, KING OF THE WEST SAXONS AND BRETWALDA

King Offa had been much concerned to ensure the continuation of his regime after his death. He knew only too well from his own experience that the succession upon the death of a king could be challenged and set aside, and he wished to be certain that the succession of his son Ecgfrith was secure. In 781 Charlemagne had arranged for his sons Charles and Pippin to be anointed by Pope Hadrian. It appears that, in imitation of Charlemagne, Offa took advantage of the presence of the papal legates in England to have Ecgfrith consecrated king by the Pope's personal representatives, thereby obtaining a spiritual sanction to Ecgfrith's succession. This is the earliest reference to the consecration of an English king. After this, Ecgfrith was undeniably king and shared power with his father. Charters were signed by both Offa and his son.[1] Offa died on 29 July 796 and despite the careful preparations Ecgfrith also died before the year was out, reigning for only twenty weeks. A letter from the scholar Alcuin, written after Ecgfrith's untimely death, attributed it to the blood shed by Offa to ensure that Ecgfrith succeeded him.[2] William of Malmesbury stated that in his short reign he studiously avoided the cruel path trod by his father and restored the privileges of all the churches, which his father had abridged, including those of the monastery at Malmesbury.[3]

Ecgfrith was succeeded by Coenwulf, a descendant of Coenwalh, brother of Penda. There is no evidence that he was in any way responsible for Ecgfrith's early death, but given the record of ruthlessness in Mercian politics, this possibility cannot be completely excluded. Coenwulf inherited Offa's position of power over England south of the Humber. Northumbria continued actively to resist Mercian domination and there were strong movements in the southern kingdoms

---

[1] Birch, *Cartularium Saxonicum.* item 237. Whitelock, *English Historical Documents.* item 76.

[2] Whitelock, *English Historical Documents.* item 202

[3] Malmesbury, *The Kings before the Norman Conquest.* para. 94.

to throw off the Mercian yoke. Coenwulf continued to prosecute Offa's expansionist policies. Upon ascending the throne his main tasks were to maintain and strengthen Mercian authority over the kingdoms south of the Humber, and to continue attempts to establish sovereignty over Northumbria.

A political crisis developed in Kent as a result of the death of Elric, son of King Wihtred, in 796. He is generally considered to be the last of the Oiscing kings. This may be true of the descendants by the direct male line, but a descendant by the female line had already succeeded to the throne in 784, when Ealhmund, descended from the spouse of Ingeld, was reported to be one of the kings of Kent. Elric appears to have passively accepted Offa as his overlord, after his defeat in battle probably in 785. He apparently died without a direct heir and the Kentish throne was claimed by an exile, who had found a refuge from Offa in the land of the Franks. He was a monk named Eadberht Praen. Nothing is reported about his antecedents, but his first name indicates that he could have been a member of the Kentish royal family and the use of the surname Praen shows that his descent was through the female line. It has been suggested that he had entered holy orders to preserve his life.[4] But when the throne became vacant he returned to Kent in 796 and in disregard of his monastic vows became king of Kent. By this action he was considered an apostate. Aethelheard, Archbishop of Canterbury, a Mercian, fled from the city. For two years Kent remained independent of Mercian rule. During this period King Coenwulf came under pressure from his clergy to revoke Offa's decision to establish a third archiepiscopate at Lichfield. He was willing to do so, but his loss of the physical control of the city of Canterbury was an obstacle. He, accordingly, wrote a letter to Pope Leo in 798, explaining that King Offa had split the southern province because of the enmity he had formed against Archbishop Jaenberht and the people of Kent and requesting that the southern province should be re-united, but under London instead of Canterbury.[5] The ostensible reason was that St Augustine's original intention had been to base the southern province at

---

[4] Whitelock, *English Historical Documents*. item 197.

[5] Whitelock, *English Historical Documents*. item 204.

London. The proposed transfer to London would bring the seat of the southern province to a city within Coenwulf's realm. In his reply Pope Leo wrote: 'As for what was said in your letter asking us if the authority of the supreme pontificate could by canonical consent be situated in the city of London, where Augustine received the dignity of the pallium sent by St Gregory, we by no means dare to give to them the authority of the supreme pontificate; but as that primacy was established at Canterbury, we concede and pronounce it by our decree the first see.' In this letter he also dealt with the problem of Eadberht Praen: 'As regards that apostate cleric who mounted the throne, we, accounting him like Julian the Apostate, excommunicate and reject him, having regard to the safety of his soul.' [6]

King Coenwulf finally decided to resolve the problem of Kent by military intervention. The Chronicle stated in its annal for 798 that King Coenwulf wasted Kent and Romney Marsh. He seized Eadberht Praen, the Kentish king, and took him in chains to Mercia, had him blinded and his hands cut off. Coenwulf took the Kentish crown for himself and also invoked the Kentish practice of multiple kingship by appointing his brother Cuthred to share the Kentish (but not the Mercian) throne with him. The arrangement had the advantage that he had his representative on the spot in Kent, where he could take immediate steps against any signs of revolt. When Cuthred died in 807 Coenwulf continued to rule Kent as sole king. With Mercian rule re-established in Kent, Archbishop Aethelheard was able to return to Canterbury. Archbishop Hygeberht resigned his see at Lichfield and in 802 the Pope confirmed that Aethelheard held the full powers of the archbishopric of Canterbury. Archbishop Aethelheard died in 805 and was succeeded by Wulfred, who enjoyed Coenwulf's confidence for many years until they quarrelled in 817. From his position as king of Kent Coenwulf was able to impose a settlement, which Wulfred had no choice but to accept.

The East Angles may also have rebelled against Mercian rule at about the same time as the men of Kent. The evidence from coins shows that between the East Anglian coins of Offa and those of

---

[6] Whitelock, *English Historical Documents.* item 205.

Coenwulf, the mint had struck coins for a king Edwald, apparently independent of Mercia.

Within Northumbria there were three 'parties' competing for power at the time of King Coenwulf's accession. Firstly, those supporting the legitimate royal line descended from Ida; secondly, those patriots who opposed Mercian interference under the leadership of Eardwulf; thirdly, the survivors of the Moll party, taking their instructions from Mercia. The first two parties came to blows in the aftermath of the murder of King Aethelred. Simeon of Durham reported in the annal for 798: 'Ealdorman Wade, entering into a conspiracy formed by the murderers of King Aethelred, fought a battle against king Eardwulf, in a place called Billington near Whalley; and many on both sides being slain, ealdorman Wade, with his men, was put to flight and King Eardwulf royally gained the victory over his enemies.' This account may be interpreted to indicate that Eardwulf himself was not implicated in the murder of Aethelred, but had earned the enmity of Aethelred's murderers, who had been denied the fruits of their action by the accession of Eardwulf. Whalley (SD 7335) is located six miles northeast of Blackburn. In the following year Simeon of Durham reported: 'Ealdorman Moll was slain by the urgent command of King Eardwulf. Also at the same time Osbald, once ealdorman and patrician and for a time king, after that abbot, breathed his last; his body was buried in the church of the city of York. Ealdorman Ealdred, the murderer of King Aethelred, was slain by Ealdorman Thortmund, in revenge of his lord, the same king.' Eardwulf continued to eliminate all possible claimants to his throne. The same source reported in the annal for 800: 'Alhmund, son of King Alhred, as some say, was seized by the guardians of King Eardwulf and by his order put to death with the companions of his flight.'

By 801 Eardwulf had disposed of his opponents within Northumbria sufficiently to enable him to turn his attention to those opponents who were sheltering within Mercia. Simeon of Durham reported that in 801: 'Eardwulf, king of the Northumbrians, led an army against Coenwulf, king of the Mercians, because he had given an asylum to his enemies. He also, collecting an army, obtained very many auxiliaries from other provinces, having made a long expedition among them. At length, with

265

the advice of the bishops and chiefs of the Angles on either side, they made peace. . . an agreement of sure peace was made between them.' This peace treaty, with the backing of the church, was another important turning point in early English history. It spelled the end of all Mercian attempts to bring Northumbria under the supreme rule of the historic Anglian royal dynasty.

Although King Eardwulf had eliminated the Moll party, there was still opposition to his rule within Northumbria and it came to a head in 806 or 808. Under the date 808 Roger of Wendover reported in his *Flores Historiarum* that King Eardwulf was driven out of the kingdom by Aelfwold, who reigned for two years as king. The identity of Aelfwold and his right to the throne is not explained: perhaps he was the legitimate descendant of Ida and leader of the royalist party. Eardwulf went into exile, first to the court of the Emperor Charlemagne and then to the Pope in Rome. Both supported him as the rightful king of Northumbria. When Aelfwold died two years later, Eardwulf returned and was accepted again as king, but died very soon afterwards. He was succeeded by his son Eanred. He had a long reign of thirty years, about which little has been reported, which may suggest that it was a period of peace and stability.

In the south Mercian ambitions suffered a great set-back in 802, when Beorhtric, the puppet king of Wessex died, according to Asser by accidentally taking a poisonous drink prepared by his Mercian wife, Eadburh. The anti-Mercian party, outraged by her scandalous behaviour, succeeded in proclaiming as king Ecgberht, son of Ealhmund. As explained above, he had a legal right to both the West Saxon and Kentish thrones and because of this had been exiled by Offa and Beorhtric. At the time of Ecgberht's accession a quarrel broke out between the Hwicce and the men of Wiltshire. The Chronicle stated that Aethelmund, ealdorman of the Hwicce, led an incursion across the border at Kempsford into Wiltshire. Ealdorman Weohstan led the men of Wiltshire into battle against the invaders. Both ealdormen were killed in the fighting, but the men of Wiltshire were victorious. Kempsford (SU 1596) is located on the upper Thames, which at this point formed the border between Mercia and Wessex and still forms the border between Wiltshire and Gloucestershire. Ealdorman Aethelmund was the Mercian nobleman, who succeeded Ealdred, the last sub-king of the Hwicce. The purpose of the Hwiccian incursion is not explained. The Hwicce may have had ancient claims to possession of territory south of the Thames and were hoping to take advantage of an occasion when there was a change of rule in Wessex by regaining disputed territory. The incident shows that the Hwicce were content to go into battle under the leadership of their Mercian ruler. It is noteworthy that Coenwulf did not make use of this outbreak as a pretext for a general attack on the West Saxons.

The Anglo-Saxon Chronicle reported in its annal for 815 that King Ecgberht wasted Cornwall from east to west. This activity shows that hostility between the West Saxons and the West Welsh continued undiminished, but Ecgberht failed to destroy the independent Dumnonian regime.

During his reign Coenwulf developed Winchcombe in the Hwiccian province as an important centre. This place had been the site of a nunnery established by Offa in 787. King Coenwulf started building an abbey there in 798. It was dedicated on 9th November, 811 by Wulfred, Archbishop of Canterbury, in the presence of Coenwulf and twelve bishops. Coenwulf probably had a palace at Winchcombe and much Mercian government business was transacted there.

Throughout his reign Coenwulf was troubled by wars with the Welsh, as were his predecessors. The Welsh Annals for 798 stated that Caradog, king of Gwynedd, had been strangled by the Saxons. In 816 a Mercian force penetrated as far as Snowdonia and in 818 the Mercians harried in Dyfed. In 821 Coenwulf died at Basingwerk on the Dee estuary. This place stood on the Mercian frontier, where it is crossed by the Roman road leading from Chester into North Wales. It appears that Coenwulf was preparing an assault on the Welsh kingdoms when he died.

There was no direct heir. Coenwulf had had a son, Coenelm or Kenelm, who had predeceased him soon after 811, although there was an older daughter, Coenthryth. Actually the succession went to Coenwulf's brother Ceolwulf. A myth grew up that Kenelm had been murdered while out hunting in the Clent Hills on the instructions of Coenthryth by one of her retainers, so that she could obtain the succession (although reigning queens are unknown in the Mercian royal dynasty). The murdered prince came to be regarded as a martyr and some time later a cult developed for the boy-saint Kenelm. A shrine and church was built at Romsley (SO 9679), where he had been murdered and pilgrims flocked there and to Winchcombe, which prospered as a result. But at the Dissolution of the Monasteries, the abbey at Winchcombe was completely dismantled. Two stone coffins were subsequently recovered from the site, one for an adult, the other for a child, and removed to St Peter's parish church, where they may be seen. It is suspected that they contained the bodies of Coenwulf and his son Coenelm.

The entry in the Welsh Annals for 822 records the destruction of the fortress of Deganwy by the Saxons and adds that they seized control of the province of Powys. The fortress of Deganwy (SH 7779) stands on the north bank of the Conway estuary and commands access along the Conway valley into North Wales. The Mercian forces would almost certainly have advanced from Basingwerk along the Roman road to the Conway valley. It is clear that the war against the north Welsh, which was prepared by Coenwulf, was continued and brought to a successful conclusion by his brother. The victory at Deganwy was to be the last major military achievement of the Mercian kings. Ceolwulf continued to rule Kent, using the title *rex Merciorum vel etiam Cantwariorum* – king not only of the Mercians but also of the people of Kent.

Despite his victory against the Welsh, Ceolwulf was deposed in 823 for an unknown reason. His successor was Beornwulf, about whom and his claim to the throne there is little information. The name suggests that he could have been a descendant of the Beornred, who succeeded Aethelbald, but was ousted by Offa in 757. In that case, Ceolwulf's deposition was the result of another internal dynastic feud and represented the return of the branch of the royal line displaced by Offa. Beornwulf continued traditional Mercian policies. He exercised authority as ruler of Kent, but there appears to have been a return to the practice of joint kingship, as one Baldred was also acting as king of Kent from 823. Perhaps, like Cuthred, he was the brother of the Mercian king.

Since the accession of Ecgberht to an independent Wessex, a clash with Mercia seemed inevitable and it finally took place in 825. Two years after ascending the Mercian throne King Beornwulf decided that the time was ripe to bring the West Saxons again under Mercian rule. The Anglo-Saxon Chronicle reported two battles during 825. One was at Galford between the Britons and the men of Devon. The other was a great battle at Ellendun between the armies of Ecgberht and Beornwulf, resulting in the defeat of the latter. Ellendun is the former name of Wroughton (SU 1481), south of Swindon. Galford is in the parish of Lew (SX 4487) in West Devon, five miles east of the river Tamar. The simultaneous outbreak of fighting in Devon and Wiltshire is a further example of the Mercian strategy of initiating war against its neighbours on two fronts. In the west the battle took the form of an armed incursion across the Tamar, probably following the route of the modern A30 road. The fighting probably took place on the slopes of Galford Down. The West Welsh were halted by the men of Devon after they had penetrated no further than five miles beyond the Tamar. The men of Somerset were engaged with the main West Saxon army at Ellendun, where, indeed, their ealdorman fell in combat. The two defeats in 825 were a further stage in the decline of Mercia and constituted the first blow in a campaign, during which Ecgberht established his regime, based on the union of the West Saxon and Kentish dynasties, as the dominant power in Britain.

The defeat at Ellendun weakened the Mercian hold on the subject kingdoms. The Chronicle reported that after the battle Ecgberht 'sent from the army his son Aethelwulf and his bishop (of Sherborne) Ealhstan and his ealdorman Wulfheard to Kent with a large force and they drove King Bealdred north across the Thames.' It then made an important statement, which throws considerable light on the strategic situation in the southeast and the struggle against Mercian domination. 'And the people of Kent and of Surrey and the South Saxons and the East Saxons submitted to him, because they had been wrongfully forced away from his kinsmen.' This statement is consistent with earlier evidence that Ecgberht had inherited from his father Ealhmund the right to occupy the Kentish throne. But it goes further than this by implying that the people of Surrey, Sussex and Essex also owed allegiance to him, apparently as king of Kent, and that these kingdoms, previously under Mercian rule were now transferred to Kentish suzerainty. The take-over of Kent by Aethelwulf on behalf of Ecgberht in 825 was the successful culmination of a long-standing Kentish ambition to dominate their immediate neighbours. The first sign of such an ambition was reported by the *Historia Brittonum*, when Hengist sought the cession of adjacent areas. In 568 King Aethelberht's invasion of Surrey was halted at Wimbledon. Under the supreme authority of Oswy as Bretwalda the first King Ecgberht was given tutelage over Surrey and southern Essex in 664. The Kentish occupation of London in 674 lasted only two years. A Kentish attempt to take over Sussex in 685-6 was defeated by Caedwalla.

Ecgberht, son of Ealhmund, had obtained his West Saxon inheritance when he was appointed king of the West Saxons in 802, but his Kentish inheritance, based upon his descent from Ingeld's Kentish marriage, was denied him until 825 because Kent continued under Mercian rule. His victory at Ellendun enabled him to obtain his Kentish inheritance and he became the legitimate king of Kent and overlord of Essex, Surrey and Sussex. No opposition was offered by these small kingdoms to the change of overlord, because they had been kept militarily impotent by the Mercian kings. The changed status of Kent is not to be regarded as the annexation of Kent and its dependant areas by the West Saxons. Wessex and Kent continued as separate kingdoms, but now ruled by the same dynasty. Ecgberht made an important decision, which underlined the separateness of his two kingdoms. As he now had a large area to govern, he decided to share it with his son, Aethelwulf. The latter became king of Kent and overlord of Essex, Surrey and Sussex. He remained, however, subordinate to Ecgberht in his position as head of the royal dynasty. This arrangement kept the government of Wessex separate from the government of Kent and its dependant territories. It was an arrangement which worked satisfactorily and was continued after Ecgberht's death by Aethelwulf, when he succeeded to the West Saxon throne. Ecgberht had already followed the Kentish tradition of names with an initial Eh sound by naming his son Aethelwulf. This tradition was continued consistently by Aethelwulf and his successors until Edward the Confessor and although their West Saxon descent was through the male line they did not revive the distinctive West Saxon style of name reminiscent of Cerdic.

With Ecgberht and Aethelwulf poised to take over Essex, the king of the East Angles appealed to Ecgberht for protection against the Mercians. The Mercian army, although defeated at Ellendun, had not been totally destroyed and Beornwulf led it against the East Anglian insurrection. During the fighting in East Anglia Beornwulf was killed in 826 and was succeeded by Ludeca, about whom little is known. He had appeared as an ealdorman in one of Beornwulf's charters. For a short while he re-established Mercian rule in East Anglia, as the mint there struck coins in his name. In 828 Ludeca was killed together with five of his ealdormen. Ecgberht allowed the East Angles to appoint their own kings, as the East Anglian mint struck coins in the names of Aethelstan and Aethelweard. In 829 Ecgberht was ready to take the war into Mercia, where Wiglaf had succeeded to the throne. The Chronicle stated that Ecgberht conquered Mercia and brought all the lands south of the Humber under his rule. He was the eighth king to be given the title of Bretwalda. It is remarkable that after an interval of 149 years during which Aethelbald and Offa had refused the title, the post was revived and filled by Ecgberht. In Mercia Wiglaf was deposed and Ecgberht issued coins as *rex Merciorum* – king of the Mercians.

The annal for 829 reported that Ecgberht led his army to Dore, where he confronted the Northumbrians, but they submitted peacefully to him. Dore (SK 3181) is five miles southwest of Sheffield; now on the border between Yorkshire and Derbyshire, it would have been on the border between Mercia and Northumbria in 829. This account indicates that Ecgberht had no need to invade Northumbria, because the Northumbrians recognised his superior power and submitted without offering any armed resistance. Roger of Wendover, however, offers a different version in his *Flores Historiarum*. He states that Ecgberht's army pillaged in Northumbria and that King Eanred was obliged to pay tribute.

By the year 830 Mercian military power had been destroyed and the situation was not dissimilar from that in 655 after the battle of Winwaed. Ecgberht had gained military domination of Mercia, but the civil administration and maintenance of law and order had to be continued. As in the case of Oswy in 658, Ecgberht, who may have had Oswy's experience in mind, re-instated the former ruling dynasty, but

271

now governing as his subordinates. The annal for 830 reported that Wiglaf obtained the kingdom of Mercia again. William of Malmesbury stated that in his second reign Wiglaf ruled only as a tributary prince of Ecgberht. He wrote: 'Wiglaf, subjugated in the commencement of his reign by Ecgberht, governed thirteen years, paying tribute to him and to his son, both in his person and his property'; and 'Wiglaf, first driven from his kingdom by Ecgberht and afterwards admitted as a tributary prince, augmented the West Saxon sovereignty.'[7] The military defeat of Mercia affected the military balance along the sensitive frontier with Wales and may have given encouragement for the Welsh kings to advance their cause. The chronicler reported that in 830 Ecgberht led his army into Wales and brought the Welsh kings to submission. By 830 Ecgberht had imposed a new political settlement in the west, which subordinated Wiglaf and the Welsh kings to Ecgberht's rule, thereby ensuring peace along the Welsh-Mercian frontier.

Although Echberht had gained military dominion over all of England and Wales, he encountered prolonged opposition to his assumption of power from the archbishop of Canterbury. The mint at Canterbury ceased to issue the coinage of Archbishop Wulfred and in its place issued the coinage of Ecgberht. A charter of 836 granting privileges to the monastery at Hanbury (SO 9663, 4 miles east of Droitwich) throws light on the political alignments of the period. The grant was made at a synod or council held by King Wiglaf at Croft (SP 5195, 7 miles southwest of Leicester), but the list of signatories of the charter shows that those present included not only the Mercian bishops, but also Ceolnoth, who had succeeded Wulfred as archbishop of Canterbury, and the bishops of London, Rochester, Selsey and Sherborne plus two unidentified bishops.[8] Ecgberht did not confirm this grant and his absence from such a large gathering indicates that the archbishop supported by most of his bishops had combined with Wiglaf to take independent action within Mercia. But Ecgberht disposed of supreme temporal power and Ceolnoth finally had to come to terms with him. He did this in 838 in a council at Kingston-on-Thames. A document drafted at Canterbury reported some

---

[7] Malmesbury, *The Kings before the Norman Conquest*. paras. 96, 107.

[8] Whitelock, *English Historical Documents*. item 85. Birch, *Cartularium Saxonicum*. item 416.

details of the agreement concluded at Kingston. Ecgberht agreed to restore an estate at Malling (NM 6796) to Christ Church, Canterbury, and in return Archbishop Ceolnoth recognised Ecgberht and his heirs as the protectors of monasteries in the kingdom. A document using the same words granted land to the see of Winchester in return for the recognition of Ecgberht and his heirs.[9] Subsequent developments revealed that despite his subordinate position, Wiglaf succeeded in retaining within his kingdom not only the historic Mercian lands, but also Berkshire (acquired by Offa in 779), Middlesex and the city of London. The ultimate sovereignty over all the territories administered by Wiglaf remained, however, in the hands of Ecgberht.

In the southwest the Dumnonians still maintained their independence in Cornwall, but King Ecgberht had gained a foot-hold west of the Tamar. This was referred to in a letter from Archbishop Dunstan to King Aethelred in the period 931 – 8. It stated that when the West Welsh rose against Ecgberht he put down the rebellion, and gave a tenth of the land to the church. Three estates at Pawton, Caellwic and Lawhitton were granted to the abbey at Sherborne.[10] Pawton is in St. Breock parish (SW 9771). Caellwic is probably Kelly in Egloshayle (SX 0071). Lawhitton (SX 3593) is 2 miles southeast of Launceston. The location of these places shows that Ecgberht had secured control of north east Cornwall as far as the river Camel during his campaigns in 815 and/or 825.

By the year 830 Ecgberht had imposed peace on his enlarged domain, but his subjects had only a few years in which to enjoy freedom from strife. A new enemy from across the North Sea was threatening and had, indeed, already struck. The first warning of Viking activity had been given in a raid on the Dorset coast in 789 during Beorhtric's reign. It was followed by hit and run raids on the monasteries at Lindisfarne in 793 and at Hartness and Tynemouth in 794. There was an intermission until 835, when the Danes ravaged the Isle of Sheppey. The Danish menace had now assumed a much more serious character. In 836 the Chronicle reported a Viking force of twenty-five (or thirty-five) ships at

---

[9] Birch, *Cartularium Saxonicum. item* 421, 423.

[10] Whitelock, *English Historical Documents. item* 229

Carhampton (ST 0142). King Ecgberht took an army there and a major battle took place, in the course of which two West Saxon bishops and two ealdormen perished. The Vikings, however, remained in possession of the battlefield. Carhampton stands a short distance inland from Blue Anchor Bay. It is remarkable that after his succession of military victories Ecgberht had failed to expel or destroy the invaders and had suffered serious losses in attempting to do so.

Ecgberht was more successful in 838, when the enemy struck again in Cornwall. On this occasion they combined with the West Welsh against the West Saxons. Ecgberht pursued them with his army and defeated both the Welsh and the Danes on Hingston Down (SX 3972), which lies eight miles northwest of Plymouth. Ecgberht's response to an attack on this area west of the Tamar suggests that his rule had extended into the southeastern corner of Cornwall.

In 839 Ecgberht died after a reign of thirty-seven years. He can certainly be considered one of the great Anglo-Saxon kings. He ruled at a crucial time, when Britain was about to be stormed by the northern invaders. From his position as head of the united West Saxon/Kentish dynasty he established a powerful regime in the south, which became the bastion of English resistance to the new threat. It was his descendants, particularly the great Aelfred, who provided the necessary military leadership against the Viking onslaught.

GENEALOGICAL TABLE

The Union of the West Saxon and Kentish Royal Dynasties

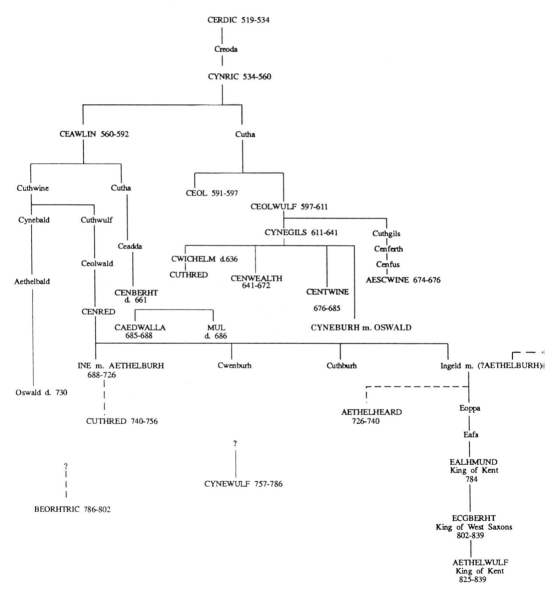

CERDIC 519-534

Creoda

CYNRIC 534-560

CEAWLIN 560-592 — Cutha

Cuthwine — Cutha

CEOL 591-597

CEOLWULF 597-611

Cynebald — Cuthwulf

CYNEGILS 611-641 — Cuthgils

Cenferth

Ceadda — Cenfus

CWICHELM d.636 — AESCWINE 674-676

Ceolwald — CUTHRED

Aethelbald — CENWEALTH 641-672

CENBERHT d. 661 — CENTWINE 676-685

CENRED

CAEDWALLA 685-688 — MUL d. 686 — CYNEBURH m. OSWALD

INE m. AETHELBURH 688-726 — Cwenburh — Cuthburh — Ingeld m. (?AETHELBURH)

Oswald d. 730

CUTHRED 740-756

AETHELHEARD 726-740 — Eoppa

Eafa

?

CYNEWULF 757-786

EALHMUND King of Kent 784

?

BEORHTRIC 786-802

ECGBERHT King of West Saxons 802-839

AETHELWULF King of Kent 825-839

276

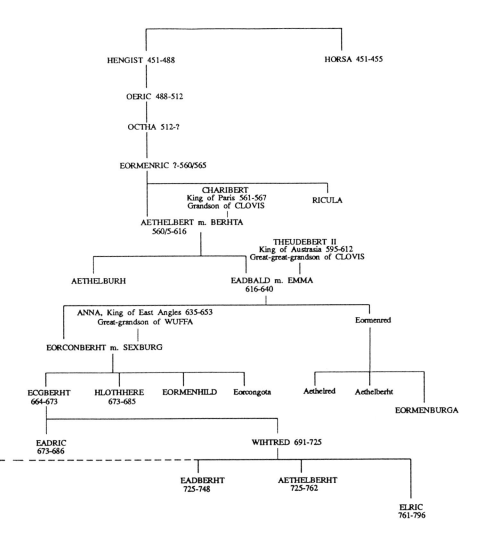

HENGIST 451-488 HORSA 451-455

OERIC 488-512

OCTHA 512-?

EORMENRIC ?-560/565

CHARIBERT
King of Paris 561-567
Grandson of CLOVIS RICULA

AETHELBERT m. BERHTA
560/5-616

THEUDEBERT II
King of Austrasia 595-612
Great-great-grandson of CLOVIS

AETHELBURH EADBALD m. EMMA
616-640

ANNA, King of East Angles 635-653
Great-grandson of WUFFA Eormenred

EORCONBERHT m. SEXBURG

ECGBERHT HLOTHHERE EORMENHILD Eorcongota Aethelred Aethelberht
664-673 673-685

EORMENBURGA

EADRIC WIHTRED 691-725
673-686

EADBERHT AETHELBERHT
725-748 725-762

ELRIC
761-796

The names of Kings and Queens are shown in capitals.

277

BIBLIOGRAPHY

Anderson Marjorie O. *Kings and Kingship in Early Scotland.* Scottish Academic Press. 1973.

Alcock Leslie. *Arthur's Britain.* Pelican Books. 1987.

Asser. *Life of Alfred.* Trans. S. Keynes & M. Lapidge. Penguin. 1983.

Barker Philip, Ed. *Wroxeter Roman City Excavations.* Dept. of the Environment.

Bassett Steven, Ed. *The origins of Anglo-Saxon Kingdoms.* Leicester U.P. 1989.

Venerable Bede. *History of the English Church and People.* Trans. L. Shirley-Price. Penguin Classics. 1984.
The Age of Bede. Penguin Classics. 1988.
Eddius Stephanus. *Life of Wilfred.* Penguin Classics. 1984.

Birch, *Cartularium Saxonicum.*

Bradley S.A.F. Trans. *Anglo-Saxon Poetry.* Dent Everyman's Library. 1982.

Brooke Christopher. *The Saxon and Norman Kings.* Batsford 1963.

Campbell James Ed. *The Ango-Saxons.* Phaidon. Oxford 1982.

Clapham Sir Alfred. *St. Augustine's Abbey,* Canterbury. English Heritage.

Clark John. *Saxon and Norman London.* Museum of London.

Clemens Peter. *The Anglo-Saxons.* Bowes & Bowes 1959.

Crossley-Holland Kevin. *Beowulf.* Boydell Press 1987.

Ekwall Eilert. *Concise Oxford Dictionary of English Place Names.*

Evans Angela Care. *The Sutton Hoo Ship Burial.* British Museum Publications. 1986.

Finberg H.P.R.   (i) *The early charters of the West Midlands.* Leicester U.P. 1961.
(ii) *The early charters of Wessex.* Leicester U.P. 1964.
(iii) *The Formation of England.* Paladin. 1984.

Florence of Worcester. *A History of the Kings of England.* Reprint Llanerch Enterprises.

Frere Sheppard. *Britannia: A History of Roman Britain.* Routledge & Kegan Paul. 1978.

Garmonsway G.N. Trans. *The Anglo-Saxon Chronicle.* J.M. Dent & Sons Ltd. 1954.

Gildas. *The Ruin of Britain.* Ed Michael Winterbottom. Phillimore. 1978.

Hart C.R. *The Early Charters of Eastern England.* Leicester University Press 1966.

Haslam, Ed. *Anglo-Saxon Towns in Southern England.* Phillimore. 1984.

Heighway Carolyn. *Gloucester: a History and Guide.* Alan Sutton. 1985.

Hope-Taylor Brian. *Yeavering.* H.M.S.O.

Henry of Huntingdon. *The History of England.* Trans Thomas Forester 1853. Reprint Llanerch Press. 1991.

Jackson Robert. *Dark Age Britain.* Book Club Associates. 1984.

James Edward. *The Franks.* Basil Blackwell Ltd. 1988.

Jarman C.E. *Chester: Cathedral and City.* Jarrold & Sons Ltd. Norwich. 1982.

Johnson J.S. *Richborough and Reculver.* English Heritage.

Johnson Stephen. *Later Roman Britain.* Routledge & Kegan Paul. 1980.

Lloyd Laing. *Celtic Britain.* Paladin Books. 1984.

Major Albany. *The early wars of Wessex.* Blandford Press. 1978.

Malmesbury William of. *The Kings before the Norman Conquest.* Trans. Joseph Stephenson. Reprint Llanerch Enterprises. 1989.

Marsden John. *Northanymbre Saga* BCA. 1992.

Millward Roy & Robinson Adrian (i) *The Welsh Marches.*
(ii) *The Welsh Borders.* Eyre Methuen. 1978.

Morris John. *The Age of Arthur.* Phillimore. 1974.

Myres J.N.L. *The English Settlement.* Clarendon Press. Oxford. 1986.

Nennius. Trans. Morris John. *Historia Brittonum.* Phillimore. 1980.

Ordnance Survey. (i) *Britain in the Dark Ages.* Second Edition.
(ii) *Map of Roman Britain.*
(iii) *Guide to Castles in Britain.* 1988.

Oxford University Dept. External Studies. *Dorchester through the Ages.* 1985.

Pannel J.P.M. *Old Southampton Shores*. David & Charles 1967.

Peers Sir Charles *Pevensey Castle*. English Heritage.

Putnam Bill. *Roman Dorset*. Dovecote Press. 1984.

Salway Peter. *Roman Britain*. Clarendon Press Oxford. 1981.

Sawyer P.H. *From Roman Britain to Norman England*. Methuen & Co. Ltd.

Simeon of Durham. *History of the Kings of England*. Reprint Llanerch Enterprises. 1987.

Stenton Sir Frank. *Anglo-Saxon England*. Oxford University Press. 1971.

Trinder Barrie. *A History of Shropshire*. Phillimore. 1983.

Whitelock Dorothy. *English Historical Documents*. Volume 1 Eyre Methuen. 1979.

Webb J.F. (Tr) *The Age of Bede*. Penguin Classics. 1988.

Weinreb Ben & Hibbert Christopher. *London Encyclopedia*. Book Club Associates. 1987.

Webber, Ronald. *The Devon and Somerset Blackdowns*.

INDEX

286